PRAISE FOR THE 1ST I

This is the book we've a
has been the inspired lead quality
financial planning to the m market. Now she tells us how to do it, soup to nuts, in her book, *Garrett's Guide to Financial Planning.*
George D. Kinder, CFP, author of <u>The Seven Stages of Money Maturity</u>.

This book, written by one of the industry's most innovative thinkers, is the ultimate guide to serving the largely untapped Middle Market efficiently and profitably.
Joel P. Bruckenstein, CFP, CFS, CMFC, co-author of <u>Virtual Office Tools for a High-Margin Practice: How Client-Centered Financial Advisors Can Cut Paperwork, Overhead, and Wasted Hours</u> and <u>Tools & Techniques of Practice Management</u>

Sheryl Garrett worked in every type of financial services environment and then came up with a business model to do something no one thought could be done: provide fee-only financial advisory services to the middle class while making a good living. Her book tells you not only why the less-than-semi-affluent are great clients, but exactly how to find them and keep them satisfied.
David J. Drucker, MBA, CFP, co-author of <u>Virtual Office Tools for a High-Margin Practice: How Client-Centered Financial Advisors Can Cut Paperwork, Overhead, and Wasted Hours</u> and <u>Tools & Techniques of Practice Management</u>

Sometimes the best clients are right under our nose: working Americans, whose financial decisions can be more critical to their future than the wealthy. Helping this market achieve financial independence is something every financial advisor can be proud of. For everyone who has ever wondered where to find new clients, Sheryl Garrett has come to the rescue. Here is a remarkably smart and solid plan to helping Americas retire with confidence.
Katherine Vessenes, JD, CFP, national speaker, and author of <u>Protecting Your Practice</u>

Sheryl Garrett is a pioneer, visionary and hero to middle Americans and the planners who serve them. This book is a gift.
Randy Gardner, LLM, CPA, CFP, MBA, co-author of 101 Tax Saving Ideas

The Financial Industry and the Financial Planning business are both in the clutches of enormous change. Organizational realignment of structures and skills to better meet the public's needs is the order of the day. Sheryl Garrett's book is a common sense, clear view of the issues of the day, followed by a Peter Drucker-like analysis of Middle Market opportunities and practice management concepts. No one should miss this wonderful addition to the industry's body of knowledge.
Richard R. Lee Jr., CFP, CFA

Americans are searching for affordable financial guidance that is completely objective and relative to their particular needs. Sheryl is a pioneer in advocating and offering this kind of financial planning advice. Her book shares these years of experience and offers practical insights on how to offer hourly-based, affordable financial advice to anyone seeking such direction. The time has come for qualified financial planners to follow Sheryl's example and her book is the perfect "bridge" to that new practice model. This is a "must read" for any financial planner who wants to stay on the '"cutting edge" of the profession.
Paul Lemon, Integrated Financial Planning PC

Sheryl Garrett has revolutionized the financial advisory profession. She has taken the as-needed, fee-only financial advice model to the mainstream and proven that it works. This book paves the way for new models like ours and the tens of thousands of financial advisors who want to get quality, objective and affordable financial advice to all Americans.
Ron Peremel, CEO, myFinancialadvice.com

Sheryl Garrett makes a compelling case for financial advisors to serve middle American clients. Better yet, she goes on to teach you how to be successful in this huge market. A must-read for every financial advisor, especially those advisors new to the business.
Warren J. Mackensen, CFP, MBA, MS

One of the keys to the advancement and growth of the financial planning profession are new practice models to serve more people more efficiently. As a leader in this area, Sheryl has found some ways of building a

profitable practice to serve the Middle Market. She freely shares her substantial knowledge and experience in a practical and useable way. For someone wanting to build a new practice today, this book is invaluable. The market she identifies is ready to harvest and she shows how to do it. The book is well organized and readable and is a road map to success!
J. Jeffrey Lambert, CFP

Sheryl is a leading financial services authority having built a successful firm of networking RIAs across the U.S to serve the Middle Market. Through this book she is passing her expertise on to other financial service professionals. A must read for those trying to understand the industry and interested in serving the Middle Market.
Richard Sincere, www.sincereco.com

Finally! Sheryl Garrett fills a gaping hole in the financial planner's bookshelf with her comprehensive, no-nonsense guide to fee-only financial planning for middle America. Drawing on her many years of experience successfully serving this market, insight from industry leaders, and market data, Ms. Garrett makes a compelling argument that the future of financial planning lies on Main Street, not just with the wealthiest 10% of America traditionally served by the industry. But the book doesn't stop there! Chock full of tips, one-pagers, and pointers to valuable outside resources, *Garrett's Guide to Financial Planning* also provides the tools that financial planners need to tap this underserved market profitably. It outlines the needs, preferences, and buying patterns of this new target client, and describes the practice model best suited for meeting them. Plus it includes Sheryl's time-tested best practices for getting noticed despite the marketing clutter constantly facing today's consumer. I devoured the entire book in two sittings, and I'm sure I saved myself months, if not years, of effort.
Sherrill St. Germain, www.newmeans.com

2nd Edition

sheryl garrett, CFP®

garrett's guide to financial planning

How To Capture The Middle Market and Increase Your Profits

The All-American Planner

ISBN: 978-0-87218-919-5

Library of Congress Control Number: 2007928643

This publication is designed to provide accurate and authoritative information in regard to the subject matter covered. It is sold with the understanding that the publisher is not engaged in rendering legal, accounting or other professional service. If legal advice or other expert assistance is required, the services of a competent professional should be sought. — **From a Declaration of Principles jointly adopted by a Committee of the American Bar Association and a Committee of Publishers and Associations.**

The National Underwriter Company
P.O. Box 14367, Cincinnati, Ohio 45250-0367

2nd Edition

Printed in U.S.A.

Dedication

To my parents, Jack and Barbara Garrett, for their unconditional love and devotion. Thank you for giving me my entrepreneurial spirit – you gave me both the wings and the courage to fly.

To all those who have shared in and supported my life's passions. You know who you are and how much I appreciate you.

CONTENTS

ACKNOWLEDGEMENTS

The first edition of *Garrett's Guide to Financial Planning* would not have been possible without the contributions and dedication of my marketing communications consultant and friend, Marie Swift. Her influence permeates this edition as well. Marie is the author of the marketing chapter of Garrett's Guide, and she is a major force in the field of marketing communications for the financial services industry. Marie, it has been a sincere pleasure and honor to work with you all of these years.

I also owe a debt of gratitude to Jamie Breeden, CFP®. Jamie was instrumental in gathering and compiling research for the first edition. At that time, she was attending the Kansas State University's financial planning degree program. That was six years ago. Now, Jamie is Director of Member Services for the Garrett Planning Network. Jamie, you showed great potential then and have proved it every day since.

In this second edition the staff at The National Underwriter Company gave me the opportunity to "fill in the blanks" that I wished I had covered in the first edition, and to provide necessary updates and revisions. I am extremely grateful for this opportunity and to be working with such an extraordinary team of professionals. Thank you Debbie Miner, J.D., CLU, ChFC for your support and specifically, the greatest editor in the world, Sonya King, J.D., LLM. Sonya took me by the hand from day one and never let go. I also wish to express my appreciation to John Fenton, J.D. and Joe Stenken, J.D., CLU, ChFC for their help in editing this edition.

One of the new additions in this volume is an incredibly important chapter on business planning contributed by my dear friend and colleague, Mary Lacey Gibson, CFP®, financial planner and small business consultant. Mary, your thoughtfulness, leadership and tenacity are always on the mark. Thank you for your contributions to this edition, the Garrett Planning Network, and me personally.

And finally, to the clients who taught me what really matters, and the staff and members of the Garrett Planning Network. Thank you for sharing my passion, and your insights, enthusiasm and support for me and for one another. You are the greatest group of people anyone could have the honor to lead. And to my colleagues and friends in and around the financial planning industry thank you for your invaluable insights and ongoing support. Your wisdom, passion and generosity continue to awe and inspire me.

FOREWORD

In an age of instant gratification, and with a buy-on-demand mentality, middle America is facing its biggest crises yet: the ability to continue operating the type of lifestyle these individuals have grown accustomed to during the '90s. With this prolonged bear market, and in a world where things are as uncertain as ever, middle America is facing a pressing need as we travel down the road of the 21st century — the continuance of staying power. How will middle Americans continue to pursue their habits of providing for themselves, their kids, their extended families, their employers and so forth? How will middle America find the right solutions to allow qualified individuals to help them pursue their financial necessities in order to ensure a better life for all of us?

In my practice, we focus on middle America. These clients have different wants and needs than other types of clients planners focus on. They are deeply concerned about the current financial environment and are beginning to display a fearful attitude for the first time in many years. They want answers now. They want the "perceived" certainty that has been missing since the end of the bull road for the foreseeable future. When advisors were earning 20% and higher annually for their clients, almost on a routine basis, their concerns were never immediate issues. Yet the world that we've been living in is far less certain for all of us. Much of what went on pre-9/11 is not necessarily valid anymore. I find myself constantly assuring my middle American clients to continue holding firm on the same principles that got them there in the first place. A properly diversified portfolio, a long-term buy and hold strategy, dollar-cost-averaging, slow and steady growth towards wealth accumulation, and proper financial planning are all necessary to achieve success in arriving at the objectives agreed upon during the financial planning process. Getting to Point B from where they are at now (Point A) is always the critical issue.

Well, in talking with many advisors during my financial planning fast track and practice management training sessions, I find very few advisors pursing middle America as a viable client option. They respond that the reason they have not focused on this marketplace is that if they are going to spend time to develop planning and investment strategies for clients, they might as well go after the wealthier clients who can easily afford their services. As Tom Cruise stated in the movie "Jerry Maguire, "show me the money"! These clients are different than the high-income clients advisors are notorious for going after because in many cases, the same amount of work is involved, yet the payout could be substantially less. From the typical planner's mind, with a limited amount of time and from a cost-benefit standpoint, it does not make sense. How untrue! This marketplace is yearning for information. You need to deliver true and factual financial information and educate these clients to understand the importance of future independence and planning early. They are ripe, willing and able to go the distance. Your platform should be to educate middle America.

It worked for H&R Block. They educated middle America about the importance of having qualified individuals prepare their tax returns and it worked. They're nationwide and have just added financial services to their repertoire. We can't be so short-sided as to not see the opportunity that presents itself here. This is the information age and we need to provide advice in that arena to those middle Americans who desire it. Many of them are beginning to see the value in hiring a financial advisor. They know that in order for them to receive value added services, these clients are going to have to ante up for that service, like other professionals charge for theirs. Financial service professionals are another source of competent advisors that clients need to regularly deal with, just like CPAs, attorneys, and physicians. The numbers are showing that more middle Americans are paying for financial services and advice than ever before. Studies from the major planning membership and licensing organizations will confirm this.

In my mind, middle America holds the key to more successful planning opportunities for financial planners long-term. That's because they represent a significant number of potential clients. Just think about it – with 285 million Americans, and roughly 70% of them being classified as middle Americans, that translates into 105 million households. With 40,000 Certified Financial Planner® (CFP®) licensees nationwide, and another 200,000 self-proclaimed financial advisors serving the public, the odds of building up a practice are pretty strong. But the daunting question remains, why are planners continuing to ignore this marketplace?

With a void in the number of planners addressing middle America, there are many opportunities for all of us as financial advisors servicing this marketplace. They need help in all of the basic areas of insurance planning, education planning, investment planning, income tax planning, employee benefit and retirement planning, and estate planning. They will also be willing to compensate planners on a fee-only, commission-only, or some type of combination. Many large firms have already discovered this niche by providing the requisite training and resources necessary to get their reps up to speed on this market and this, in turn, has proved to provide a fine living servicing this clientele. It does take longer, but over time, the constant source for referrals and renewability factors is there. And I find that these clients are more likely to help their friends and family to get to the financial level they need than other types of clients.

Up to this point, no qualified advisor has written on how to aggressively penetrate this marketplace. It has truly been the lone missing educational component in our vast advisor encyclopedia of knowledge. However, after reading Sheryl Garrett's manuscript discussing this untapped market, and knowing about the high profile turn-key program she runs in Kansas City for advisors nationwide, I am convinced that by learning to fully understand this marketplace and instituting the appropriate game plan spelled out in this book, financial advisors will be able to tap into this hidden and potentially lucrative marketplace, before it becomes too widespread, and with today's advisors reaping the benefits from helping this important, yet overlooked, segment of our society.

Jeffrey H. Rattiner, CPA, CFP®, MBA, RFC
JR Financial Group, Inc.
Englewood, CO
August 25, 2002
Author of:
Getting Started as a Financial Planner (Bloomberg Press, 2005).
Rattiner's Financial Planner's Bible (John Wiley & Sons, 2002).

Preface

Press On –

Nothing in the world can take the place of persistence. Talent will not, nothing is more commmon than unsuccessful men with talent. Genius will not; unrewarded genius is almost a proverb. Education alone will not. The world is full of educated derelicts. Persistence and determination alone are omnipotent.

– Calvin Coolidge

In the five years since this book was originally published, I have been determined to learn and observe as many "best practices" in the financial planning industry as well as potentially similar professions. My philosophies and approaches have evolved and crystallized since the original publication of *Garrett's Guide to Financial Planning: How to Capture the Middle Market and Increase Your Profits* in 2002. I am pleased to provide in this fully updated and expanded version the philosophies, characteristics, and procedures of successful middle market practitioners that I have learned from throughout my career, but most significantly over the last few years.

I retired as a personal financial planner at the end of 2004. However, I remain very much involved in financial planning through my work as the founder and spokesperson for the Garrett Planning Network and the Garrett Financial Education Alliance, expert witness work, and through various volunteer activities with our professional associations.

The nearly 300 members of the Garrett Planning Network (Garrett), colleagues in the National Association of Personal Financial Advisors (NAPFA), the Life Planning Institute, and the Financial Planning Association (FPA) have been instrumental in exploring, distilling, and sharing these strategies and wisdom. Over the last five or six years I have had the honor and benefit of speaking with thousands of practitioners, while studying the industry and marketplace, in my determination to find more efficient and effective ways to help our clients meet their goals while we achieve ours.

I have incorporated these observations into the second edition of *Garrett's Guide to Financial Planning*. Many of these tips I utilized in my financial planning practice; other great ideas, strategies, and techniques were learned from other professionals—and I would use these today if I were starting out all over again.

Some feedback I received on the first edition was that while the reader thoroughly appreciated *why* I believe they should target the middle market, they stressed that the first volume failed to deliver as much explanation of *how* to work efficiently and profitability with this particular market. Consequently, in this volume you will find not only commentary on the need and opportunity in this market, and how to market to it, but you will also find substantially more real life, hands-on examples in all areas of operating a financial planning practice—from business plan development, to streamlining your workflow, to your client deliverables. This volume fills in those essential gaps. *(However, please note that step by step details of some of these strategies and processes introduced in this text are reserved for the exclusive use of members of the Garrett Planning Network. If you want to know more, visit our website.)*

Our overriding purpose as I see it, is to affect positive change in peoples' financial lives. One of our primary responsibilities is to serve as "accountability coach" for our clients. Helping our clients achieve their most cherished objectives—that is what we do. What an awesome opportunity and responsibility! As you read *Garrett's Guide to Financial Planning: How to Capture the Middle Market and Increase Your Profits,* I hope you'll benefit from learning about my practice and current thoughts on most effectively and efficiently serving Middle Market clients.

Sheryl Garrett, CFP®
www.GarrettPlanningNetwork.com
info@GarrettPlanningNetwork.com
April 30, 2007

Introduction

My firms' mission statement is "to help make competent, objective financial advice accessible to all people." As I share how and why I established my hourly, as-needed financial planning practice, it will become clear that I am passionate about spreading the word:

> *Middle Americans, do-it-yourselfers, and people from all walks of life need and want to work with a competient, objective financial adviisor!*
>
> *– Maybe you are the one they are looking for?*

As you read my thoughts and digest the information, please take the time to reflect on your *own* needs, goals, and dreams. Consider the possibilities and do not overlook this great opportunity. By tapping the abundant market I call "Middle America" (which is actually much, much broader than you may be thinking now), not only could you make a *huge* difference for a host of appreciative clients, but you could also gain better balance in your own life while enjoying a professional lifestyle and virtually no competition in building a sustainable business that you love.

That doesn't mean this work is easy. Starting any business, or working as a financial planner under any delivery model, requires a significant commitment of time, energy, and to a lessor extent, money. All new business adventures involve risks. The more time you spend researching and planning *how* and *for whom* you wish to establish your service offering and design your business in advance, the more time, energy, money, and heartache you'll save in the long run.

As an advisor and consultant involved in the financial planning profession since 1987, I've had the privilege of knowing thousands of financial planning practitioners and financial services professionals. As a staff planner, registered representative, advisor to high net worth clientele, middle market advisor, coach and mentor to hundreds of financial advisors, and most recently, consumer advocate and expert witness, I've had exposure to most traditional financial services distribution channels and have had to discover for myself what business model fit me best and the clients I wanted to serve.

After serving a variety of client markets in these assorted professional settings and roles for over a decade, I finally came to the conclusion regarding how *I* needed and wanted to deliver financial advice—and to whom. I knew that I not only wanted to become a truly independent financial planner, I needed to be self-employed to fully execute my optimal financial life plan. I knew I wanted to be able to serve all people, regardless of net worth, income level, or investable assets; and as a professional, I wanted to be in control of my worklife and workproduct.

In 1997, while equal partner in wealth management firm Stepp & Garrett, Inc., a Kansas City-based financial planning firm specializing in serving high net worth clients, I became determined to make a change. While I had enjoyed success on many levels, I eventually became convinced that the firm's focus on serving affluent clients, on a comprehensive wealth management basis, *only*, was too narrow to meet my personal objectives. We offered one total package of services, and the prospective client was free to choose whether to take it or leave it. Whether to hire us for more limited scope or shorter-term engagements was not an option. This service model is very appropriate for many practitioners and their clients, but it was too narrow to meet my personal and professional objectives.

I always felt a sense of remorse when I had to turn potential clients away because they did not meet our client profile or account minimums. I grew up in a modest home and inherited strong, working-class values from my parents. While I'd achieved what some would consider an enviable position, there was always a tug at my heart when regular folk —like my friends, family and neighbors—called to inquire about our services and I had to turn them away.

It was very hard to tell the hair stylist, postman, grocery store employee, church secretary, and video storeowner, "Sorry, but you don't meet our minimums." Worse yet, I had no proven resource or other professionals to whom I felt comfortable referring them.

Is a photographer, plumber, or teacher less important than a highly paid corporate executive? Doesn't the freelance writer need my help as much (or more) than the dot-com millionaire? Who would help my parents, family, friends, and neighbors with their most important financial decisions?

Obviously, they needed, wanted, and were willing to pay for help. Sometimes they just had a single pressing question or issue. Other times they needed validation and advice regarding key decisions they were facing. In some cases they needed one or two subjects addressed, rather than a full financial plan; at other times, they needed and were willing to pay for more comprehensive financial planning services. But I was unable to provide the assistance they needed in the most effective manner under the service models of my past.

While working for clients on an annual retainer basis I began to feel increasingly burdened by the amount of responsibility and high level of ongoing commitment required to provide financial concierge level services. I'd carry a mental to-do list and felt that I was on call 24/7, even when I was on "vacation."

Eventually, I came to the realization that I wanted to serve "regular folk" and do-it-yourselfers, like me—and maybe you, too—who I knew were being overlooked and/or underserved by the financial services industry. I knew I'd need to be extremely efficient with my time and service delivery, and effectively adapt my marketing strategy to reach this huge, untapped market.

But since 1998, I've proven that it can be done—and with stellar success both personally and professionally. I fell in love with my chosen vocation. Prior to this time, I tried to leave financial planning on three different occasions. The service models I had worked under in the past didn't fit me or the clients with which I preferred to work. But with my new service model and practice focus in place, not only did I become happier with the balance in my personal and professional lives, I also helped people who *truly appreciated me and the advice I provided.* I generated a professional standard of living, similar to that of other financial services professionals, attorneys, and business consultants yet I also have enough time and flexibility to fully enjoy life with my friends and family.

Join me, as we explore the boundless opportunities and joys of working with the Middle Market and do-it-yourselfer client. Regardless of how far you decide to eventually go to make competent, objective advice accessible to *all* people, by reading this book you will:

- gain some fresh perspectives on the financial planning industry and the profession's evolution;
- learn about different practice models and opportunities;
- discover "best practices" tips and techniques employed by some of the most successful Middle Market practitioners in service today;
- be exposed to a host of financial planning resources; and
- glean key business planning, marketing and practice development insights.

I love hearing from other practitioners and would welcome your comments once you've completed reading the book.

So, let's get started – go to Chapter One now!

Sheryl Garrett, CFP®
Shawnee, Kansas
www.GarrettPlanningNetwork.com
info@GarrettPlanningNetwork.com

Chapter 1

The Evolution of Financial Planning

In a few hundred years, when the history of our time will be written from a long-term perspective, it is likely that the most important event historians will see is not technology, not the Internet, not e-commerce. It is an unprecedented change in the human condition. For the first time—literally—substantial and rapidly growing numbers of people have choices. For the first time, they will have to manage themselves. And society is totally unprepared for it.

Peter F. Drucker

Client centered financial advisors of today help clients make smarter financial decisions and address issues in all major areas of their clients' lives—family (biological and chosen), career, and leisure pursuits.

When we speak of family goals and responsibilities, I think of the following examples: homes; expenses for activities and responsibilities for our children and ourselves (e.g., summer camp, cars, college and professional education, health insurance, long-term support); older parents caring for a disabled sibling, one whom we may need to care for at some point; older parents personally needing financial or physical assistance; and support of other family (biological or chosen), or a best friend temporarily down on their luck.

A clients' career is the "in-flow" or resource-generating category (i.e., money one makes to spend in the other two major areas of family and leisure). The single biggest asset most of us have is our ability to make money. Unfortunately, our single biggest liability is our penchant for spending all of our money. As financial advisors, we frequently advise clients regarding the pro and cons of taking a new job offer, starting a business, investing in one's career, transitioning from one career to the next, and remaining active and productive in later years. But when do when we ask ourselves these same questions? The primary objective of this book is really two-fold: (1) to help the financial planner earn more money; and (2) to help the financial planner enjoy what he or she does even more.

Leisure pretty much covers all other financial objectives (dining out, movie tickets, country club membership, golf, sports cars, boating, fishing, cabin at the lake)—essentially anything that falls outside of the realm of necessities.

As financial planners, we help people make better, more informed financial decisions. The subject matter is now very broad, touching on all aspects of our personal and professional financial lives. This broader view of the role of the financial planning, while still relatively new, is rapidly evolving.

To help put things into perspective—financial planning was born out of the insurance industry in the late 1960's as a means to further identify clients' financial needs and to fulfill those needs with additional product offerings. Life insurance companies began to expand their proprietary product offerings to include mutual funds, retirement plans, and variable annuities. Over time, many of the major life insurance companies evolved into the major financial services companies we know today.

In the early years, financial services professionals were generally captive agents of national insurance companies or brokers with major wire house broker-dealers. Investment and insurance products were limited to those branded by the respective company, and advisors were restricted to the products offered by their employer. Commissions received on the sale of insurance and investment products compensated these advisors. In an attempt to better address the broad range of client financial planning needs, and to cross-sell additional products to their clients, advisors began to employ consulting and analysis techniques now known as the "financial planning process."

According to the CFP Board of Standards (see Figure 1.1), today's financial planning process consists of the following six steps:

1. Establishing and defining the client-planner relationship;

2. Gathering client data, including goals;

3. Analyzing and evaluating the client's financial status;

4. Developing and presenting financial planning recommendations and/or alternatives;

5. Implementing the financial planning recommendations; and

6. Monitoring the financial planning recommendations.

Figure 1.1

THE FINANCIAL PLANNING PROCESS
CFP BOARD OF STANDARDS (MODIFIED TO THIRD PERSON)

1. **ESTABLISHING AND DEFINING THE CLIENT-PLANNER RELATIONSHIP** – The financial planner should clearly explain or document the services to be provided to the client and define both the planner's and the client's responsibilities. The planner should explain fully how she will be paid and by whom. The client and the planner should agree on how long the professional relationship should last and on how decisions will be made.

2. **GATHERING CLIENT DATA, INCLUDING GOALS** – The financial planner should ask for information about the client's financial situation. The client and the planner should mutually define the client's personal and financial goals, understand the client's time frame for results and discuss, and if relevant, how the client feels about risk. The financial planner should gather all the necessary documents before giving the client the advice needed.

3. **ANALYZING AND EVALUATING THE CLIENT'S FINANCIAL STATUS** – The financial planner should analyze the client's information to assess her current situation and determine what she must do to meet her goals. Depending on what services she has asked for, this could include analyzing her assets, liabilities and cash flow, current insurance coverage, investments, or tax strategies.

4. **DEVELOPING AND PRESENTING FINANCIAL PLANNING RECOMMENDATIONS AND/OR ALTERNATIVES** – The financial planner should offer financial planning recommendations that address the client's goals, based on the information she provides. The planner should go over the recommendations with the client to help her understand them so that the client can make informed decisions. The planner should also listen to the client's concerns and revise the recommendations as appropriate.

5. **IMPLEMENTING THE FINANCIAL PLANNING RECOMMENDATIONS** – The client and the planner should agree on how the recommendations will be carried out. The planner may carry out the recommendations or serve as the client's coach, coordinating the whole process with the client and other professionals such as attorneys or stockbrokers.

6. **MONITORING THE FINANCIAL PLANNING RECOMMENDATIONS** – The client and the planner should agree on who will monitor the client's progress towards her goals. If the planner is in charge of the process, the planner should report to the client periodically to review her situation and adjust the recommendations, if needed, as her life changes.

As more agents and brokers began using the financial planning process with their clients, they felt hampered by the limited product offerings available through their captive broker-dealer relationships and they began to seek the freedom offered by independent broker-dealers. To this day, the majority of financial services professionals are affiliated with independent broker-dealers.

Along with the variety of product offerings that became available to the independently registered financial advisors came the flexibility to charge clients fees in addition to commissions. Advisors could receive compensation for their time and advice, regardless of whether products were sold or not. However, the majority of their compensation still came from commissions.

For more than a decade, there has been a major movement within the financial services industry to increase fees as a percentage of revenues. Sales commissions for many products have declined substantially during this period. Independent financial advisors are finding that charging fees in addition to receiving commissions normalizes their cash flow and allows them to focus their energies on providing financial advice on any issue for which their clients need assistance. Client engagements are no longer based on transactions alone. Transactional engagements have evolved into long-term client-advisor relationships.

There has also been increased concentration on providing comprehensive financial advice. Many financial services representatives are evolving into financial planning professionals. They are embracing the value of comprehensive financial planning as a means to provide clients with better financial advice and more holistic solutions. Rather than providing advice and solutions for just one area of the financial planning process, they are focusing on clients' needs and objectives in all aspects of their financial lives.

One segment of the financial planning industry has migrated completely away from commissions. In this service model, 100% of the advisor's compensation is paid directly by the client. The "fee-only" compensation model is currently the fastest growing segment of the financial planning industry, and the trend is escalating. The primary reason for the popularity of fee-only advice is the relationship the advisor has with his or her clients. Consumers are becoming increasingly aware of the potential conflicts of interest between the compensation interest and affiliated business interests of their professional advisors. In recent years, the media has also been a strong advocate of the benefits of fee-only advice for consumers. This enhanced media coverage has fueled consumer interest in learning more about how their advisors are compensated and fee-only planning options.

Fee-only advice is available for the traditional financial planning issues, such as goal setting, cash flow planning, tax planning, investments and risk management, retirement planning, and estate planning. However, many fee-only practitioners have expanded their services and now include ongoing asset management, tax return and estate document preparation, trust services, and in some cases, concierge services, too.

In many cases, fee-only financial planners and independent advisors have become so successful and comprehensive in their service offerings that they have continually raised their minimum fees or assets under management requirements. As a result, most fee-only planners (in addition to a growing number of fee-based advisors) now target affluent and semi-affluent clients exclusively. Many of these practitioners are no longer able to take on new clients, and their success is drawing more competition to this end of the marketplace. The competition consists of larger financial advisory firms with vast resources, brand names, and relationships that facilitate the advisor's efforts to compete and serve the needs of more clients.

In two highly touted research papers by Undiscovered Managers, the authors addressed these issues and concluded that, "the business of providing financial advice to semi-affluent investors—is on the brink of a major evolution."[1]

The Undiscovered Managers' studies have been highly controversial. One of the fundamental controversies has centered on the definition used by the researchers concerning the financial advisory business. The Undiscovered Managers' reports concentrated solely on the investment advisory aspect of the financial planning process. Their research went on to compare the current climate in the financial advisory industry to that of the institutional money management industry 20 years ago. They concluded that the same trends that occurred within the institutional money management industry would most likely unfold in the next five to 10 years within the financial advisory industry.[2]

Unfortunately, the Undiscovered Managers' research equated *financial* advice with *investment* advice. This is a common misunderstanding for the public and the media alike. The financial planning industry also confuses *investment management* with *financial planning*. Investment advice is clearly a very important component of financial planning, but too many advisors and consumers confuse the two subjects. Investment advice and financial planning advice are not synonymous. Therefore, the conclusions drawn from this research should be taken only in the context they relate to the delivery of investment advice.

I fundamentally disagree with the statement in the Undiscovered Managers' report that reads, "[t]he financial advisory business — the business of providing financial advice to semi-affluent investors — is on the brink of a major evolution."[3] In my opinion the authors' contention that the financial planning business is the business of providing investment advisory services to semi-affluent investors is also flawed.

Actually, I see the financial advisory business as an evolving profession whose mission should be to provide the appropriate level of competent, objective financial advice to *any* individual seeking assistance. All consumers have the need to consult with a financial planning professional at one time or another. Competent, objective financial advice should not be reserved only for the wealthy.

The Undiscovered Managers' research leads to the conclusion that the future of the financial advisory business will be dominated by just a few large, institutional wealth management firms providing extremely comprehensive, one-stop-shopping advisory services to wealthy consumers. While this service model may be an important component of the future of financial services industry—based on the limited number of Americans desiring and able to afford this level of service and the significant competition in this marketplace—we are still left with a vast, untapped opportunity to serve segments of the population that do not fit this model.

In this book, we'll explore these untapped markets, and answer such questions as:

- Who are these consumers?
- What services do they seek from financial planners?

- What business models effectively and profitably serve this marketplace?
- How do we build a viable and sustainable business to serve this marketplace?
- How do we market to these consumers?
- What are the specific financial planning needs and the appropriate strategies for serving these clients?

Let's begin by looking at the factors affecting the evolution of the financial planning industry, and how the desires and demands of the consumer are a fundamental part of this evolution.

What's Driving the Evolution?

Factors driving the evolution in the delivery of financial advice include the strong economy that we've been experiencing over the last several years, the availability and popularity of mutual funds, the 401(k) plan, and the insecurity of the Social Security system. The bull markets of the 1980's and 1990's also caused many consumers to become more interested in taking a proactive role in their personal finances.

There is significantly more publicly available information regarding personal finance than ever before. In fact, the two hottest topics in consumer journalism are personal health and personal finance. Personal finance publications such as *Kiplinger's Personal Finance*, *Smart Money*, and *Money* have made it possible for all consumers to learn more about their personal finances and to take a more proactive role in the management of their own financial affairs.

The Internet has also made a significant impact in the availability of and access to financial information for all consumers. One report has stated that 70% of investors with at least $1,000,000 of investment assets get some of their investment news online.[4] The use of the Internet by average Americans is similarly popular.

Our society is busier than ever. We want to have more control, to make things simpler, more convenient, and more efficient. The Internet has provided us with tools that can quickly and easily simplify our financial lives and provide us with greater control.

One area where we have seen tremendous growth is in investment assets in online brokerage accounts. Assets grew from $27.7 billion dollars in 1995 to $754.4 billion dollars in 1999. In 2000, there were more than 11,500,000 online brokerage accounts. In 2004, the total dollars in online brokerage accounts was expected to reach $2.2 trillion dollars according to Cerulli Associates.[5]

Services such as Morningstar enable consumers to analyze individual mutual funds and portfolios of funds. Web-based services such as Financial Engines provide very sophisticated, yet user-friendly asset allocation tools that incorporate some of the most advanced financial simulation models available today. Software applications (e.g., Intuit's Quicken, Quicken Financial Planner, and Turbo Tax) have empowered consumers by providing them with highly sophisticated tools to analyze and manage their personal finances. The result of the improvements in technology and access to information is that the cloak of mystery has been removed from the financial advisory business. *The playing field has been leveled.*

Many advisors in our industry were concerned about consumers' increased access to information. Although financial advisors were once the gatekeepers of financial information, we are no longer the only ones with access to the volumes of information, tools and resources needed by consumers. But professional advisors need not worry about job security—consumers still need help. They have more options and opportunities available to them today than at any time in the past. They need trusted advisors that will work in their best interests to help them sort through the vast (and often confusing) amount of information, and help them make the best decisions for their personal situations.

The plethora of information available in the popular press, on the Internet, and through publicly available financial software applications has actually provided financial advisors with *more*, not fewer, opportunities to assist clients. For example, the quality of the output from financial calculators or software programs is no better then the initial assumptions used in preparing the analyses. Most consumers are unskilled in determining appropriate assumptions to be used in these analyses (e.g., inflation rates, rate-of-return assumptions on asset classes, and mortality expectations), let alone determining risk tolerance.

Most software applications utilize static averages in projecting cash flow over life expectancy. An educated advisor, on the other hand, has access to and knowledge of probability analysis and modeling tools, such as Monte Carlo simulation. The output from a Monte Carlo simulation may reveal a low probability that the client would achieve success based on the assumptions they might employ in their projections. This is just one of the many areas where the advice of a qualified financial professional can be extremely beneficial to a client.

The amount of subject matter to be mastered in personal finance is enormous. It often takes professionals years to develop a level of expertise in most areas. The average consumer cannot be expected to understand, stay current on, or be able to incorporate the many appropriate options and strategies that may be available to them (presuming they even wanted to).

Consumers are rapidly recognizing the need for access to a trusted adviser—one who can help them weigh options and opportunities regarding their personal finances, and assist them in appropriately planning their financial futures.

The Undiscovered Managers' research states that, "clients are better informed than in the past and are demanding better advice for their money." The report goes on to state that clients "still might not feel comfortable or capable of managing their own investments, but they will be far more able to evaluate the quality of service that they receive." [6]

As clients' needs and expectations of their advisors evolve, our industry and service offerings must evolve as well. Financial planning practitioners who embrace service models that meet the needs of informed consumers will benefit from "the information age."

Investment implementation options are also evolving. A growing number of consumers are investing directly in online brokerage accounts and with no-load mutual fund companies.

Indexing is now an option available to all consumers. The benefits of indexing are low costs and the simplicity of this investment strategy.

An investor trying to replicate the returns of a market may do so simply by investing in an index fund.

Overseeing a portfolio of index funds can be simple, but determining the appropriate asset allocations may be more complex. Services such as Financial Engines now provide the average consumer with specific asset allocation strategies based on their stated tolerance for risk. Once the appropriate asset allocations have been determined, fund companies such as Vanguard and Barclay's iShares make implementation of a passive asset allocation strategy simpler and more cost-effective.

Some investors who embrace a long-term buy and hold asset allocation strategy may no longer feel it necessary to pay a professional investment advisor to implement a passive investment strategy. However, many consumers still need validation from a professional to confirm the appropriateness of their asset allocations and analytical decisions with regard to their overall financial objectives.

Other important factors that have aided in the evolution of the financial planning profession are the public awareness and professional development activities of the CFP Board of Standards, the Financial Planning Association (FPA) and the National Association of Personal Financial Advisors (NAPFA). One of the primary missions of the FPA is to raise public awareness of the need for financial planning for all Americans. Financial planning is extremely valuable for all people, regardless of whether they employ a professional advisor or whether they are do-it-yourselfers. The financial planning process is the basis for making smart financial decisions. All consumers, and our society as a whole, will benefit from making smarter financial decisions.

Traditional Financial Planning Target Clients vs. Typical American Consumers

The typical target client of the traditional financial planner may be described in broad terms as a "delegator." While the delegator's composite may not include "old money" (i.e., an inheritance), and although delegators may not necessarily be wealthy, these clients do enjoy sufficient resources as well as a desire to outsource many of the day-to-day services associated with an organized and successful life. The delegator client may happily pay for lawn mowing and gardening services, catered or convenience meals delivered to their home, a live-in nanny, custom-tailored clothing, luxury vacations, etc.

Characteristics of a "delegator" in a financial planning relationship are as follows:

- d*esires a permanent, ongoing engagement* with their advisor;
- is interested in, and willing to, *delegate management of their financial affairs* to their advisor;
- h*as money to invest* or immediate insurance needs; and
- provides their advisor with a *long-term source of revenue.*

While the above characterizations summarize the qualities of the client that most financial planners consider representative of their target market, this client is definitely not the "typical" person.

The "typical" client may be described in broad terms as a "validator." While the validator's composite may include some of the characteristics described above, validators do not have the resources or the desire to outsource many of the day-to-day services that delegators tend to outsource. The validator client may prefer to do his own lawn mowing and garden care, cook large batches of food and divvy them up in the freezer as convenience foods, create a babysitting co-op for childcare, shop sales at department stores, and purchase off-the-rack clothing. This client may also enjoy camping instead of going on a cruise, etc.

Characteristics of the "validator" in a financial planning relationship include:

- *needs professional advice, periodically*, but not on a permanent and ongoing basis;
- is *not interested in, or willing to, delegate* the management of their financial affairs to an advisor;

- is aware of, and *may be sensitive to, potential conflicts of interest*;

- is *cost sensitive*, but recognizes that there is no "free lunch" (they are willing to pay for value when they see it);

- has most of their investment assets in qualified retirement plans; *seek investment advice, but not ongoing management* of these assets; and

- seeks empowerment, education and *validation of their decisions*.

If we had to split the country into just two groups, most of America would fall into the validator category, not the delegator category. I contend that the majority of Americans do not meet the definition of the "traditional" target financial planning client—that is, the delegator described above. In the following chapters, we will explore the needs of the "typical" consumers—the validators—including what they want from a financial advisor, and the practice models that can profitably and effectively serve these clients.

Figure 1.2

Client Composites

Typical Target of Traditional Financial Advisor	Ideal Client for Planners Seeking Untapped Market
Broadly defined as a Delegator	Broadly defined as a Validator
Convenience-oriented	Value-oriented
Willing to delegate research, implementation and management of financial affairs to advisor	Willing to do some research, but does most implementation and monitoring on own
Desires and is willing to pay for a permanent, ongoing engagement with advisor	Does not desire, or is not willing to delegate management of financial affairs to an advisor
Willing to pay for services desired	Cost sensitive / thrifty
Desires some education, wants to understand process, but willing to defer to advisor	Seeks empowerment, education, validation of their decisions
Wants ongoing services; Provides advisor with a long-term source of revenue	Needs professional advice periodically; Provides advisor with one-time or repeat business
Can afford and is willing to outsource a variety of household services	Does not have desire or resources to outsource most household services
Minority of Americans	Majority of Americans

ENDNOTES

1. Hurley, *et al.*, *The Future of the Financial Advisory Business and the Delivery of Advice to the Semi-Affluent Investor*, p. 1 (Undiscovered Managers, September 1999). See also Slowik, *et al.*, *The Future of the Financial Advisory Business Part II: Strategies for Small Businesses*, (Undiscovered Managers, September 2000).
2. Id. at 3.
3. Id. at 1.
4. See HNW at: http://www.hnw.com/intelligence/market.jsp.
5. *The Internet and Financial Product Distribution*, pp. 80-82 (Cerulli Associates, Inc., 2000).
6. Hurley, *et al.*, at 17-18.

CHAPTER 2

THE FORGOTTEN MIDDLE MARKET

UPPER CLASSES ARE A NATION'S PAST; THE MIDDLE CLASS IS ITS FUTURE.

– Ayn Rand

When we say "Middle Market," what exactly do we mean? Is this term based on an income range, as in "middle income" Americans? Is it based on a mindset, as in "the middle class"? Is there a difference? Or is it something more?

While the financial services industry, economists, social scientists, and the public at large may differ in their definitions of what "Middle Market" means, when asked to describe their families' income, wealth and social status, most Americans will answer with the non-descriptive label of "middle class." But exactly what does this mean?

Actually, it may be easier to define what the Middle Market is *not*. The authors of the Undiscovered Managers' reports define "semi-affluent" as those with net worths ranging from $1,000,000 to $10,000,000. This demographic represents about 2% of American households. Given this definition, one might define the "affluent" as those with $10,000,000 to $50,000,000 of net worth, and the "wealthy" as those individuals whose net worth exceeds $50,000,000.[1] The poverty line is also definable. According to the U.S. Department of Health and Human Services, the

2002 Poverty Guideline for a family of four is approximately $18,000. This demographic makes up almost 12% of American households.[2]

According to the best-selling book *The Millionaire Next Door*, there were approximately 3,500,000 millionaire households in the United States in 1999, and 95% of these millionaires had a net worth between $1,000,000 and $10,000,000.[3] Cerulli Associates has defined clients with investable assets ranging from as low as $500,000 to as high as $5,000,000 as the "mass-affluent." Their statistics reveal that as of 1999, approximately 11.5% of all U.S. households fell within this demographic.[4]

I define "middle America" as individuals who fall somewhere between the broad definitions of poverty and semi-affluent—strinkingly, this is about 86% of all Americans. My definition utilizes net worth rather than just household income. Bert Whitehead of Cambridge Advisors, LLC (a network of fee-only financial planners who target and serve the Middle Market) defines a "middle American" as "anyone who works for a living...or anyone who *has had* to work for a living." Both definitions clearly illustrate that "middle America" is mainstream America.

Based on after-tax, annual household income, most studies agree that the middle class is grouped around the national average (with the lower and upper ends of this range representing the 20th and 90th percentiles of the population), and accounts for 70% of U.S. households. This definition includes all sources of income. But annual income is just one criterion for defining "middle class." Other factors, such as educational level, occupation, family background, and social status should also be included.

Interestingly, the National Center for Opinion Research states that 36% of people earning less than $15,000 a year consider themselves "middle class." Among those with incomes between $35,000 and $50,000 a year, 50% identify themselves as "middle class." While 71% of individuals earning in excess of $75,000 a year described themselves as "middle class," statistically those persons earning over $75,000 per year are technically high-income households.[5] Most people earning around $75,000 a year would argue that they are not high-income, but statistically they are in the top 20% of all households.

Clearly, our concept of "middle class" and the statistical definition of "middle income" are different. While middle income may be statistically defined as the middle 70% of household incomes in the United States, keep in mind this is an average of *all* households in America regardless of geography, number of wage earners, members per household, or employment status.

But from community to community and from household to household, "middle income" implies different things. For example, in rural mid-America, a widowed retiree living on $36,000 per year, who owns her own home, and has a government pension and health insurance for life is considered to be financially secure. However, that same $36,000 annual income would barely sustain a family of four living in the San Francisco Bay area.

A young professional just graduating from college may technically earn a low-to-medium starting salary, but as he matures in his career this individual may make an income of $75,000 per year, or more. This person will likely see himself as middle- or upper-middle class based on his professional credentials and reputation, rather than his income.

Clearly, "middle class" is really a *mindset*. And I am convinced that it is a very healthy mindset for our financial planning clients to have. Individuals who think of themselves as middle class often have more realistic expectations for their financial lives. Fundamentally, they want the same things as their wealthier counterparts—that is, they want to enjoy life, provide for their families, and retire with financial security someday. And while the not-yet-affluent and never-will-be-affluent may have fewer options and strategies available to them than the wealthy, typically they also have less complex financial planning situations. With the right attitude, conviction and guidance, they can—and will—achieve their financial goals.

For the purpose of building wealth, *income doesn't matter as much as how much you save and what you do with the wealth you have accumulated.* For that reason, I'd much rather work with a client who earns $40,000 a year and saves 15% of her income than a client who earns $400,000 a year and can't seem to make ends meet.

In their insightful book, *The Millionaire Next Door*, Thomas J. Stanley, Ph.D. and William D. Danko, Ph.D. reported that most of the millionaires they profiled either *think* or *have thought* of themselves as middle class Americans. The majority of those studied live in middle class neighborhoods, drive middle class vehicles, and enjoy the same hobbies and activities (and sometimes even the same occupations) as their middle class neighbors.[6] While these individuals have accumulated net worths in excess of $1,000,000, their millionaire status has not changed who they are. *Net worth is only a measure of the success one has had in managing his or her money.*

Stanley and Danko found that affluent people typically follow a lifestyle that is conducive to accumulating money. They found seven common denominators shared by those who successfully build wealth. These are:

1. They live well below their means.
2. They allocate their time, energy and money efficiently, and in ways that are conducive to building wealth.
3. They believe that financial independence is more important than displaying high social status.
4. Their parents did not provide "economic outpatient care."
5. Their adult children are economically self-sufficient.
6. They are proficient in targeting market opportunities.
7. They chose the right occupations.[7]

There are an estimated 105,000,000 middle income households in the United States in 2001. As we learned from the profiles in *The Millionaire Next Door*, most millionaires are "self-made" millionaires. Of the 105,000,000 middle income households in the United States, many of these individuals, with good financial management, will become the future "millionaires next door."

Stanley and Danko go on to report that:

> *"[M]ORE THAN TWENTY-FIVE MILLION HOUSEHOLDS IN THE UNITED STATES (APPROXIMATELY 17%) HAVE ANNUAL INCOMES IN EXCESS OF $50,000; MORE THAN SEVEN MILLION (LESS THAN 5%) HAVE ANNUAL INCOMES OVER $100,000. BUT IN SPITE OF BEING 'GOOD*

> *INCOME' EARNERS, TOO MANY OF THESE PEOPLE HAVE SMALL LEVELS OF ACCUMULATED WEALTH. MANY LIVE FROM PAYCHECK TO PAYCHECK."* [8]

Millionaires, on average, invest nearly 20% of household realized income each year. Most invest at least 15%. Most don't become millionaires until they are 50 years of age or older. Most are frugal. "And few could have ever supported a high-consumption lifestyle and become millionaires in the same lifetime."[9]

The above research shows that regardless of income, individuals who (1) live well below their means, (2) allocate their time, energy, and money efficiently, and in ways conducive to building wealth, and (3) believe that financial independence is more important than displaying high social status can achieve financial independence.

Very few practitioners in the financial services industry have elected to target clients with household incomes of $75,000, even though that group accounts for fully 20% of household income in the United States. Instead, many practitioners have set their client income threshold at $100,000. But individuals in this group account for only 5% of the population, and competition for these clients is fierce. As minimum income levels are set even higher above $100,000, there are fewer and fewer households to target, and the market opportunity drops precipitously.

Where do you what to spend your energies in developing a clientele? Targeting the same market niche that every other financial advisor in the country is targeting? Or would you rather be developing a practice that can effectively meet the needs of those Americans who are currently being ignored or underserved by the financial planning community?

My ideal clients are the "Millionaires Next Door"—but 5 to 20 years *before* they reach their millionaire status. It is their attitude and conviction that makes them my ideal clients. We will explore other characteristics that make these individuals the largest untapped market for financial advisors in America.

While middle income consumers are obviously a large segment of the untapped market, there are many more smaller segments of mainstream America that have yet to be adequately served. As we focus on the target markets of traditional financial advisors, we will uncover these untapped opportunities.

As stated in Chapter 1, most financial advisors are looking for clients who are willing to delegate management of their financial affairs. However, as Stanley and Danko revealed, most millionaires make their own investment decisions. They employ the expertise of legal and tax professionals only when necessary, and few delegate management of their personal finances.

"According to a recent survey by Forrester Research, 35% of all investors are "delegators," which means they choose to put their money in the hands of a professional.[10] Another 55% are "validators" who want to control their own finances, but occasionally need an advisor's guidance." The remaining 10% are known as "do-it-yourselfers," but many do-it-yourselfers will also seek validation when needed.

A vice-president of Schwab AdvisorSource once stated:

> *"Do-it-yourselfers have no desire to seek investment advice. They like being in control. Delegators are people who want help managing their portfolios, and are willing to give someone else discretionary control. Validators fall somewhere in between do-it-yourselfers and delegators. They kind of know what they are doing, but feel that they could use some outside help, perhaps in the form of a one-time financial planning consultation." Often, "people shift between these categories at different points in their lives."*[11]

In the December 2001 *Cerulli Edge* newsletter, Cerulli Associates reported that the volatility in the stock market was a contributing factor to an increased demand for financial planning among what they define as "mass-affluent" clients. They stated that:

> *"In the bull market of the 1990's, a significant number of investors (many of whom were new to investing) felt confident in their ability to make financial decisions on their own and adopted a self-directed approach. They opened accounts with online brokerage providers and took advantage of online financial planning tools. Evidence*

> *of investor confidence was illustrated by a 1999 survey conducted by the Certified Financial Planner (CFP) Board of Standards in which 33% of upper-income Americans felt confident that they could make financial decisions without professional help. This sentiment helped fuel the online brokerage movement, as online brokerage transactions totaled 82.3 million, accounting for 38% of total equity trades conducted on the NYSE and [the] NASDAQ at its peak in the first quarter of 2000."*[12]

One fact that isn't revealed in these statistics is that the majority of self-directed investors use mutual funds and qualified retirement plans rather than individual stocks to implement their portfolio strategies. So individual investors make up a significantly higher percentage of equity transactions then these statistics indicate. Individual investors also receive little or no guidance from professional financial advisors.

Cerulli Associates went on to report:

> *"In the second quarter of 2000, the Internet bubble burst — leaving investors not only questioning their investment choices but also reevaluating their ability to effectively manage their finances. The CFP predicts the percentage of do-it-yourself investors [will] drop, as the strategy appears to be losing popularity. This is consistent with Cerulli's long-held belief that self-service investing has plateaued and is now eroding. With the stock market continuing its downward spiral through 2000 to 2001, many financial planning firms are reporting a jump in the number of new clients seeking assistance to recover from the recent market downturn and rebuild their savings."*[13]

Cerrulli Associates continued:

> *"Investors are not just looking to diversify their portfolios and limit their exposure to technology stocks; they are* **SEEKING FINANCIAL PLANNING ASSISTANCE.** *Investors increasingly want to work with an advisor to create a plan tailored to help them reach their overall financial goals. This bodes well for advisors with financial planning*

> *EXPERTISE, AS MORE INVESTORS WANT PROFESSIONAL ADVISORS ACROSS A BROAD RANGE OF INVESTMENT TOPICS, INCLUDING STARTING COLLEGE SAVINGS PROGRAMS, MANAGING RETIREMENT PORTFOLIOS, ESTABLISHING ESTATE PLANS, AND PURCHASING APPROPRIATE LIFE INSURANCE POLICIES."*[14]

I find this excerpt from *The Cerulli Edge* newsletter to be thought-provoking, but debatable. The authors have drawn the conclusion that individuals who've had access to low-cost investment execution and who've grown comfortable with implementing their own investment decisions are now permanently scared away from their do-it-yourself strategy. I feel that this is a very narrow viewpoint of the psychology of individual investors.

Do-it-yourselfers have been empowered with information and resources that have enabled them to research and implement their investment strategies at a very reasonable cost. Many of these individuals have also learned some very important lessons over the last few years. Hopefully, they've learned that excesses in the marketplace will eventually be corrected, and that they can't predict the market. Do-it-yourself investors have discovered that they actually do need assistance in determining the appropriate asset allocations and investment strategies to fulfill their financial objectives. However, this doesn't mean that they can't implement those strategies themselves using the low-cost techniques they've discovered over the past few years.

Thus, I argue that the do-it-yourselfer will remain a do-it-yourselfer and the validator will remain a validator. Validators have recognized the need for periodic financial guidance, but they'll continue to implement the recommendations of their advisors themselves. They desire to manage their own investment portfolios. They'll seek the advice of qualified consultants to validate their approaches, strategies and decisions *when they feel it is appropriate*.

As stated in the *Cerulli Edge* article, do-it-yourselfers have recognized the need for professional guidance. Unfortunately, for many of these individuals there are very few palatable options available today for working with professional advisors because (as stated in Chapter 1) the majority of financial advisors want to work with clients who are willing to *delegate* management of their financial affairs to advisors.

The Charles Schwab Story

We can learn a great deal about the psyche of the individual investor by studying the evolution of the discount brokerage powerhouse, Charles Schwab & Company. The cover story of the May 27, 2002 issue of *Barron's* stated:

> *"When Wall Street pros muse about the financial institution of the future, they rarely fail to mention Charles Schwab. Since its founding in 1974, the broker has been at the leading edge of a series of industry transforming changes. Starting with discount commissions in the 'Seventies, the ability to trade different mutual funds in one place in the 'Eighties, and Internet-based trading in the 'Nineties, Schwab seemed to blaze the trail that competitors inevitably followed."*[15]

Charles Schwab founded his company based on a strategy of being different. He wanted to be seen as the "un-broker." His goal was to provide great service without pushing products or making specific investment recommendations. Do-it-yourselfers and many validators now had a broker who would provide them with just what they wanted and nothing more—great execution and service at a low cost.

The bull market of the 1990's saw the addition of Schwab's no-fee OneSource program. Through OneSource, investors could consolidate holdings in a number of outside mutual funds in their Schwab account. New customers arrived in droves, but many of these investors were less sophisticated than the typical Schwab account holders. In response to the needs of its expanding customer base, Schwab has continually added services and tools to assist these less sophisticated investors while at the same time providing higher-end advisory assistance to its traditional clientele.

Schwab has enjoyed continued success in determining marketplace trends and capitalizing on those trends. In just 25 years after its founding, Schwab's market capitalization surpassed that of Merrill Lynch, the long-time industry leader. Daniel Leemon, Schwab's former chief strategy officer, attributed their success to the fact that they have extensive customer research, and he stated that, "Where we're going… is the direction in which our customers are leading us."[16]

Figure 2.1

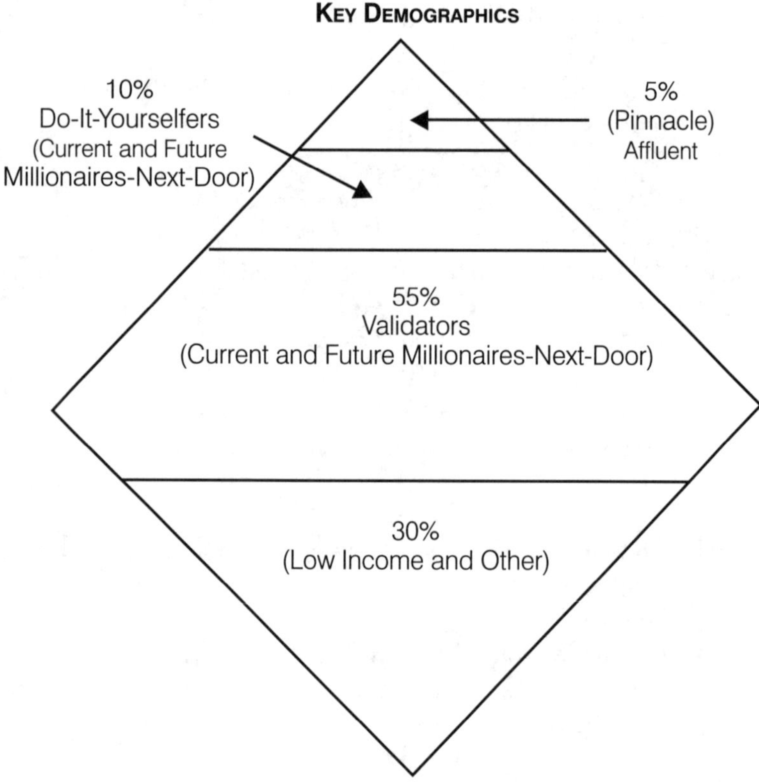

Taking a lesson from Charles Schwab & Company, we as planners should determine what the public wants from financial advisors and then deliver it to them. Remember, there are an estimated 105,000,000 middle income households in the United States. A good number of these "middle Americans" (and even some "millionaire-next-door" types) are "validators"—people who will seek out and pay for financial planning services and advice when needed to ensure they are making sound decisions. Of the 105,000,000 middle income households in the United States, many of these individuals, with your help and continued good financial management, will become the *future* "millionaires next door."

Instead of chasing the top 5% of the population, as most financial planners and advisors are prone to do, why not go where the greatest market opportunities are? Do you want to spend your energies competing in an already crowded marketplace (i.e., the affluent), targeting the same market niche that every other financial advisor in the country is targeting? Or would you prefer to develop a practice that can effectively meet the needs of those Americans who are currently being ignored or underserved by the financial planning community—and help *the rest* of America?

In Chapter 3, we will explore the various financial planning service models now prevalent with Middle Market practitioners, and for which middle Americans these service models are best suited. As we will discover, there are service models that can effectively and profitably meet the needs of virtually all consumers. Then, in Chapter 4, we will provide reasons why you should consider catering to the Middle Market and discuss why you should become an "All-American Planner."

Endnotes

1. Hurley, et al., *The Future of the Financial Advisory Business and the Delivery of Advice to the Semi-Affluent Investor*, pp. 8, 9 (Undiscovered Managers, September 1999).
2. U.S. Department of Health and Human Services, "Annual Update of the HHS Poverty Guidelines," 67 Fed. Reg. 6931 (2-14-02).
3. Thomas Stanley, Ph.D., and William Danko, Ph.D., *The Millionaire Next Door*, p. 13 (Simon & Schuster, 1996).
4. *The Cerulli Edge,* p. 13 (Cerulli Associates, Inc., December 2001).
5. *National Center for Opinion Research* (2000).
6. Stanley and Danko, pp. 8, 9-12, 302.
7. Id. at p. 4-5.
8. Id. at p. 2.
9. Id. at pp. 9, 11, 33, 34.
10. Lewis Braham, "Online Advice: Remote – and Reassuring," *BW Online* (May 28, 2001); http://www.businessweek.com/magazine/content/01_22/b3734024.htm.
11. Robert Klapper, former Vice President of Schwab Advisor Source. Marla Brill, "Do you need a financial advisor," *Brill's Mutual Funds Interactive*; http://www.fundsinteractive.com/marla4.html.
12. *The CerulliEdge* at p. 14.
13. Id.
14. Id.
15. Erin Arvedlund, "Schwab Trades Up: As It Expands With its "Lexus" Line, the Discounter's Own Shares Look Like a Buy" *Barron's*, p. 19 (May 27, 2002).
16. Jeffrey M. Laderman, "Remaking Schwab," *Business Week*, p. 122 (May 25, 1998).

CHAPTER 3

SERVING THE MIDDLE MARKET CLIENT

IT IS CHANGE, CONTINUING CHANGE, INEVITABLE CHANGE, THAT IS THE DOMINANT FACTOR IN SOCIETY TODAY. NO SENSIBLE DECISION CAN BE MADE ANY LONGER WITHOUT TAKING INTO ACCOUNT NOT ONLY THE WORLD AS IT IS, BUT THE WORLD AS IT WILL BE....

– Isaac Asimov

There are many styles, approaches, and practice models used in the financial planning industry today. As consumers' awareness of their need for financial advice has increased and continued to evolve, diverse financial advice delivery models and solutions have been created. All of the delivery models discussed in this chapter are utilized in serving the Middle Market. We will elaborate on the primary advantages and disadvantages of each model with regard to their effectiveness in meeting the needs of Middle Market financial planning clients. We will also explore growing trends in the industry and with respect to consumers.

Practice models are often defined by their compensation structure and the length, depth, and scope of the client engagement. We'll first start with the typical compensation structures and address the length and depth of the client engagement, including the pros and cons of each form of compensation.

The scope of the typical client engagement has been evolving. Early in my career, the overwhelming majority of advice that was rendered centered around retirement planning, investment analysis, portfolio design and insurance needs. While these subjects are still very integral to the typical financial planning engagement, many clients today are also seeking guidance from their advisors in areas such as major purchase and financing decisions, education and career planning, alternative investment strategies, philanthropic activities, major home improvements, and extended family issues just to name a few. Clients' need for guidance covering this broad range of subjects has fueled the growth of delivery models that are flexible enough to accommodate the clients needs, as well as the advisor's desire and ability to profitably meet those needs.

Let's begin by exploring the primary compensation structures, which include: (1) commission-only; (2) fee and commission; (3) fee-offset; and (4) fee-only. For the sake of clarification, I wish to define these compensation structures first. I will then elaborate on the commonalities of the service models and the clientele served by each model. Primary advantages and disadvantages of each model in serving the Middle Market will also be summarized.

Compensation Structures Defined

Commission-Only

Commission-only advisors receive all compensation from the recommendation and implementation of insurance and/or investment products. Sales licenses are required for investment and insurance products. Advisors are regulated by the National Association of Securities Dealers (NASD) because of their brokerage licenses, and the state insurance commissioner due to their insurance licenses.

Fee and Commission (or Fee-Based)

Planners are compensated directly by the client in the form of a fee to perform certain services, such as drafting a financial plan. They may also receive additional compensation from third parties, most commonly investment firms or insurance companies, for recommending and implementing those products. Sales licenses are required. A planner must be an RIA or an RIA Representative with their respective state or with the Securities Exchange Commission (SEC). Advisors are also regulated by the NASD because of their brokerage licenses, and their state's insurance commissioner due to their insurance licenses.

Fee-Offset

Clients are quoted a flat fee for services to be rendered. Advisors may receive compensation from third parties for implementing investment recommendations. Commissions received are applied toward the client's total fee quote. If the quoted fee exceeds the commissions received the client pays the balance of the fee directly to the advisor. Sales licenses are required. The advisor must be an RIA or RIA Representative with their state or the SEC. Advisors are also regulated by the NASD because of their brokerage licenses, and by their state's insurance commissioner due to their insurance licenses.

Fee-Only

The National Association of Personal Financial Advisors (NAPFA) defines "fee-only" as advisors who "are compensated solely by fees paid by their clients and do not accept commissions or compensation from any other source."[1] No sales licenses are required under most circumstances because no new business is provided other than by charging fees only. Broker-dealers may not want these advisors on their roster, and inactive licenses expire within two years. The advisor must be a Registered Investment Advisor (RIA) or a Registered Investment Advisor Representative with their state or with the SEC.

Service Models: Commonalities and Differences

Commission-Only

Decades ago, most financial services professionals were compensated exclusively by commissions generated from the sale of investment and insurance products. However, as discussed in Chapter 1, the financial planning profession is evolving toward more comprehensive and holistic personal financial planning and advice. Much of this subject matter falls outside of the insurance or investment arena. Professionals who offer more holistic or comprehensive advice have found it difficult to work within the constraints of a commission-only compensation structure.

In an excerpt from the *White Paper on the Regulation of Financial Planners*, Jonathan R. Macey states that a financial planner is "someone who prepares individualized analyses of financial position and family situation, who assists in determining economic goals, and who formulates plans for clients to achieve their economic goals. In short, a financial planner develops plans that address all financial aspects of the individual's life."[2] Macey goes on to state that "[t]he breadth and scope of the advice given by financial planners is what distinguishes them from other, more specialized participants in the financial services industry."[3]

Financial services professionals who are compensated on a commission-only basis most effectively are the "specialized participants" to whom Macey refers. I refer to them as specialists. This commission-only advisor's relationship with his or her client is generally transaction-based. When the client has a specific investment, insurance or financing need, the specialist implements appropriate products to fulfill specific needs.

Some commission-only professionals still provide comprehensive financial planning advice, without a fee, but their ranks are shrinking rapidly. The commission-only advisor takes the risk that their recommendations to clients will be implemented through them and they will receive compensations on these sales. If the ideas are not implemented, they are not compensated for their work. John Moshides, a Life and Qualifying Member of the Million Dollar Round Table, told sales trainer Leo Pusateri, president of New York-based Pusateri Consulting and Training, that he had spent an enormous amount of his time in insurance and planning over the years, without ever asking for a fee. "We took our chances and hoped for closure," he said. "Our hit rate is high, but we've never been fully compensated for all the hard work and true value we have been providing to our clients."[4]

Typically, specialists are happy to work with Middle Market clients, who may not meet other advisors' account minimums or requirements as long as they can be fairly compensated (assuming they are competent and capable of rendering the necessary advice). "Specialists" include financial services professionals who sell: life, health, disability and long-term care insurance products; annuities; stocks, bonds, mutual funds, other securities; and mortgages and real estate investments.

These specialists frequently work in tandem with holistic and comprehensive financial planners to assist clients in implementing their financial plans. I view the role of the financial planner as a generalist, orchestrating their clients' financial plan, much like a quarterback orchestrates his team on the football field. The quarterback needs a good team of specialists—running backs, tight ends, and defensive backs—to win the game. Specialists enable the financial planner to be the generalist, while they apply their specialized knowledge to assist clients in implementing specific recommendations provided by their financial planner. These specialized professionals may be municipal bond traders, mortgage brokers, or long-term care insurance agents. Unlike the broad general knowledge that a financial planner must possess, each specialist has specialized knowledge in their area of the financial services industry.

Essentially, there are two types of activities that clients may need or request: planning advice and the implementation of products or services. Both are separate and distinct, and both have value. The planner may do the analysis and plan formulation, and then recommend that the client either:

1. Implement the plan on his or her own;

2. Engage the planner's services to assist with the implementation of the plan; or

3. Work with specialists to implement the plan.

Commonly, a financial planner will work with a client to identify goals and develop a specific plan to meet those goals. At times, the planner may suggest that a client change their federal and state income tax withholding through their employee benefits office at their place of employment. This implementation step may be difficult to delegate; therefore, the client will usually take on this task. Other implementation steps may be more easily delegated to the financial planner, such as implementing the recommended portfolio changes. Certain implementation steps must be delegated, or outsourced, to specialists in and around the financial services industry (e.g., the recommendation to purchase an umbrella liability insurance policy or have estate planning documents drafted).

In practice, I find that a combination of the three implementation tactics is often required. Clients will have to do certain things themselves with your guidance. They may also delegate some responsibilities to you. And generally, there are additional responsibilities that need to be fulfilled by other professionals.

Pros and Cons of the Commission-Only Service Model for the Advisors

There are distinct advantages to working in the commission-only model:

- Most notable is the significant revenue opportunity that can be achieved in a relatively limited amount of time.
- The initial training and licensing required to transact business can be obtained fairly quickly.
- Minimal or no ongoing client service is required with transactional exchanges.
- Many financial services professionals prefer to specialize rather than maintain the broad knowledge base required of comprehensive financial planners.

The disadvantages of the commission-only model include:

- One is not compensated for all of the advice they render.
- Transactionally-compensated financial services professionals must continually market their products or services; thus, a significant amount of time must be devoted to prospecting for new clients on a regular basis.
- There is no compensation paid until a sale is made.
- "Cold calling" is the name of the game, at least initially. Successful sales professionals are gifted with these skills, or they must learn them.
- Most Americans are inherently distrustful of sales people.

For the financial services company representative, one of the biggest obstacles is the last point stated above—that is, most Americans are inherently distrustful of sales people. While most financial services professionals have their clients' best interests at heart, they may not have the capacity to advise clients on all areas of their personal financial situation—and they still have to overcome the negative perception that goes along with being a sales person.

In addition, competition for investment assets and insurance business is at an all-time high. Consumers are bombarded with personal finance articles and advertisements highlighting insurance and investment options with low or no commissions. Other disadvantages are that the Middle Market provides limited opportunity for large initial sales and repeat business, and competition has also caused commission rates to fall.

Consumer finance journalists often see themselves as public defenders and they have drawn attention to actual and potential abuses in our industry. Journalists often make bold statements when writing for the masses. When writing an article on selecting a financial advisor, consumers are told to inquire about education, experience, credentials, and potential conflicts of interest.

Consider this excerpt from an article in the *Washington Post* written by personal finance columnist, Jane Bryant Quinn:

> *"There's nothing wrong with commissions per se. If you get advice, you should expect to pay for it. But commissions present a conflict of interest that you should know about.*
>
> *A commissioned salesperson, for example, may sell you an expensive financial product when there are cheaper ones that would do a better job. Fee-Only people don't face that temptation—although nothing guarantees that they'll give you good advice.*
>
> *Always ask planners what they'll earn from your business, so you'll know what financial services cost. Commissioned salespeople should be willing to say.*

> *If they say you pay nothing, walk away. They do indeed earn something, and it comes from your investment in various ways. If they'll lie about that, who knows what else they'll lie about?"* [5]

As a result of the media's continued educational efforts, journalists and prospective clients are now often more comfortable with an advisor whose compensation has little or nothing to do with the implementation of recommendations.

Fee-and-Commission Based (aka Fee-Based)

As I mentioned before, advisors who are compensated only when they implement specific investment and insurance products may find it difficult to hold themselves out as financial planners and offer holistic or comprehensive financial planning services. They generally limit their advice to subjects for which they can be compensated. However, as Jonathan Macey articulated, "a financial planner develops plans that address *all* financial aspects of the individual's life" (emphasis added).[6]

To ensure that adequate time and energy can be allocated to analyzing and providing recommendations for all aspects of a client's financial life, most advisors now charge fees in addition to receiving commissions.

Adding fee revenue to the compensation structure has not been a painless transition for many practitioners. For many years, clients received financial planning advice and did not pay a separate fee for that advice. The practitioner's compensation was built into the insurance premiums and investment products purchased by clients. Many clients may not have recognized exactly how, or how much, their advisor was being compensated because they did not actually write a check to the advisor. The actual cost was not plainly—or painfully—obvious.

However, with the proliferation of no-load mutual funds, discount brokerage firms, and the direct marketing of insurance products, the financial services industry has changed drastically over the last several years. Financial services companies are now marketing directly to consumers. At the same time, there has been enormous growth in the number of consumer finance articles, publications, newsletter services, and websites providing advice to clients regarding these products and services.

Consequently, consumers are now much more aware of the availability of no-load and low-load insurance and investment products. Traditional commission rates have been falling in response to these market forces. As a result, many financial planning practitioners have added fees to their compensation structures to:

1. offset declining commission rates;

2. enable their businesses to provide a steady level of service and advice; and

3. provide themselves with compensation for all areas of their advisory practice.

Currently, the majority of financial planners are compensated through a combination of fees and commissions. However, fees represent the fastest growing portion of most practitioners' total compensation. The majority of fee revenue is charged in the form of a retainer based on a percentage of assets, which the advisor manages, or net worth. Some fee-and-commission-based financial planners charge a flat fee that is determined by estimating the number of hours required to prepare a financial plan. They also may receive commissions upon the implementation of their clients' financial planning recommendations.

This compensation model can be tailored to suit ongoing supervisory relationships or periodic engagements. An annual retainer fee is best suited for ongoing supervisory relationships, while the hourly or project-based fee is best suited for periodic or limited scope engagements. Of course, in addition to these fees, a fee-and-commission based advisor will also receive commissions on the sale of investment, insurance, or financing products.

Most practitioners prefer to work with clients on an ongoing, long-term basis because these long-term engagements provide a continual revenue stream for the advisor, which also relieves some of the marketing and prospecting burden over time.

With retainer clients, the financial planner is responsible on a continual and ongoing basis to provide oversight and advice to clients regarding their financial lives. This service can be very appropriate for clients wishing or needing to delegate the management of their financial affairs to their advisor. Conversely, most do-it-yourselfers, validators, and middle income clientele (see Chapter 1) are not interested in or willing to pay for the services of a full-time financial planner. Furthermore, most Middle Market consumers do not have enough manageable investment assets to justify the fees charged for continual and ongoing investment supervision.

Some would argue that fulltime, active portfolio management provides little or no financial benefit to the client. How many people actually have such continual and ongoing comprehensive financial planning needs that require them to delegate these responsibilities? A periodic review of a clients' financial situation is a must for maintaining optimal financial health; however full time advice is generally oversold and overpriced, in this authors' opinion.

In the *2004 FPA Financial Performance Study of Financial Advisory Practices*, the accounting firm of Moss Adams revealed that the average revenue for all solo practitioners who completed the survey was $2,468 per client per year and $4,518 for ensemble (multiple professional) practices.[7] These results were compiled from responses from financial advisors regardless of compensation structure. The majority of fee revenue came from assets under management—52% for solos and 67% of ensembles.

Fee-only members of the National Association of Personal Financial Advisors (NAPFA) were also surveyed. Moss Adams discovered that the average revenue for solo practitioners was $4,120 per client, and the average revenue in ensemble (multi-professionals) practices was $6,350 per client. Once again the majority of fee revenue came from assets under management.

Challenges of a Fee-and-Commission Practice

- To be able to accept commissions on the sale of insurance and investment products an advisor must become affiliated with a broker-dealer. Within our industry we have a number of registered representatives and agents who align with captive companies and major wire houses. However, the majority of fee-and-commission-based advisors align themselves with one of the hundreds of independent broker-dealers.

Some of the advantages of going with an independent broker-dealer versus a major warehouse or captive company include: more flexibility in the products and services offered to clients; and more autonomy, while still having the back office, due diligence, compliance, technological, and marketing support provided by a broker-dealer. But these services don't come cheap. Registered representatives share a portion of all commission revenue generated (often 10-20%) and typically a portion (often 10%) of all fee revenue generated in their work as a financial planner affiliated with a broker-dealer. The only rationale I have been given as to why broker dealers charge for activities of their reps that they are not involved with is due to the potential liability and supervisory responsibility. Do the math! Will you receive thousands of dollars per year in benefits and services from your broker-dealer? If not, consider your alternatives. You could change broker-dealers and move to a firm more accommodating to the way you do business. Or you could opt to drop your broker-dealer affiliation altogether. More on that later in this chapter.

Not only do these advisors share a substantial portion of their revenues with the broker-dealer with whom they are affiliated, but they also are under the regulatory jurisdiction of the NASD, which adds an additional layer of compliance regulation (which basically boils down to a lot of time spent doing the required paperwork to maintain compliance). Although you may be a gifted communicator and a skilled professional advisor, if you want to communicate to more than one person at a time, speak with the press, or deliver a workshop in a community, you are required to submit this material to your compliance/legal department, in advance, for their review and blessing. Many advisors who leave the jurisdiction of the NASD are pleasantly surprised to discover that their state or SEC compliance requirements merely require that they use good professional judgment, don't make false or misleading statements, or use client testimonials. Other than that, you are the professional—you be the judge. What a liberating concept!

- The majority of independent practitioners, charging both fees and commissions, seek long term contractual engagements with their clients. They typically offer this service on an annual basis. Clients retain the advisor for one year to provide them with financial planning and investment management services for a predetermined price. It often takes years for an advisor to establish and manage a profitable retainer-based practice. The labor involved in providing comprehensive financial planning and investment advisory services on an ongoing basis dictates that a typical financial planner may only be able to effectively serve 50-100 clients. These clients must be delegators, with needs that will allow the advisor to generate annual revenues averaging between $2,500 and $5,000. The survey respondents of the 2004 FPA *Financial Performance Study of Financial Advisory Practices* indicated that approximately 40% of gross revenues went toward overhead expenses.[8] This is unchanged from the 2001 survey.

- The overwhelming majority of fee-and-commission-based financial advisors offer, or exclusively provide, their services on an annual retainer basis. The advisor working on retainer must be ready, willing, and able to assist clients on a continual and ongoing basis. Some of my colleagues pride themselves on being available to their clients 24 hours a day, 7 days a week. Not me! I have a firm belief that there is no such thing as a *financial planning* emergency. However, I do believe that there are a lot of *lack of planning* emergencies. If a client seeks out and follows the advice of a competent advisor they will plan ahead for all of the desired, expected, and probable things that can and do come up in our lives. I admit that there are those rare occasions where something occurs that we did not plan for and, therefore, did not prepare for. However, identifying the most probable occurrences and the unbearable risks, we help our clients prepare through proper financial planning for those events. I don't want to be put in the role of financial fire fighter. Planning implies thought and action taken in advance of a need. Given my belief that there is no such thing as a financial planning emergency, clients did not have access to me 24 hours per day, 7 days a week—and everything has worked out just fine.

- Providing retainer services can put substantial pressure on the advisor when several clients need the advisor's attention at the same time. The advantages of continual and ongoing revenue can, at times, be outweighed by the continual and ongoing responsibilities of servicing retainer clients. As a result, most practitioners offering retainer services have found it necessary to find, hire, employ, train, and manage support staff.

- Many consumers are reluctant to enter into long-term contractual arrangements for financial planning services. Their reluctance might be due to unfamiliarity with, or distrust of, the advisor and/or possibly benefits of financial planning. They might question the value of professional financial advice. Their reluctance might be the result of the long-term contract itself. Some people are "tire kickers" – that is, they want to have professional experience with the advisor before turning over control of their investment portfolios to a planner. Others want periodic or as-needed advice, and they'll never be interested in turning over control or entering into a retainer arrangement.

Ongoing or Project-Based Services

All consumers have questions about their personal finances at one time or another. For delegators who are able to afford and justify the expense of a full-time financial advisor, there are those practitioners who offer ongoing retainer engagements. However, for the multitude of Middle Market consumers who are not the target clients for the retainer model, there are advisors who offer their services on a periodic or as-needed basis.

Few financial planners limit their practices to periodic or as-needed advice; therefore, they must balance the demands and responsibilities of managing retainer engagements while appropriately servicing their periodic or project-based engagements. I advocate using *either* the retainer service model *or* the as-needed service model, rather then trying to provide both. The clients served, the services provided, the marketing functions, and the administrative responsibilities can be unique to each model. In my experience, solo practitioners who focus on working with clients exclusively on a retainer or a project basis will be most efficient and profitable. The dual service offering is more likely to be successful in larger practices employing multiple professional advisors and a support staff.

The project-based advisor may enter into 100 or more engagements per year. I refer to these projects as "engagements" rather than "clients" because, over time, the practitioner will be re-engaged to provide services to clients they have worked for in the past. Services are provided on an as-needed basis rather than on a continual and ongoing basis. Clients are responsible for contacting the advisor with questions or service issues for which they need the advisor's guidance. However, it is highly recommended that clients meet with their advisors periodically for a "check up" to maintain their financial health, just as individuals should get a regular physical and dental check up to maintain their physical and dental health.

Project-based advisors do not need to require minimum revenues per engagement; this greatly expands their prospective client base. However, given that no minimum revenue per client is required, the advisor must generate a significant volume of engagements each and every year. Initially, the marketing activities required to develop this practice model will be substantial. However, referrals are also much more plentiful for the project-based advisor then the retainer-based advisor. Established project-based financial planning practitioners receive the majority of their new business by referrals from existing clients, and word of mouth in general. Because the project-based advisor has worked with substantially more people as clients then the retainer-based advisor, they have more potential referral sources.

I have also discovered that clients of retainer-based advisors may be reluctant to refer their advisor to others. This reluctance may be a result of the minimum fees imposed by the advisor. Clients may be concerned that those whom they would refer may not qualify for, need, or elect to pay for the services they themselves deem appropriate and justified. A few clients might be concerned that they could offend someone by even suggesting that they need a full-time financial advisor.

Again, the media has played a large part in increasing consumer awareness of the costs associated with employing a full-time financial advisor and paying for ongoing services. Consider this excerpt from an article in the *Wall Street Journal* by popular personal finance columnist and author, Jonathan Clements entitled, "Some Advice Worth Paying For: Most Planners Cost Too Much."

> *"You need a hand, but you don't want to pay an arm and a leg.*
>
> *The bull market of the 1990s gave many folks the confidence to invest on their own. Now that confidence has collapsed*

> *ALONG WITH SHARE PRICES, BATTERED INVESTORS ARE LOOKING FOR HELP.*
>
> *BUT EVEN IF YOU HIRE A TALENTED ADVISOR, YOU COULD DO MORE HARM THAN GOOD, BECAUSE THE COST OF THE ADVISOR MAY OFFSET ANY IMPROVEMENT IN YOUR PORTFOLIO'S PERFORMANCE.*
>
> *INDEED, IF YOU'RE GOING TO USE AN ADVISOR AND STILL EARN HEALTHY GAINS, I BELIEVE YOU NEED TO STICK WITH ONE OF THE LOW-COST ALTERNATIVES. TRUE, YOU MAY MISS OUT ON THE HEAVY-DUTY HANDHOLDING THAT TRADITIONAL ADVISORS OFFER. BUT GIVEN THE COST SAVINGS, THAT SEEMS LIKE A SMALL PRICE TO PAY."*[9]

Mr. Clements then goes on to list several low-cost options for obtaining financial planning services and/or investment management and advice.

In general, and as a tie-in to Mr. Clements' thoughts, I believe that the project-based advisor incurs less resistance securing engagements and referrals due to the fact that this type of advisor requires less commitment on the part of the client. A consumer can hire the advisor for a limited engagement and, if satisfied, they can re-engage him or her for additional services as needed. In a project-based scenario, the client does not need to feel that he or she is captive to the advisor's services. It's like visiting the dentist. If the dentist does a good job and the client has grown to like and trust him, the client will return periodically and re-engage his services. Clients who are happy with the service they have received will tell their friends about the professionals on their service team.

Project-based advisors are able to tailor their services to the specific, immediate needs of the client. They cater to beginners, middle income individuals, do-it-yourselfers, and validators desiring periodic, as-needed advice.

Most practitioners embracing this compensation and service model provide specific investment advice, but few of them manage money. This may appeal to the consumer who is either unwilling, or reluctant, to delegate the management of their investment portfolio.

However, fee-and-commission-based advisors, regardless of whether they work under a retainer or on a project-basis, are still receiving a portion of their compensation from commissions. Thus, they must still overcome the inherent distrust many consumers have of the advisor whose compensation is directly impacted by implementation decisions.

Pros and Cons of Broker-Dealer Affiliations

Commission-and-fee-based advisors are typically independent financial services entrepreneurs who affiliate with independent broker-dealers (e.g., Financial Network Investment Corporation, Linsco/Private Ledger, Raymond James Financial Securities, Investor's Capital, or Securities America) for back office and corporate level support such as:

- securities and insurance analysis/recommendations;
- training and conferences;
- marketing support and ideas; and
- securities, custody, and transaction clearing services.

These independent, fee-and-commission-based advisors operate their own practices. In order to provide fee-based services to their clients, they need to be registered as their own investment advisory firms with their state's Department of Corporations or the Securities and Exchange Commission (SEC). (Alternatively, they may be required to register as investment advisors through their broker-dealers and their broker-dealers' SEC registration, depending on their broker-dealers' rules.)

In order to offer their clients a range of insurance, securities, and investment vehicles and accept the corresponding commissions, these fee-and-commission-based advisors must also pass various securities licensing examinations and become "registered representatives" of their broker/dealer. The broker-dealer screens and approves for sale a host of products (typically, there are ample choices, but not the whole range of the marketplace). The broker-dealer commonly will require a sales or production minimum that must be satisfied to maintain registered representative status.

Once the client has purchased the recommended product, the planner's commissions are debited from the client's total investment or insurance premium. The investment or insurance company pays the commission to the broker-dealer, who then passes down a portion of the commission to the registered representative. The percentage of the commission and/or fee that the broker-dealer pays to their registered representatives is called a "payout." Securities and insurance transactions clear trades through third-party resources, such as Pershing, which may provide additional reporting and online account viewing services. (The third-party resource is chosen and approved by the broker-dealer.)

Because broker-dealers are exposed to liability for the communications and activities of their registered representative, these advisors are required to run all of their advertising, marketing materials, and client communications through their broker-dealer's compliance department for review, comment, and approval. Most broker-dealers also require advisors to pay a portion (commonly 10%) of their fee revenue back to the broker-dealer for supervisory expenses. There are branch office inspections by the broker-dealer's compliance department, in addition to any other inspections and compliance audits that proceed from routine or other triggers from the SEC or the state's Department of Corporations.

Clearly, the requirements for being a registered representative of a broker-dealer include both advantages (e.g., back office support, marketing assistance, compliance supervision) and disadvantages (e.g., corporate level rules, sales/production quotas, "selling away" conflicts, burdensome compliance rules, payout rates on product implementation, and fee revenue sharing). These are the trade-offs that exist if the advisor wishes to provide both independent, fee-based services and to accept commissions when his recommendations are implemented.

Fee-Offset

In theory, this compensation structure seems like the best of all worlds. The commissions received upon the implementation of investment advice are applied toward the total fee for all services rendered. However, the apparent simplicity of this model breaks down when you get into the details. It may be one of the most equitable compensation structures, but it can also be very difficult to explain to clients. Commissions received from the sale of insurance products may not be "rebated" to the client. Exact "payouts" (commission received by the advisor) on many investment products cannot be determined in advance. Therefore, upon the initial engagement, the client does not know the amount for which they might have to write a check.

The few financial planners who work on a fee-offset-basis generally work with clients on a retainer basis when managing money. They may also provide project, or as-needed, advice on a very limited basis.

As explained above in the fee-and-commission-based section, these individuals are usually independent financial services professionals on the financial planning side of their business, and registered representatives with one of the independent broker-dealers on the product implementation side of their business.

The major disadvantage of this business model (in addition to needing to overcome potential objections from clients concerning the acceptance of commissions) is that it is a fairly complex compensation structure that may be difficult to explain to clients.

Fee-Only

There are as many different ways to determine a fee as there are ways to receive a commission. Planners working under the "fee-only" model may employ a formula approach, such as 1% of assets under management, 0.75% of net worth, 2% of income, or any combination of the above. Commonly, fee schedules decline as assets, net worth, or income rises. Occasionally, fee schedules decrease, and then level off over time to represent the additional work involved in the early years of the relationship.

Other practitioners provide their services for a flat-fee that is determined based on the anticipated time involved and complexity of the case. These are the most common types of fee structures utilized by those offering retainer services on a fee-only basis.

Determining the appropriate fee for services to be rendered over time can be quite challenging. No one formula will be equitable for all clients. However, fee schedules do have their advantages. During the initial meeting with a prospective client, the practitioner will have access to the information required to plug into the formula and quote a fee. The quoted fee may or may not be representative of the complexity of the client's situation or the amount of time required to prepare the plan. The advantage is the simplicity of coming up with a number/quote because it's a formula and the planner has the variables that go into the calculation.

The fee-only approach has earned praise from the American Association of Retired Persons (AARP), the Consumer Federation of America, and leading journalists, all of whom regard the fee-only structure as being good for consumers. Quotes from journalists posted on NAPFA's web site[10] include:

> *"Financial Planners who take commissions have a built-in conflict of interest...even with disclosure, my choice would be a Fee-Only planner."*
>
> **Jane Bryant Quinn, *Newsweek***

> *"Start with the general practitioner...a Financial Planner (whose) compensation should be from fees alone."*
>
> ***Money***

> *"The most important matter is how the planner is compensated. Hire the planner who...has no financial stake in (your) investments."*
>
> ***Forbes***

> *"Think of financial planners as money consultants. Their job is to look out for your money's best interests, not to sell you stuff. You should pay a planner for her time, either an hourly rate or a flat fee. They are called Fee-Only planners, and they have no financial incentive to recommend one investment over another."*
>
> **Barbara Loos, author of *I Haven't Saved a Dime, Now What?!***

Fee-only planners pride themselves on minimizing conflicts of interest regarding compensation. However, opponents of the fee-only method of compensation argue that basing one's fee on the percentage of assets under management will motivate the advisor to take control over as many of the client's assets as possible. For instance, a planner could face the dilemma of providing objective advice regarding the merits of funding a Section 529 college savings plan or paying off one's mortgage with investment assets. This decision will impact the advisor's compensation just as much as the advisor who is compensated by commissions upon the sale of an investment or insurance product.

While the media has been a big proponent of fee-only planning in recent years, they have also voiced their concerns about the value of assets under management scenario. Consider these excerpts from respected consumer journalists:

> *"For years, fee-only financial planners have disparaged commission-charging brokers and planners. Their argument: Commissions give advisors an incentive to trade clients' accounts and to recommend those products that pay the fattest commissions.*
>
> *But as much as I agree with fee-only financial planners, these folks have a problem of their own. They are just way too expensive. Fee-only advisors typically snag 1% of a client's account each year, equal to $10,000 on a $1 million portfolio.*
>
> *Moreover, these advisors often recommend mutual funds, which might charge 1% in annual expenses, bringing the total cost to 2% a year. Result? If your pre-cost annual return is 8%, you will lose a quarter of your gain to investment costs."*[11]
>
> **Jonathan Clements, *Wall Street Journal***

> *"No-commission advice is a good idea, but it's possible to overpay a fee, too. Many planners charge 1 percent of the value of your assets a year: $5,000 a year on a $500,000 portfolio, for example. If all you are getting is asset allocation, ...1 percent is pretty darned pricey."*[12]
>
> **Linda Stern, *Newsweek***

I have yet another concern with respect to basing fees on a percentage of assets under management. If we tie our fees to investment portfolios, we are sending the message to clients that we are money managers instead of financial planners. Comprehensive financial planners must have knowledge of all subject matter relating to personal finance. Many financial planners don't have the time or expertise to successfully compete against professional money management firms with regard to the management of investment portfolios.

The majority of financial advisors who provide asset management services also perform labor-intensive portfolio accounting functions for their clients. They often produce quarterly investment portfolio performance reports. Along with these performance reports, advisors include their quarterly invoice. Quarter after quarter clients receive the message that they are paying for investment advice, rather than for financial planning services. As financial planners, we educate our clients that our objective is to assist them in achieving their financial goals over the long term. Yet quarter after quarter, we focus their attention on the short-term performance of their investment portfolios.

Fee-Only, Hourly or Flat-Fee

Some fee-only financial planners charge a flat fee for a specific project to be preformed. Others charge by the hour. Most hourly planners provide clients with an estimated fee range when quoting fees. Project-based and hourly fee models can provide a very equitable engagement for both the client and the advisor. However, the practitioner must have experience and full knowledge of the scope of the project in order to accurately estimate the amount of time required to complete the project. Practitioners new to hourly billing often underquote because they do not adequately estimate the complexity of the case or the amount of time that will be involved. On the other hand, the engagement rate for new practitioners is often very high, and this provides them with a lot of experience. Experience is, of course, how we all learn and grow. Presuming the advisor accurately tracks and monitors her time, she will become proficient at estimating and quoting fees under the hourly model.

In recent years, the media has been advocating fee-only *hourly* planning as a cost-effective option for the Middle Market and do-it-yourselfers. Consider these article excerpts:

> *"...A NEW BREED OF PLANNER OFFERS SOPHISTICATED, À LA CARTE ADVICE AT REASONABLE HOURLY RATES, ALLOWING EVEN NEW INVESTORS THE OPTION OF LOW-COST ANSWERS TO SPECIFIC QUESTIONS."*[13]
>
> **Mary Rowland, *MSN Money Central***

"I THINK HOURLY PLANNERS MAKES A LOT OF SENSE FOR BEGINNERS AND OTHERS WHO CAN'T AFFORD THE UP-FRONT COST OF A COMPLETE PLAN, AS WELL AS FOR DO-IT-YOURSELFERS AND OTHERS WHO WANT TO GET A FINANCIAL EDUCATION."[14]

Mary Rowland, *Bloomberg Wealth Manager*

"[F]INANCIAL ADVISORS ARE A QUIRKY BUNCH, AND THEIR INVESTMENT RECOMMENDATIONS TEND TO REFLECT HOW THEY'RE COMPENSATED, WHAT THEIR BACKGROUND IS AND WHAT SORT OF A COMPANY THEY WORK FOR. ... I WOULD SHY AWAY FROM USING COMMISSIONS TO COMPENSATE A BROKER OR PLANNER. ... MANY BROKERAGE FIRMS AND FINANCIAL PLANNERS WILL INSTEAD MANAGE A CLIENT'S ACCOUNT FOR AN ANNUAL FEE, EQUAL TO MAYBE 1% OF THE ACCOUNT'S VALUE. ... IF YOU PAY A PERCENTAGE OF ASSETS, YOUR ADVISOR NO LONGER HAS AN INCENTIVE TO CHURN YOUR ACCOUNT OR PUT YOU IN INVESTMENTS THAT GENERATE THE HIGHEST COMMISSIONS. THESE FEE ARRANGEMENTS, HOWEVER, DON'T ELIMINATE ALL CONFLICTS OF INTERESTS. ... IF ADVISORS CHARGE A PERCENTAGE OF ASSETS, THEY CAN SEE THEIR INCOME SLASHED IF CLIENTS MOVE MONEY INTO 529 COLLEGE-SAVINGS PLANS OR BUY AN IMMEDIATE ANNUITY. ... WITH AN HOURLY FEE, YOU ELIMINATE VIRTUALLY ALL CONFLICTS OF INTEREST. ... IF YOU CAN FIND AN ADVISOR WHO CHARGES JUST AN HOURLY FEE, THAT MAY BE THE BEST WAY TO GO."[15]

Jonathan Clements, *Wall Street Journal*

"THE PAST DECADE HAS SEEN A BIG PUSH AMONG PLANNERS TO TARGET HIGH-NET-WORTH CLIENTS. THEREFORE, MANY PLANNERS HAVE A MINIMUM ASSET REQUIREMENT – TYPICALLY, $100,000. CONSIDERING THAT U.S. HOUSEHOLDS HAVE A MEDIAN NET WORTH OF $40,000, THAT LEAVES A LOT OF FOLKS IN THE COLD. LUCKILY, MIDDLE CLASS CLIENTS HAVE ALTERNATIVES ...PLANNERS WHO WORK PRIMARILY WITH THE $100,000-AND-UNDER INCOME SET, CHARGING HOURLY FEES FOR PERIODIC ADVICE."[16]

Smart Money

Trends in Fee-Only Planning

All in all, fee-only financial planning is the fastest growing compensation model in the planning profession. The majority of fee-only financial planners also manage money on a continual and ongoing basis for their clients. There are also many fee-only advisors who manage money exclusively.

The FPA indicates that approximately 20% of their members are fee-only advisors. Unfortunately, we have found no statistics on the actual number of fee-only financial planners. NAPFA is the largest group of purely fee-only practitioners in the country, with approximately 1300 members. Their definition of "fee-only" (stated above) drastically limits the number of potential members. One of the criteria for membership in NAPFA is that all compensation must be paid directly by the client. No third party compensation is permitted. Also, to become and remain a NAPFA Registered Financial Advisor one must continue to offer and provide, when appropriate, comprehensive financial planning services to their clients. Therefore, fee-only investment managers who do not offer financial planning services to their clients are not eligible to become a NAPFA Registered Financial Advisor.

The statistics provided by the FPA (indicating that 20% of their members are fee-only) probably include fee-only money managers and fee-based financial planners who offer a fee-only option. Financial planners who offer both a fee-only option and fee-and commission-based services are tailoring their compensation structures in an attempt to satisfy the needs and desires of clients. However, I feel the most significant reason for charging on a fee-only basis is the removal of potential conflicts of interest related to compensation. Therefore, offering fee-only as an *option*, rather than *exclusively*, leads some clients to question the objectivity of the compensation structure as well as the recommendations.

Consumers engage financial planners to help them simplify their financial lives and attain their financial goals. They want trusted advisors who will listen to them, objectively evaluate their situations, and develop affordable and easy to follow financial plans. Some clients need and want to delegate the implementation and monitoring responsibilities of their financial plans and investment portfolios to their advisors. However, many clients, particularly those in the Middle Market, do not have financial situations complex enough to justify paying for this full-time oversight. Unfortunately, there are not nearly enough competent, objective advisors offering their services on a periodic or as-needed basis to meet the demands of the general public.

As stated above, the fastest growing segment of the financial planning industry is fee-only. One indication of public demand for fee-only advice is the volume of consumer inquiries received by the National Association of Personal Financial Advisors (NAPFA). In 2001, NAPFA received almost 30,000 inquiries to their consumer response program. On the other hand, the Financial Planning Association (FPA), with nearly 30,000 members, received only slightly more than NAPFA. Both organizations are very active in public awareness. However, the public appears to be responding much more favorably to NAPFA's message.

As noted earlier, the press also carries the fee-only torch. Over the last few years, the publishers of *Worth*, *Mutual Funds* and *Medical Economics* magazines have produced lists of top financial advisors in the country. The majority of the advisors named in these publications are fee-only planners. I am not implying that these lists are scientifically compiled or in any way exhaustive. However, consumers are obviously getting the message that the majority of the best financial advisors in the country work exclusively on a fee-only basis.

Many fee-only financial planners select this compensation structure for philosophical reasons. Others feel that they have an overwhelming marketing advantage by working on a fee-only basis. We all know outstanding financial advisors who are compensated in many different ways. But, it's becoming apparent that many consumers seeking a financial planner are actively seeking out fee-only advisors. All financial advisors must market their services and themselves. However, most fee-only planners I know report that their marketing activities are minimal or nonexistent; instead, consumers are seeking them out.

I frequently receive phone calls and e-mails from consumers stating they sought advice from a fee-only advisor only to discover that they did not meet the advisor's client profile. Middle Market consumers frequently do not have adequate assets or income, or sufficiently complex financial situations to justify the minimum fees imposed by many fee-only advisors. These consumers have read the same publications discussing the advantages of working with a fee-only advisor as their affluent counterparts. Unfortunately, there are not enough fee-only financial planners offering services on a periodic or as-needed basis to meet the needs of the general public. Herein lies the greatest opportunity for reaching these "untapped Middle Markets."

In order for our industry to truly evolve into the profession of financial planning, I feel we must separate our compensation from the implementation of insurance and investment products and the investment portfolio. Our still-emerging profession must develop practice models that will enable *all* consumers to benefit from professional financial advice.

Middle Market consumers are seeking out fee-only financial planners and this trend will continue. However, most Middle Market consumers do not qualify for, will not justify the costs of, and possibly don't need the services of a full-time financial advisor. But *all* people periodically have questions about their personal finances and need access to competent, objective advisors who can work with them on their terms.

These are the reasons I so strongly advocate the fee-only, hourly, as-needed service model. To me, it is simply the most effective and equitable way to serve people at all levels of income and net worth, while meeting the widest variety of client needs.

Whether or not you choose to serve your clients on a fee-only hourly basis as I advocate, my primary mission in writing in this book is to increase mainstream America's access to competent, objective financial advice that is tailored to meet their specific needs and budgets. I hope to inspire other practitioners to become "All-American Planners." In the following chapters we will explore ways to efficiently—and profitably—serve the Middle Market.

In Chapter 4, we'll explore whether serving the Middle Market and do-it-yourselfers is an appropriate fit for you. I'll also present reasons why more financial planners are choosing to cater to this appreciative, and still virtually untapped, Middle Market. We'll get into "Debunking Myths" regarding serving Middle Market clients in Chapter 5, and later move on to discussing business plans for effectively serving this market in Chapter 13.

Endnotes

1. *Why Select a Fee-Only* Advisor, National Association of Personal Financial Advisors (NAPFA), at: http://www.napfa.org/ConsumerServices/whyfee.htm.

2. Jonathan R. Macey, *White Paper on the Regulation of Financial Planners*, Financial Planning Association, pp. 4-5 (April 2002), *quoting* John P. Moriarty & Curtlan R. McNeilly, *Regulation of Financial Planners*, §§2.01, 2-1 (West Group, Vol. 29 Securities Law Series, 2001).

3. Id.

4. Bill Pusateri, guest columnist, "A Fee-Based Journey – Too Old for New Tricks?," *The Referral Minute* (Bill Cates, Referral Coach International, 2002), at: Bill Cates@ ReferralCoach.com. The Million Dollar Round Table is the premier association for the world's best sales professionals in the life insurance-based financial services business. The Top of the Table designation is reserved for the top producers from the MDRT group.

5. Jane Bryant Quinn, "Don't Get Burned by Fee-Only Planners," *Washington Post* (January 28, 1997) at http://www.washingtonpost.com/wp-srv/business/longterm/quinn/columns/012897.htm.

6. Macey, at p. 5.

7. Moss and Adams, LLP, *2004 FPA Financial Performance Study of Financial Advisory Practices*. pp. 6, 11.

8. Id. at p. 5.

9. Jonathan Clements, "Some Advice Worth Paying For: Most Planners Cost Too Much," *The Wall Street Journal*, p. D1 (August 7, 2002).

10. See http://www.napfa.org/Media/Press/ar_misc.htm; and http://www.napfa.org/ConsumerServices/consumers_brochures.htm.

11. Jonathan Clements, "Some Advice Worth Paying For: Most Planners Cost Too Much," *Wall Street Journal*, p. D1 (August 7, 2002).

12. Linda Stern, "It's Time for a Checkup," *Newsweek*, p. 67 (April 1, 2002), *quoting* NAPFA member, Gary Schatsky.

13. Mary Rowland, "Financial Advice for the Little Guy," MSN Money Central (April 1, 2002), at: http://www.moneycentral.com/content/P20066.asp?.

14. Mary Rowland, *Bloomberg Wealth Manager* (July 3, 2002).

15. Jonathan Clements, "Think Picking Stocks is Tough? Try Selecting a Financial Advisor?" *Wall Street Journal*, p. D1 (May 22, 2002).

16. Nkiru Asika Oluwasanmi, "Ten Things Your Financial Planner Won't Tell You," *Smart Money* (December 18, 2001) at: http://www.smartmoney.com/consumer/index.cfm?story=tenthings-january02.

CHAPTER 4

WHY YOU SHOULD CONSIDER CATERING TO THE MIDDLE MARKET

MY BASIC PRINCIPLE IS THAT YOU DON'T MAKE DECISIONS BECAUSE THEY ARE EASY; YOU DON'T MAKE THEM BECAUSE THEY ARE CHEAP; YOU DON'T MAKE THEM BECAUSE THEY ARE POPULAR; YOU MAKE THEM BECAUSE THEY'RE RIGHT!

– Fr. Theodore Hesburgh, Former President, University of Notre Dame

---

There are tons of reasons why I advocate that more financial planners serve the Middle Market on an hourly, fee-only basis. Strategic business factors include:

- **Vast Opportunity:** The truly untapped opportunities in financial planning today are in the Middle Market. The overwhelming majority of the American population – 70%-88% of all Americans – falls within the Middle Market definition, they need periodic financial advice from a trusted advisor, and they are willing to pay for it. There is no competition - other than a few large financial sales organizations - and we have just discussed the inherent limitations with that compensation model.

- **Ease of Marketing:** Marketing efforts are aided greatly by the fact that the media loves to work with and quote fee-only financial advisors who relate well with and cater to their readers (most of whom are Middle Americans). Referrals from other advisors are another major benefit in structuring your service model to complement, rather than compete. Independent financial advisors who target the affluent delegator type exclusively can become your best allies and referral sources. We are a helping profession. We want to be of assistance, if not personally, to at least be able to refer to another trusted advisor who may be a better fit for the individual.

While the strategic business factors noted above are important, the most important qualities that most practitioners cite as the reasons they serve middle market clientele on an hourly, as-needed, basis is because of the:

- **Professional Satisfaction**: The sense of satisfaction knowing that you have made an enormous contribution to someone's life who might not otherwise have had any comparable options is the greatest honor and responsibility I can imagine of any professional.

- **Personal Satisfaction – Work and Life Balance:** What a concept? After 11 years in financial planning I finally discovered the most effective way for me to design my work life to complement my personal life. I needed more control over my work load, my service offering, delivery methods, and my calendar. Rather then dealing with "financial planning emergencies" or the responsibilities of ongoing supervision I needed to control my work schedule. I wanted to be able to work with anybody I felt I could help, so long as they were willing to pay my hourly rate. If I elected to spend the summer in Alaska on a nature expedition – I could. Once my client projects have been fulfilled, I am done.

  I also thought I wanted to work solo. (I later discovered that was not the case, but I did enjoy the option.) Many independent planners enjoy working solo and possibly from a home office. As I mentioned earlier, I feel that to live up to our fiduciary responsibly, with regard to most effectively serving clients on a continual and ongoing basis, we are well advised to build a business employing other professionals and support staff.

You Can Work With Any Kind of Client and Get Paid For All That You Do

The following are examples of clients in very unique situations who I was able to help and be fairly compensated. The purpose of these examples is to illustrate how charging hourly fees is a viable and very effective way to work with a huge untapped market; mainstream Americans, wealthy validators and do-it-yourselfers.

The first untapped market segment is what I call, "Beginners." All too often we think of beginners as young people just starting out in the accumulation stage of life, but unfortunately, millions of Baby Boomers are in the exact same situation. They have not yet begun to seriously accumulate assets. Yet they fully expect to retire in their 60s.

My ultimate "Beginner" was a 17-year-old son of clients. The young man approached his parents asking for their support in opening an online brokerage trading account. He had $1,800 to invest. His parents made a deal with him that they would support his request if he spent one hour with me first. Of course, his mom and dad paid my $180 fee for this one hour consultation. Within an hour I had this young man convinced that a Roth IRA was the only way to go. And instead of purchasing individual high-tech stocks, he decided to invest in the NASDAQ 100 Index (QQQ). I introduced him to the NASDAQ Heat Maps and he was jazzed. This was one of the most enjoyable engagements I've ever had, and it may just have been the most rewarding $180 that couple will ever spend.

Once again, "Beginners" can be of any age. Although my story was about a 17 year old, it is still an excellent illustration of the kind of things we can do for clients in just one hour. And think about how many questions the average Baby Boomer has regarding their money life. The opportunities are endless. Our biggest challenge is getting people to recognize that they have questions and letting them know how to find professional financial advisors who are willing and able to serve them.

The next untapped market, I'll refer to as those with "Modest Income". One of my earliest engagements in my hourly-only practice involved a Baby Boomer couple. Their situation was not good, but also not complicated. Ten years prior, they bought a seller financed home. At the time they purchased the home these clients had a very poor credit. However, that was 10 years before; their credit had risen to above-average. My initial reaction was that they would be best served by refinancing their mortgage. But, it was more than that. They lived in a very tiny house, with no garage and always longed for a larger, yet modestly priced home, with a garage and workshop, and some acreage. Amazingly, their tiny home in the city was worth considerably more than they knew, and because their current high interest rate mortgage made their monthly payments very high, they could have their new home, with no additional monthly cash outflow. We realigned where their money was going. Instead of to the mortgage holder, their money went into their new "dream home." My services cost these clients approximately $750, and we were done…with that engagement. And I was paid for all of my time.

By far, the largest segment of the untapped market for financial advisors is Middle-Income individuals and couples. I'm a big fan of the book, *The Millionaire Next Door*.[1] The authors illustrate in this book that the majority of millionaires were once middle-income wage earners and most still consider themselves middle-income. It may just be that the middle-income mentality and frugality caused these individuals to become millionaires. My perfect client has always been the millionaire next door, 5 to 20 years before they achieve their millionaire status.

One couple that I worked with since before I opened my hourly-only practice was a middle income couple, with both spouses employed by the government. They were diligent savers, contributed regularly to their TSA accounts, and made annual IRA contributions. They helped put their children through college. They sought my advice to validate what that they were saving enough, in the right places, and if they were missing out on any obvious opportunities. Because the overwhelming majority of their investment assets were in the government-sponsored retirement plans, with very limited investment options, I did not feel that it was prudent for them to hire me to manage their very low maintenance portfolio on an ongoing basis. However, the couple and I both agreed that periodic checkups would be extremely prudent. We scheduled a regular financial checkup for every six months and the couple called me if they had any questions or concerns in the interim. Their initial review cost approximately $1,500. Subsequent checkups typically ran approximately 2 to 3 hours and therefore cost about $360-$540 each. Even phone calls, e-mails, follow-up questions etc. were charged in six minute increments, at my billing rate. All work is billable. Regardless of the subject matter, whether it was running a retirement scenario, providing advice regarding financing a vehicle, or whether to sell their rental property, I was paid for my professional financial advice and time strictly on an hourly basis.

Another large untapped market segment is the "Do- it-Yourselfer" or "Validator." The majority of traditional financial advisors are not interested in working with a prospective client who is only looking for a one-time review or a limited engagement. Traditional advisors generally require, or at least desire, ongoing revenue streams – from all of their clients. Many advisors require comprehensive financial planning, including ongoing portfolio management. Full service – that is what we did at my prior firm. There is nothing at all wrong with that service model. There are clients who absolutely need and can afford that level of service.

However, I find that a lot of people, who could afford that level of service, are not comfortable entering into a long-term contractual obligation, before "trying on" their new advisor. Prospective clients seeking validation have difficulty finding a competent, objective advisor willing to work with them, on their terms.

A glaring example of a wealthy client seeking validation, on their terms, was a couple with combined annual income of over $500,000 and an investment net worth approaching $5 million. This couple called me at my former practice. At that firm we provided comprehensive financial planning and ongoing investment management services, exclusively. Based on our fee schedule their first year annual fee would have calculated to nearly $20,000. These individuals were extremely savvy money managers. They were not about to turn over the control of the investment portfolio to anyone. And they were not about to pay our ongoing annual financial planning fee. They are the epitome of the millionaires next-door. As soon as I started offering my services by the hour, I started seeing these clients at least annually. They built into their budget that they would spend $2,000 a year in financial advisory fees with me. They had done and continue to do the majority of the leg work. Yet they sought out validation for certain issues with which they had little or no experience and for second opinions on what they were doing. One time, they hired me to do a significant cost basis research project. That engagement cost them $1,100. Another time, these savvy, money managers wanted to hire me to run Monte Carlo analysis on their retirement projection. They wanted to know with a high degree of certainty whether or not they would be able to retire as planned. That engagement cost just under $1,000. These clients were more than happy to pay my hourly rate, to have access to a competent, objective advisor, but it had to be on their terms. Hourly, as-needed advice was precisely what they were looking for.

You can see in each of the above examples, I was compensated for all the financial advice I gave, regardless of the subject matter. It did not matter whether the individual had extremely modest resources, whether there was an investment portfolio that I could manage, whether there was a need to secure any insurance or investment products, or whether the client was looking for an ongoing relationship, I was paid.

I would much prefer working with these untapped market segments, as I have described above, and be paid for all of my work, then to chase the same few prospective clients that most every other financial advisor is after. This is a marketing decision as well as a business decision. All professionals must be paid - for all of their work.

Endnotes

1. Stanley, Thomas J. and William D. Danko, *The Millionaire Next Door* (Pocket 1998).

CHAPTER 5

DEBUNKING THE MYTHS

MY BASIC PRINCIPLE IS THAT YOU DON'T MAKE DECISIONS BECAUSE THEY ARE EASY; YOU DON'T MAKE THEM BECAUSE THEY ARE CHEAP; YOU DON'T MAKE THEM BECAUSE THEY ARE POPULAR; YOU MAKE THEM BECAUSE THEY'RE RIGHT!

– Fr. Theodore Hesburgh, Former President, University of Notre Dame

In the previous chapters, I have highlighted a number of opportunities and benefits in working with the Middle Market on an hourly or project fee only basis. In case your were not sure – I am a huge proponent of the service model I refer to as, "hourly, as-needed." However, because this is far from traditional in financial planning, there are a lot of naysayers out there.

Some of the primary declarations that come to mind follow.

1. "YOU CAN'T MAKE A LIVING."

I will concede that you can make more money, or the same money easier, delivering financial advisory services and being compensated partially or fully by commissions. I also concede that gathering assets under management, or working exclusively with the wealthy, can be a very lucrative way of doing business. We also must admit that this is where the competition is and the multitudes of clients are not.

So, on one end of the spectrum we have a very successful life insurance and annuity salesperson or an owner of a fairly large independent wealth management firm, each making $500,000 a year. These examples represent the "high" earners in our industry.

A Moss Adams survey revealed that the average earnings of all financial services professionals completing the survey earned about $75,000 per year. With fee only planners the number was about $51,000 per year.

So somebody is definitely bringing down the averages. However, *who* you choose to serve need not have much impact on your earning potential compared to *how* you go about running your business.

The following are examples of various financial planning practices structures, that are "making it," while serving the Middle Market on an hourly basis.

Remaining Solo

Ah....the freedom of being truly independent. With that independence comes a lot of responsibilities. We are the rainmaker and the coffee maker; the receptionist and the compliance officer; the financial advisor and the business owner. Many advisors are not cut out for this. One may be a technically excellent advisor, yet a poor manager of time and resources. Successful solo practitioners must become masters in the art of running a small business, as well as providing financial advice.

We all recognize that there are only so many hours in a day. Working solo significantly limits the amount of work that can be produced by solo practitioners, which directly affects the amount of money they can make.

Example Practice:
One Professional
Charging: $240/hour
Billing: 800 hours per year
Gross Revenues: $192,000
Overhead: Minus 1/3
Net: $128,000 to the practitioner

Figure 5.1

REVENUE MODEL FOR HOURLY SOLE PRACTITIONERS

	Avg Hours	Avg Revenues	Year 1	Year 2	Year 3	Full Capacity	Goal
Principal's Compensation			$24,120	$32,160	$48,240	$80,400	**2/3rd**
Overhead/admin (office space, supplies, etc.)			$11,880	$15,840	$23,760	$39,600	**1/3rd**
Total Revenue Needed			$36,000	$48,000	$72,000	$120,000	
Hourly Billing Rate			$150	$150	$150	$150	
Percentage Billable Time			15%	20%	30%	50%	
Working Hours in the Year			1600	1600	1600	1600	
Billable Hours per Year			240	320	480	800	
Engagements:	**Avg Hours**	**Avg Revenues**	**Target Number of Engagements**				**Average # of Meetings per Week**
Initial Engagements	8	$1,200	30	35	48	80	**1.7**
Check Ups	3	$450	0	(apx 50%) 15	(apx 50%) 32.5	(apx 50%) 56.5	**1.2**
Billable Hours:			240	325	481.5	809.5	**2.8**

If you adjust the hourly rate, you get the following results:

@ $180/hour, $96,000 net to practitioner

@ $150/hour, $80,000 net to practitioner

Even at $80,000 per year, I doubt that the majority of America would deny that this is a professional living.

The solo practitioner is a special breed. These are people who recognize that they work best alone. They cherish their independence. Quality of – and balance in – life are phrases commonly expressed by these practitioners working on an hourly or project basis with Middle America. Their calendar controls their workflow. When they are done with a project they are done. No employees to train, manage, pay or keep busy. The solo practitioner places extreme value on this freedom.

The solo practitioner must be disciplined, focused and highly efficient. Consider solo attorneys: What is their hourly rate? What is their overhead? How many hours can they bill in a year? Do people need them? Are they happy? Are they professionals?

Simply Expanding

As a way to free up more time for billable work, and eliminate or minimize the things we do not enjoy or are not efficient at doing, many practitioners are using a combination of some of the following outsourcing techniques. (I have included names of some providers you could consider.)

VIRTUAL STAFF

- Receptionists/Phones/Appointments (AnswerNet, GotoVMail)
- Data Entry/Back Office Administration (Total Office)
- Scanning/Document Management (Total Office)

OTHER OUTSOURSCING

- Website Development and Maintenance (AdvisorSites, Custom E-Advisor Pages)
- Mailings (Total Office)
- Compliance (National Compliance Services, Compliance Advisory Services)
- Computers and Networking (ICCA, Geeks on Call, Geek Squad)
- Accounting (Quicken, QuickBooks)
- Human Resources Management (PayChex, ADP)
- Payroll (PayChex, ADP)
- Employee Benefits (PayChex, ADP, First HSA)
- Portfolio Management (Portfolio Solutions, FTJ FundChoice, FOLIOfn)
- Investment Account Setup (Local Discount Brokerage Reps, Total Office)
- Specialty Advice (NATP – tax, Advisors Intelligence – investments)

EXAMPLE PRACTICE:
One Professional
Charging: $240/hour
By outsourcing, able to bill out 10% more time
Billing: 960 hours per year
Gross revenues: $230,000
Overhead: Minus 1/3rd + $15,000 additional cost
for outsourcing services
Net: $139,000 to the practitioner

If you adjust the hourly rate, you get the following results:

@ $180/hour, $100,000

@$150/hour, $81,000

As you can see, the fixed costs involved with the majority of the outsourcing solutions do not make a huge difference at the lower hourly rates, compared with the solo solution, above. Nevertheless, this simple way to expand your practice is highly attractive to planners. Most of us would love to be able to spend the majority of our day doing what we enjoy and do best. Imagine if you could retain the pleasures of working by and for yourself but not have to do every single thing yourself.

Building a Business

I see the natural progression for many independent financial advisors to start out as a solo practitioner, and as the demand for their services grow, to begin outsourcing certain services. Many of these options were not available when I wrote the first edition of this book. This area of our industry, with technology, is making things possible that we could not possibly imagine just a few years ago.

By outsourcing everything that we can and should, we can focus on what we do best, meeting with clients and providing financial advice. We can focus on billable work – yet everything critical to running our practice gets done.

Regardless of how much we are able to outsource, there is still a limit to how much quality work a solo practitioner can produce over any given period of time. Once you have mastered your workflow processes (more on that later in this book), and have delegated as much as possible to various outsource solution providers, you may find that you have the opportunity to take on substantially more clients than you single-handedly can serve.

The traditional next step for practitioners facing this opportunity is to hire a full-time employee. Some of the things we must keep in mind regarding hiring employees involve the fixed costs, such as additional office space, furniture, equipment, licenses, wages, and benefits. There is also a time demand: interviewing, hiring, training, managing, and supervising employees. However, we must invest this time to glean the benefits employees can provide us.

I recommend the first hire be a paraplanner. Personally, I have never had a secretary or an administrative assistant in my hourly practice. I found that I could hire a paraplanner, for approximately the same wage as an administrative assistant, and the paraplanner could provide entry-level assistance and assist me directly with client work.

I don't mind at all if this paraplanner does not have experience working with another financial planning firm. I do care, however, that this person have an educational background in financial planning, is eligible (and is planning) to sit for the CFP comprehensive examination, and is self-motivated.

I have had very good success hiring top graduates from local area colleges that offer a CFP Board-registered financial planning degree program. These talented young people are looking for opportunities to learn from veteran advisors, but often they are not interested in being the rainmaker at this point in their careers. Given that fact, I have found that there are substantial numbers of talented, motivated, yet inexperienced, college graduates looking for this type of opportunity.

As the paraplanner's skills develop, they require less direct supervision and they begin to take on more and more responsibility. I find that within two years, a talented and motivated paraplanner can begin taking on the role of a staff planner. In time, many staff planners desire to expand their opportunities and develop their own clientele. At that point you may give them the title of "lead planner.'

Paraplanners are paid a modest salary, but staff planners and lead planners are paid strictly based on a portion of their billable hours. This fee-splitting arrangement is traditional with law firms. Staff planners are typically CFP professionals, they have no marketing responsibilities, and they are paid 1/3 of the creditable hours they bill. Lead planners, on the other hand, are CFP professionals, and do have marketing responsibilities. They are paid 2/3 of the creditable hours they bill. This compensation structure works out very well for the business owner. Staff planners and Lead planners do not get paid unless the boss gets paid. And the more the boss makes, the more the Staff and Lead planners make.

The more work we can delegate to competent professional staff, the more work can be completed, and the greater the total revenues of the firm. This leverage has a direct impact on the owners' net income, on the firms' ability to serve more clients, and provides great opportunity to expand and eventually sell the business.

Think attorneys….

Solo attorneys are extremely limited in the amount of work they can complete and the amount of money they can make. A small law firm can be highly effective – providing that small business, entrepreneurial environment, yet utilizing the leveraging quality of professional staff to maximize opportunities to serve and be compensated. Now, imagine a large regional law firm. That is where I see this trend heading for many energetic entrepreneurs.

2. "Clients Won't Pay For It."

Some people won't, that's a fact. But there are plenty of people who will. Middle Market practitioners offering their services for a fee report that consumers do indeed pay for advice. In fact, those practitioners are thriving! Middle Market consumers may be very conscious of *how much* they pay, but do *not* deny the fact that they have to pay. They recognize that there is no "free lunch," and they are willing to pay a professional advisor for expertise and objectivity. The media is making great strides in educating the public.

> *[F]inancial advisers are a quirky bunch, and their investment recommendations tend to reflect how they're compensated, what their background is and what sort of a company they work for. … I would shy away from using commissions to compensate a broker or planner. … Many brokerage firms and financial planners will instead manage a client's account for an annual fee, equal to maybe 1% of the account's value. … If you pay a percentage of assets, your adviser no longer has an incentive to churn your account or put you in investments that generate the highest commissions. These fee arrangements, however, don't eliminate all conflicts of interests. … If advisers charge a percentage of assets, they can see their income slashed if clients move money into*

Figure 5.2

REVENUE MODEL FOR HOURLY MULTI-PROFESSIONAL PRACTITIONER FIRM

	SOLO Year 1	SOLO Year 2	PRINCIPAL + PT PARA Year 3		PRINCIPAL + Year 4	STAFF PLANNER Year 4		TOTAL	
Professional's Compensation	$36,180	$48,240	$86,832		$77,184	$35,640		$112,824	**Principal**
Overhead/admin (office space, supplies, etc.	$17,820	$23,760	$24,768		$20,016	$35,640		$55,656	**Overhead**
Staff Compensation			$18,000	PT Paraplanner	$18,000	$35,640	**	$53,640	**Staff**
Total Revenue Needed	$54,000	$72,000	$129,600		$115,200	$108,000		$223,200	**Revenues**
Hourly Billing Rate	$180	$180	$240		$240	$150	***		
Percentage Billable Time	15%	20%	30%		30%	40%			
Working Hours in the Year	2000	2000	1800		1600	1800			
Billable Hours per Year	300	400	540		480	720			

Engagements	Avg Hours	Avg Revenues		Target Number of Engagements (Year 1)	(Year 2)	(Year 3)	Average # of Meetings per Week	Target # of Engagements (Year 4)		Average # of Meetings per Week	
Initial Engagements	8	$1,440	*	38	43	60	1.3	120		2.5	
Hours Breakdown by Pro:								Division of Hourly Billings			
Initial Engagements								3	5		8
Check-Ups								1.5	1.5		3
Check-Ups	3	$540	*	0	19 (apx 50%)	21.5 (apx 50%)	0.4	80 (C/U apx 50% + limited engmnts)		1.7	
Billable Hours:				304	401	544.5	1.7	480	720	4.2	

* At $180/hr average

** Staff Planners paid 1/3 of their gross billings

*** Weighted average billing rate

> *529 College-Savings Plans or buy an immediate annuity. ... With an hourly fee, you eliminate virtually all conflicts of interest. ... If you can find an advisor who charges just an hourly fee, that may be the best way to go.*[1]

3. "We Won't be Able to be Compensated for the Value We Provide."

Frequently, the most valuable services planners provide to clients are intangible. We confirm whether clients are on track to achieve their objectives and we validate and improve upon their strategies and approaches. We help make whatever adjustments are necessary along the way. How can we put a dollar figure on the intangible values we provide?

I use the example of a visit to the doctor's office. Should you pay more for an office visit that reveals a life threatening illness? If so, how do you place a value on it? Of what value is an office visit to a patient who discovers they do not have a life threatening illness, when they couldn't sleep for days worrying they might have something seriously wrong with them?

In my opinion determining the appropriate value for the broad range of services we provide is nearly impossible. We can adjust the fee we charge for a specific project, based on complexity as well as time involved. I charged for my time, energy, and wisdom – that is easy to communicate and it is easy to understand. Yes, many advisors I know (myself included) have, and continue to, under price their services.

This "deal" we offer to our clients must be a win-win proposition. However, too many practitioners, whether due to lack of confidence or an overwhelming desire to help clients (even if it kills them) drastically under charge for their services. We have this subconscious drive to make certain that if someone has to get the "short end of the stick," it is definitely not going to be one of our clients. If the client cannot "comfortably afford" your services, consider prioritizing the services and delivering only those services critical at the current time. Do not do all the work that would be nice to provide; if the client can't or won't value your services and advise and choose to pay for it in the first sitting.

Get your hourly rate right in the beginning, raise it every couple of years and bill for all of your work with and for your clients. We may never be fully compensated for the value we provide, but we will be fairly compensated.

(See Figure 5.3 at the end of this chapter for a copy of my "Client Service Agreement – Hourly Engagement" form.)

4. "Implementation Won't Get Done."

The most enjoyable part of my job is working *with* clients and providing *advice*. The thing I least liked about some of my previous roles in financial planning was all the paperwork (filling out forms, transferring money, etc.).

I still provided specific advice and recommendations, as well as step-by-step instructions so that clients could implement those recommendations on their own. In rare circumstances, we would assist special needs clients with certain stages of the implementation process (such as an elderly client who needed assistance in securing a bond portfolio, or transferring or re-titling assets; or clients who are unable or unwilling to complete the implementation steps themselves).

An important key to success for hourly, as-needed practitioners is to increase the percentage of billable hours. You can't bill a client accurately if you don't properly estimate the time involved when you give them your fee quote. It is common to underestimate the amount of time it takes to carry out various implementation steps (primarily because there are so many variables involved). However, if I were to transfer the implementation responsibility to the client, while continuing to serve as their guide or coach, I could continue to do what I do best – provide advice and coaching – and I could bill for it. This drastically reduces my fee to the client, and it allows me to focus on the parts of my job that I love.

Virtually all of my recommendations were implemented – by the clients themselves. Part of the reason for this high success rate was my approach. When clients came to me, I stressed that I would supply them with advice, guidance, and clear instructions on how to implement my recommendations. They knew going into the relationship that they will be responsible for carrying out their plan. Set thorough and appropriate expectations from the beginning: This is what I do – This is what I don't do.

Imagine at your next annual physical your physician says, "you have high blood pressure, high cholesterol, and you need to go on a special diet and start exercising." He writes out prescriptions for your blood pressure and high cholesterol and recommends a specific nutritionist and exercise therapist. You went to the medical expert for advice about your physical well being. You (and your insurance company) paid a considerable amount of money for this analysis and the recommendations. But don't you bet for one minute that your physician is going to lose one moment of sleep worrying about whether you did what he told you to do. You are a grown up. You sought out advice and paid good money for it. If you chose to ignore that advice, it is your prerogative.

What is the difference between us and the physician? We know how things work and what to expect. Clients might have had experience with another financial services person, but many of us work very differently. Planners may assume clients understand how we operate when they don't. We need to make our expectations clear from the first moment we consider working together. (There is more on setting client expectations throughout the balance of this book.)

In my personal experience, the majority of my clients were validators or do-it-yourselfers (see Chapter 1), and they have never worked with another advisor (or at least no one they considered their trusted advisor). They managed their personal finances on their own prior to our meeting, but later realized that it was appropriate (or necessary) to have a professional occasionally review their situation. So, establishing clear and appropriate expectations with most of my clients was very easy. In fact, one of my earliest hourly clients said that she thought that all financial advisors worked like I did – until she tried to find one.

Most of my clients had been managing their personal financial affairs on their own – good, bad, or indifferently until we met. They were looking for guidance, clarity, validation, and great ideas, but they didn't need me to take over the management of their affairs for them. I provided the direction – they provided the leg work.

5. "Don't You Worry About Liability Exposure?"

Due to the fact that most of my engagements were limited in scope, rather than promoted and sold as comprehensive financial planning services and I documented my services specifically on my website, through my marketing materials, FAQ sheet, initial interview, client contract, Form ADV, Part II, presentation materials and notes to my internal file, I feel that I have minimized my liability exposure as much as reasonably possible.

I don't manage money, transfer assets or place investment trades, in all but very rare cases. Handling transfers and transactions are where a lot of mistakes are made. I transferred that responsibility to my client. (I will have more on the specifics of that in the chapter on investments.)

Endnotes

1. Jonathan Clements, "Think Picking Stocks is Tough? Try Selecting a Financial Adviser?" *Wall Street Journal*, p. D1 (May 22, 2002).

Figure 5.3

GARRETT FINANCIAL PLANNING, INC.
CLIENT SERVICE AGREEMENT - HOURLY ENGAGEMENT

Please review this Agreement carefully as it sets forth the understanding between you ("Client") ______________________ and Garrett Financial Planning, Inc. ("GFP") regarding the services GFP will provide you. If you have any questions about the content of this Agreement we should discuss them before you sign this Agreement.

1. **Initial Services**. GFP will provide consultations addressing the specific issue or issues you request as indicated below. GFP will provide you with a detailed financial analysis and recommendations to guide you toward the achievement of your objectives. GFP will limit its analysis to the specific areas indicated below. You understand that information regarding specific issues not revealed to or analyzed by GFP may have a direct impact on the suitability or accuracy of specific recommendations given.

2. **Specific Services Requested**. Please initial below to indicate the specific services you are requesting from GFP:

   ___ Cash flow analysis
   ___ Current portfolio review or analysis
   ___ Portfolio allocation and investment recommendations
   ___ Estate plan review
   ___ Retirement capital needs analysis
   ___ Insurance review
   ___ College education funding
   ___ Income tax planning

   Other services:

   ______ ________________ ______ ________________

   ______ ________________ ______ ________________

   Estimated Fee Range for Services: ______________________

3. **Future Services**. In addition to the specific services requested pursuant to this Agreement, GFP may provide you with financial advisory services in the future upon specific request from you. The scope of such services will be determined at the time such services are requested. Such additional services will be subject to the provisions of this Agreement, including the provisions relating to payment of fees and the limitations on GFP's duties and liabilities.

Figure 5.3 (Cont'd)

4. **Fees**. GFP's fees for advisory services, including future services, will be based primarily on the amount of time expended on your behalf and on the billing rate for each consultant devoting time to this matter. GFP's billing rates are currently $180 per hour for Lead Certified Financial Planners™, $150 for Staff Certified Financial Planners™, and $75 per hour for Paraplanners. These billing rates are subject to change upon written notice to you.

5. **Payment of Fees**. You agree to submit the lesser of $500 or one-half of the low end of the estimated fee range (as indicated in paragraph 2, above) upon signing of this Agreement. The balance of actual fees for initial services provided will be due and payable to GFP immediately upon presentation of recommendations to you. GFP will invoice you for the amount of fees for any future services performed. Payment of such invoices shall be made within twenty (20) days of the date of the invoice.

6. **Client Representations**. You represent to GFP the following and understand and agree that GFP is relying on these representations as an inducement to enter into this Agreement:

   - You agree that you will provide GFP with the necessary information to provide the agreed upon services.

   - You understand that the responsibility for financial decisions is yours and that you are under no obligation to follow, either wholly or in part, any recommendation or suggestion provided by GFP.

   - You understand that GFP obtains information from a wide variety of publicly available sources and cannot guarantee the accuracy of the information or success of the advice which it may provide. The information and recommendations developed by GFP are based on the professional judgment of GFP and the information you provide to GFP. You agree that GFP will not be liable for errors of fact or judgment as long as it acts in good faith; provided, however, that securities laws impose liabilities under certain circumstances on persons who act in good faith, and nothing in this Agreement shall in any way limit or waive any rights you may have under federal or state securities laws.

   - You understand and agree that due to the limited nature of this engagement GFP is under no obligation to contact you to recommend changes to your financial plan or any of the recommendations and advice provided under this Agreement in the future.

Figure 5.3 (Cont'd)

- You understand that all investments involve risks and that some investment decisions will result in losses. You understand that GFP cannot guarantee that your investment objectives will be achieved.
- You understand and agree that, except as otherwise provided herein, GFP will not be liable for any loss incurred as a result of the services provided to you by GFP.
- You understand and agree that GFP performs services for other clients and may make recommendations to those clients that differ from the recommendations made to you. You agree that GFP does not have any obligation to recommend for purchase or sale any security or other asset it may recommend to any other client.

7. **Confidentiality of Information**. GFP will regard any information provided by you as confidential.

8. **Termination**. This Agreement may be terminated at any time upon written notice to either GFP or you. If this Agreement is terminated by either party all fees due at time of termination will be due and payable by you immediately. GFP will immediately refund any unearned, prepaid fees.

9. **Implementation**. Upon the mutual contractual agreement of Client and GFP, GFP will assist with the implementation of investment and other recommendations. The fee quoted in this agreement does not include implementation unless clearly stated under section 2, above. Our services do include whatever specific recommendations and details needed for Client to follow through with recommendations provided under this contract. Should Client wish or need to delegate any implementation to GFP, we will not, under any circumstance, initiate a transaction in any investment account without prior approval of Client.

10. **Multiple Clients**. In the event Client is more than one individual, GFP is authorized to accept the direction of either party and such direction will be binding on all parties.

11. **Commissions**. The Client understands GFP will not receive commissions on transactions that may result from the implementation of the Client's financial plan.

12. **Assignment**. GFP will not assign the Agreement to any other party without your written consent.

Figure 5.3 (Cont'd)

13. **Governing Law.** This Agreement shall be governed by the laws of the State of Kansas.

CLIENT HEREBY ACKNOWLEDGES RECEIPT OF GARRETT FINANCIAL PLANNING'S FORM ADV PART II ON ____________________.

ACCEPTED this ___ of ________, _____ Client________________
(day) (month) (year)

Client________________

____
Signature on behalf of Garrett Financial Planning, Inc.

CHAPTER 6

THE INITIAL CLIENT MEETING

Let's step back just a moment and discuss the initial inquiry (call or meeting) that lead up to the Initial Client Meeting. Most frequently a prospective client would hear about me through a colleague at work or read about me in the local newspaper's personal finance section. They would visit my website or just phone me directly to schedule an initial meeting to explore working together. I call these Get Acquainted meetings.

The goals of a Get Acquainted meeting are to:

- get acquainted with the prospective client and they with you—Hopefully the majority of information they need to know about you, your services, etc. has already been obtained by the prospective client from your website before this meeting.

- assess the scope of services needed—What work needs to be performed? What work must be performed now? There generally is a big difference and helping clients determine what work must be performed now – in our opinion as professionals – is one of the keys to being able to successfully work with the Middle Market.

- determine what information will be needed—What questionnaires do we need clients to complete? What data do we need from them or others to enable us to do the job we are being hired to do?

- when can you get the work done?—Based on your workflow calendar, when can you complete and deliver the final work product to the client?

- and how much it will cost?

    - My estimation, based on experience, of the time it will take me to review data, run my analyses, determine and then draft my conclusions and recommendations, and present the findings to the client

        - Multiplied by my hourly rate to arrive at my low end estimate
        - Plus 20% - equals the high end of my estimate.

    - Then I keep track of all billable time. (Every moment working with or for the client) and that will be the actual cost the client will pay – not to exceed the high end of my estimate. The purpose of the fee quote provided as a range is to give the client a very clear idea of what the project will cost, and also the maximum amount it will cost them.

I tried to schedule a Get Acquainted meeting no sooner than 10 to 14 days from the initial inquiry, unless the prospective client had a pressing issue that I could and wanted to accommodate more quickly.

I stress to prospective clients that I want them to check out my website, which is really my mega-brochure about me and the services I offer, and to download a copy of my Confidential Questionnaire. I ask them to complete the questionnaire to the best of their ability and bring it with them to our first meeting. We will spend about 30 minutes going over their questionnaire at that meeting. At the conclusion of that meeting I will be able to tell them what I think they need to do right now, what I will need from them to do the work, when it will be done, and how much it will cost.

The desired outcome of the initial inquiry telephone call is to schedule a Get Acquainted meeting with people you may be able to help. We don't want to, nor can we afford to, spend more than 5 to 10 minutes on the phone with each inquirer. Let your web site tell your whole story. A well done web site can leverage your time at this stage of the client acquisition process tremendously.

And don't think that a relatively short initial telephone contact is a bad thing either. I believe an effective and brief phone conversation at this juncture is appropriate. Regardless of the stage of your career – whether you are just beginning to work with clients on a professional basis, or you have been doing so for years – you need not answer the telephone just because it rings, or talk with someone just because they called.

You are a busy professional working on your business or working in your business at all times. You are very conscientious about your time – since time is literally money. You don't want to have to tell the same story over and over again, about yourself and your services to every potentially interested party. Let your web site tell those stories.

If you design your practice to accommodate the needs of the middle market client, you must leverage your time and energy most efficiently. As a middle market planner you can rest assured that there are very few people that you can not help. Feel confident that a Get Acquainted meeting is warranted, if the prospective client has already been to your website and took the initiative to call you. If they have not yet spent quality time on the website I encourage them to do so.

Hopefully, they will do as suggested and visit your web site to find out: who are you, your background, qualifications, and services provided, how do you package your services, and how much do you charge for those services. If the prospective client discovers this information in advance, through your web site, you will save a lot of time on the phone and during your initial meeting with the prospective clients by not needing to talk about yourself, your philosophies, and your services. Your time with the prospective client should be focused on them, their issues, concerns, goals and needs.

THE GET ACQUAINTED MEETING

At the appointed time, I greet prospective clients in my lobby and escort them into my office for our Get Acquainted meeting. My desk is clear, except for a legal pad and a pencil and pen. In almost every case, prospective clients have brought additional documents with them. This is a very good sign that they are in the market for a financial advisor, and since they are in my office, I have the opportunity to become their trusted advisor – presuming I don't screw it up.

The most common ways I see the "deal" getting "screwed up" is when the advisor pitches a project or engagement that is much larger in scope (and the quoted fee) than the prospective client was prepared for in the initial engagement. Remember, financial planning is a process, not a product. We can not and should not, in most cases, do everything known to CFP® in the initial engagement. The subject matter is too broad for the average American, or wealthy person for that matter, to justify obtaining and paying for every analysis, scenario, and strategy we could perform. We must put our fiduciary hat on and ask ourselves, what is the smartest, most appropriate way I would have these prospective clients allocate their resources to best accomplish what they need and want.

The marketing communications coach of the Garrett Planning Network, Marie Swift, gives the illustration of a comprehensive financial planning as that of a sliced loaf of bread. A comprehensive financial plan is the entire loaf. Some people need and know they need the whole loaf of bread right now and are willing and able to pay for it. The greatest majority of people that you meet with know they need a slice or a hunk of bread right now and maybe additional pieces as time, needs, and cash flow allows. I would love it if all people had a comprehensive financial plan, however they don't. If I can help get them going with any segment of their financial planning, we have made significant progress, and through time, I should have the opportunity to touch each critical subject comprising their comprehensive financial planning needs.

Recognizing that most Americans can't justify or will choose not to pay for a comprehensive financial plan at our initial engagement helps us to "pitch" an initial engagement to which that they can say yes. Often the motivating event that caused them to pick up the phone and call you in the first place is part of the initial engagement. Rarely, is it the only advice needed or warranted however. In every case, all prospective clients go through the same routine and line of questioning regarding the Confidential Questionnaire. This process helps to reveal other important issues and give us an idea of when they should be addressed.

We spend the majority of our first 30 minutes together focusing on page one of my four page Confidential Questionnaire. Page one is all about the client(s), their children and extended family, what they do for a living and/or what they want to do for a living, and what they want to do when they no longer have to make a living.

Page 2 is pretty quick. I want to know who prepares their tax return, what estate planning documents they may have and when those were drafted, and the client(s) responses to some questions about their attitudes and beliefs about money. I don't need to absorb this information during our Get Acquainted meeting, however I do need to address anything that could be construed as a conflicting belief or goal. The final question, "How were your current investment assets selected?" can reveal a tremendous amount. Some responses I've seen include: "by the seat of my pants," "I subscribe to Bob Brinkers' Newsletter," "those are the only investment options in my 401(k)," and "I am a student of the markets."

The third page of the questionnaire starts out by asking about the degree of satisfaction the prospective client has had with various financial services providers, if applicable. I want the prospective client to elaborate on any "1 = Dissatisfied" or "5 = Very Satisfied." I want to make certain that the reason they became dissatisfied with a previous service provider is not because of something that I would also do. For instance, I once asked a lady I met with for a Get Acquainted meeting why she was so dissatisfied with her stock broker. She replied that she was unhappy with him because he never called her. My flag immediately went up, because I didn't proactively call clients, so if that is what she was looking for in her advisor, she would not be pleased with my approach either. We discussed this issue for a few moments. She shared with me that her former broker had promised to call her if she needed to make any changes in her portfolio, but he never called. When she called him he would call her back and explain that he was not recommending any changes at this time. She still wasn't satisfied, because he never proactively called her… even to tell her to do nothing differently. Fortunately, she and I had the opportunity to discuss this issue before it became a problem or misunderstanding for us.

I also find a lot of value in knowing about other financial services providers who many clients really find excellent. I put together a fairly lengthy list of professional referral sources. These are some of

Figure 6.1

Date of Completion: ____________

Garrett Financial Planning, Inc.
Confidential Questionnaire

Client Name (1):	________	**Client Name (2):**	________
Home Address:	________	Home Address:	________
City, State, Zip:	________	City, State, Zip:	________
Home Phone:	________	Home Phone:	________
Work Phone:	________	Work Phone:	________
Fax: (Home or Work)	________	Fax: (Home or Work)	________
E-mail:	________	E-mail:	________
Birthdate:	________	Birthdate:	________

Primary Contact Person during business hours?____________ Contact me by (circle one) E-mail or Phone

Family Members (Please list children and other dependants.)

Name	Relationship	Date of Birth	Dependent	Resides? (City & State)
________	________	__/__/__	**Y N**	________
________	________	__/__/__	**Y N**	________
________	________	__/__/__	**Y N**	________
________	________	__/__/__	**Y N**	________

Client Employer (1):		**Client Employer (2):**	
Title/Job:	________	Title/Job:	________
Number of years with this employer?	________	Number of years with this employer?	________
Anticipated employment changes?	________	Anticipated employment changes?	________
When do you plan to retire?	________	When do you plan to retire?	________
Salary:	________	Salary:	________
Self Employment Income:	________	Self Employment Income:	________
Bonus/Commissions:	________	Bonus/Commissions:	________
Other Earned Income:	________	Other Earned Income:	________
TOTAL (Current Yr) =	________	**TOTAL (Current Yr) =**	________

Figure 6.1 (Cont'd)

Who prepares your tax return?

- ❑ Self
- ❑ Paid Preparer

Name ____________________

Address ____________________

Phone (__) ____-__________

Fax (__) ____-__________

Do you have estate planning documents?
When and in what state were they drafted?

Wills	Y N	____________
Living Trusts	Y N	____________
Power of Attorney	Y N	____________
Living Will	Y N	____________
Other Documents	Y N	____________

How were your current investment assets selected? ____________________

____

____

Indicate which of the following statements summarize your attitudes or beliefs using a scale of 1-5.
(1 being most true and 5 least true)

____ I would rather work longer than reduce my standard of living in retirement.
____ I feel that I/we can reduce our current living expenses to save more for the future if needed.
____ I am more concerned about protecting my assets than about growth.
____ I prefer the ease of mutual funds over individual securities.
____ I am comfortable with investments that promise slow, long-term appreciation and growth.
____ I don't brood over bad investment decisions I've made.
____ I feel comfortable with aggressive growth investments.
____ I don't like surprises.
____ I am optimistic about my financial future.
____ My immediate concern is for income rather than growth opportunities.
____ I am a risk taker.
____ I make investment decisions comfortably and quickly.
____ I like predictability and routine in my daily life.
____ I usually pick the tried and true, the slow, safe but sure investments.
____ I need to focus my investment efforts on building cash reserves.
____ I prefer predictable, steady return on my investments, even if the return is low.

Rate your working relationships with each of the following advisors that apply:

			Satisfaction Rating			
Adviser	Dissatisfied		-	Very Satisfied		Not Applicable
Financial Planner	1	2	3	4	5	X
Broker	1	2	3	4	5	X
Broker	1	2	3	4	5	X
Accountant	1	2	3	4	5	X
Tax Preparer	1	2	3	4	5	X
Attorney	1	2	3	4	5	X
Insurance Agent	1	2	3	4	5	X
Insurance Agent	1	2	3	4	5	X

Figure 6.1 (Cont'd)

Insurance

	Client (1) Coverage/Cost	Client (1) Group	Client (1) Individual	Client (2) Coverage/Cost	Client (2) Group	Client (2) Individual
Health	________	❑	❑	________	❑	❑
Disability	________	❑	❑	________	❑	❑
Disability	________	❑	❑	________	❑	❑
Life	________	❑	❑	________	❑	❑
Life	________	❑	❑	________	❑	❑
Life	________	❑	❑	________	❑	❑
Homeowners	________	❑	❑	________	❑	❑
Auto	________	❑	❑	________	❑	❑
Auto	________	❑	❑	________	❑	❑
Umbrella Liability	________	❑	❑	________	❑	❑
Professional Liability	________	❑	❑	________	❑	❑
Long Term Care	________	❑	❑	________	❑	❑

Have you ever been turned down for Insurance? ❑ Yes ❑ No

Assets

(If you have this information in a format of your own design please feel free to omit this section. Please attach necessary documentation.)

Bank Accounts

Bank Name	Checking [C], Savings [S], or Money [MM]	Ownership	Avg. Balance
________	________	________	$________
________	________	________	$________
________	________	________	$________

CD's

Where Held?	Interest Rate	Maturity Date	Ownership	Apx. Value
________	________%	________	________	$________
________	________%	________	________	$________
________	________%	________	________	$________

Attach a copy of your most current brokerage, mutual fund and retirement statements.

Please list below and estimate a value for any other investment assets not appearing on the list above or the statements provided:

____

____

____

Personal Property

	Estimated Value
Primary Residence	________
Furnishings (Liquidation Value)	________
Vehicle ________	________
Vehicle ________	________
Other ________	________
Other ________	________

Figure 6.1 (Cont'd)

LIABILITIES

Credit Cards	Interest Rate*	Average Monthly Payment	Current Balance
________	____%	$____	$____
________	____%	$____	$____
________	____%	$____	$____
________	____%	$____	$____

*If not paid in full each month

Debts (Residence, Auto, Business, School)	Term	Interest Rate	Payment	Current Balance	Original Balance
________	____	____%	$____	$____	$____
________	____	____%	$____	$____	$____
________	____	____%	$____	$____	$____
________	____	____%	$____	$____	$____

Have you received a copy of your credit report recently? **Yes** **No**

Please comment on the advice you seek.

____

____

____

____

____

____

____

____

____

THESE ITEMS MAY BE NEEDED, SHOULD YOU ENGAGE OUR SERVICES:

- Prior Year Tax Return
- Brokerage Account Statements
- Trust Account Statements
- Retirement Plan Account Statements
- Loan Documents
- Paycheck Stubs
- Mutual Fund Account Statements
- Employee Benefits Booklet
- Legal Documents
- Insurance Policies

If you will be coming to our office for your financial consultation, please bring this completed form with you.

If we will be teleconferencing with you, please (1) keep a copy of your completed form, (2) fax or mail a copy to us at the following address:

Garrett Financial Planning, Inc. • 12700 Johnson Drive • Shawnee, KS. 66216-1643
Phone: (913) 268-1500 • Fax: (913) 268-6195
Email: info@gfponline.com

Visit us on the web at **www.GarrettFinancialPlanning.com**

the specialists I call on or to whom I may refer clients. Many of these specialists were introduced to me by our mutual clients.

The next area of the questionnaire focuses on insurance. It is designed to be ambiguous because I don't want clients to have to go to the trouble of trying to gather every detail I might need to know about their insurance coverages at this stage in our relationship. I'll ask for the declaration pages and/or policies of what I need, when and only if I need it.

At the bottom of page three I ask about bank accounts and CDs. At this point I just need to know if the current balance(s) in back accounts are abnormally high or low and if so, why? This will reveal whether there are excess funds available to redirect toward goals, whether funds need to be replenished after paying taxes or for the annual family vacation, or if the balance currently is typical. If the client tends to maintain a steady balance in the cash accounts and is not building up debt, they are probably living on 100% of their net paychecks. (More on this subject in the next chapter.)

On the final page of the Confidential Questionnaire we cover other investment assets, personal use assets, liabilities, and credit reports. The final question, placed last intentionally, asks the prospective client to "Please comment on the advice you seek." This question is positioned last, after the prospective client has had the opportunity to think through all the other subjects first. Sometimes prospective clients provide a bullet pointed list of items they want to cover, other times their response is very generic, such as, "general financial overview," or "are we on the right track?" I other words, the prospective client is open to my suggestions regarding what is needed at this time.

At this time, I do not need to review a detailed inventory of the investment assets, the intricate details of their insurance coverages, nor their debts, to be able to arrive at an assessment of what services ought to be performed now, what additional data I would need, when I could get the work done, and how much it might cost the client.

During the line of questioning I use while going over the Confidential Questionnaire I will pull out a Data Request form and start marking items that I will be requesting from the client should we decide to work together. After we complete the discussion involving the questionnaire,

I have pitched the scope of services, listed the data needed, and quoted the fee range, I conclude the meeting by attempting to schedule the Presentation meeting. Regardless of whether the prospective client elects to schedule the Presentation meeting at this moment, or needs to talk about it with their spouse or partner and call me back, I move forward in the exact same fashion.

All prospective clients are sent home with a copy of my Data Request form, my client services agreement, valid for 90 days, two copies of my Risk Tolerance questionnaire (if a couple), if I'm providing investment advice, a copy of my Form ADV, Part II.

I target scheduling Presentation meetings with new clients approximately 30 days from the date of our Get Acquainted meeting. This gives the clients about two weeks to get their homework together and gives me two weeks with their data.

Approximately 60% of prospective clients verbally engaged my services at the conclusion of our Get Acquainted meeting. Another 15-25% engaged within six months following that initial meeting.

Figure 6.2

Data Request Form

GARRETT PLANNING NETWORK

Client Name____________________ **Date** ___/___/___

- ❑ Cash Flow Worksheet
- ❑ Credit Card Statement(s)
- ❑ Credit Card Report(s)
- ❑ Social Security Benefit Report(s)
- ❑ Pension Benefits Information ____________________
- ❑ Bank Statement(s) ____________________
- ❑ Brokerage Account Statement(s) ____________________
- ❑ Mutual Fund Account Statement(s) ____________________
- ❑ Retirement Plan Account Statement(s) ____________________
- ❑ Retirement Account Investment Option(s) ____________________
- ❑ Paycheck Stub(s) (with cumulative year to date information) ____________________
- ❑ Employee Benefits Booklet(s) ❑ Specifically ____________________
- ❑ Tax Returns for last ____ years
- ❑ Insurance Policies ❑ *Homeowners* ❑ *LTC* ❑ *Life* ❑ *Umbrella* ❑ *Auto* ❑ *Disability*
- ❑ Declarations Pages ❑ *Homeowners* ❑ *LTC* ❑ *Life* ❑ *Umbrella* ❑ *Auto* ❑ *Disability*
- ❑ Loan Documents ❑ *Home* ❑ *Auto* ❑ *Other* __________
- ❑ Trust Documents ❑ *Client 1* ❑ *Client 2*
- ❑ Wills ❑ *Client 1* ❑ *Client 2*
- ❑ Risk Tolerance Questionnaire
- ❑ Other Questionnaire(s)____________________
- ❑ Service Agreement
- ❑ Other ____________________
- ❑ ____________________
- ❑ ____________________

Return data by:

___/___/200___

Next Appointment:

___/___/200___

Time __________

Location ❑ *Office*

❑ *Teleconference*

❑ *Other*

Figure 6.3

Garrett Financial Planning, Inc.
Client Service Agreement - Hourly Engagement

Please review this Agreement carefully as it sets forth the understanding between you ("Client") ______________________ and Garrett Financial Planning, Inc. ("GFP") regarding the services GFP will provide you. If you have any questions about the content of this Agreement we should discuss them before you sign this Agreement.

1. **Initial Services**. GFP will provide consultations addressing the specific issue or issues you request as indicated below. GFP will provide you with a detailed financial analysis and recommendations to guide you toward the achievement of your objectives. GFP will limit its analysis to the specific areas indicated below. You understand that information regarding specific issues not revealed to or analyzed by GFP may have a direct impact on the suitability or accuracy of specific recommendations given.

2. **Specific Services Requested**. Please initial below to indicate the specific services you are requesting from GFP:

   ___ Cash flow analysis
   ___ Current portfolio review or analysis
   ___ Portfolio allocation and investment recommendations
   ___ Estate plan review
   ___ Retirement capital needs analysis
   ___ Insurance review
   ___ College education funding
   ___ Income tax planning

   Other services:

   _____ ______________ _____ ______________

   _____ ______________ _____ ______________

   Estimated Fee Range for Services: ____________________

3. **Future Services**. In addition to the specific services requested pursuant to this Agreement, GFP may provide you with financial advisory services in the future upon specific request from you. The scope of such services will be determined at the time such services are requested. Such additional services will be subject to the provisions of this Agreement, including the provisions relating to payment of fees and the limitations on GFP's duties and liabilities.

Figure 6.3 (Cont'd)

4. **Fees**. GFP's fees for advisory services, including future services, will be based primarily on the amount of time expended on your behalf and on the billing rate for each consultant devoting time to this matter. GFP's billing rates are currently $180 per hour for Lead Certified Financial Planners™, $150 for Staff Certified Financial Planners™, and $75 per hour for Paraplanners. These billing rates are subject to change upon written notice to you.

5. **Payment of Fees**. You agree to submit the lesser of $500 or one-half of the low end of the estimated fee range (as indicated in paragraph 2, above) upon signing of this Agreement. The balance of actual fees for initial services provided will be due and payable to GFP immediately upon presentation of recommendations to you. GFP will invoice you for the amount of fees for any future services performed. Payment of such invoices shall be made within twenty (20) days of the date of the invoice.

6. **Client Representations**. You represent to GFP the following and understand and agree that GFP is relying on these representations as an inducement to enter into this Agreement:

   - You agree that you will provide GFP with the necessary information to provide the agreed upon services.

   - You understand that the responsibility for financial decisions is yours and that you are under no obligation to follow, either wholly or in part, any recommendation or suggestion provided by GFP.

   - You understand that GFP obtains information from a wide variety of publicly available sources and cannot guarantee the accuracy of the information or success of the advice which it may provide. The information and recommendations developed by GFP are based on the professional judgment of GFP and the information you provide to GFP. You agree that GFP will not be liable for errors of fact or judgment as long as it acts in good faith; provided, however, that securities laws impose liabilities under certain circumstances on persons who act in good faith, and nothing in this Agreement shall in any way limit or waive any rights you may have under federal or state securities laws.

   - You understand and agree that due to the limited nature of this engagement GFP is under no obligation to contact you to recommend changes to your financial plan or any of the recommendations and advice provided under this Agreement in the future.

Figure 6.3 (Cont'd)

- You understand that all investments involve risks and that some investment decisions will result in losses. You understand that GFP cannot guarantee that your investment objectives will be achieved.
- You understand and agree that, except as otherwise provided herein, GFP will not be liable for any loss incurred as a result of the services provided to you by GFP.
- You understand and agree that GFP performs services for other clients and may make recommendations to those clients that differ from the recommendations made to you. You agree that GFP does not have any obligation to recommend for purchase or sale any security or other asset it may recommend to any other client.

7. **Confidentiality of Information**. GFP will regard any information provided by you as confidential.

8. **Termination**. This Agreement may be terminated at any time upon written notice to either GFP or you. If this Agreement is terminated by either party all fees due at time of termination will be due and payable by you immediately. GFP will immediately refund any unearned, prepaid fees.

9. **Implementation**. Upon the mutual contractual agreement of Client and GFP, GFP will assist with the implementation of investment and other recommendations. The fee quoted in this agreement does not include implementation unless clearly stated under section 2, above. Our services do include whatever specific recommendations and details needed for Client to follow through with recommendations provided under this contract. Should Client wish or need to delegate any implementation to GFP, we will not, under any circumstance, initiate a transaction in any investment account without prior approval of Client.

10. **Multiple Clients**. In the event Client is more than one individual, GFP is authorized to accept the direction of either party and such direction will be binding on all parties.

11. **Commissions**. The Client understands GFP will not receive commissions on transactions that may result from the implementation of the Client's financial plan.

12. **Assignment**. GFP will not assign the Agreement to any other party without your written consent.

Figure 6.3 (Cont'd)

13. **Governing Law.** This Agreement shall be governed by the laws of the State of Kansas.

CLIENT HEREBY ACKNOWLEDGES RECEIPT OF GARRETT FINANCIAL PLANNING'S FORM ADV PART II ON ______________________.

ACCEPTED this ___ of ________, _____ Client__________________
(day) (month) (year)

Client__________________

____
Signature on behalf of Garrett Financial Planning, Inc.

Figure 6.4

CLIENT:

JOE AND SARA SAMPLE DATE: 04/01/2007 FEE ESTIMATE

	Time	Total
Cash Flow		
Tax Projections		
Investment Portfolio	2.5	$600.00
Retirement Projections		
Base Case	1.5	$360.00
Scenarios	0.5	$120.00
Specific Goal Funding		
College Planning Projections		
Strategies	0.5	$120.00
Investments		
Insurance		
Life	0.5	$120.00
Disability		
Health		
Long Term Care		
Property & Casualty	0.5	$120.00
Estate Planning		
Summary Report Development	1.0	$240.00
Interactive Session		
Presentation Meeting	2.0	$480.00
Follow-Up		
Meeting	1.0	$240.00
Implementation Assistance		
Notes:	Estimated Total:	$2,400.00

ESTIMATED FEE RANGE (20.0%)
$2,400.00 to $2,880.00

Figure 6.5

EXAMPLE OF AVERAGE TIME SPENT PER TASK

TOPICS	Specific Tasks	Average Time Spent Based on Complexity of Case: Basic	Average	Complex
Cash Flow	Develop Cash Flow Spending Plan	0.50		
Debt Management	Develop Debt Repayment Plan	0.50		
Income Taxes	Income Tax Projection	0.20	0.30	0.50
	Adjust Withholding or Estimated Payments	0.20	0.20	0.30
	Tax Reduction Strategies		0.20	0.50
Education	Calculate Funding Requirements	0.20	0.20	0.20
	Funding Options		0.30	0.50
Retirement Planning	Calculate Base Retirement Projection	0.70	1.20	1.50
	Run Retirement Scenarios	0.20	0.50	1.00
	Distribution Planning		1.00	1.50
Investments	Review Current Portfolio	0.70	2.00	4.00
	Recommend Changes	0.50	1.00	3.00
Insurance	Review Current Coverages	0.30	0.50	1.00
	Run Needs Analyses	0.30	0.30	0.50
	Provide Quotes on Replacement Coverages	0.20	0.20	0.50
Estate Planning	Estate Planning Projections	0.20	0.30	0.50
Meeting Time	Interactive Data Gaithering / Goal Setting			1.50
	Presentation	2.00	2.00	2.00
	TOTAL ESTIMATED HOURS	6.70	10.20	19.00
	X $150 / HOUR	$1,005	$1,530	$2,850

Figure 6.6

RISK TOLERANCE QUESTIONNAIRE

SHOW HOW MUCH YOU AGREE OR DISAGREE WITH EACH OF THE FOLLOWING INVESTMENT STATEMENTS BY MARKING THE APPROPRIATE BOX AT THE END OF EACH SENTENCE.

Statement	DISAGREE			AGREE	
I CAN ACCEPT MINOR FLUCTUATIONS IN MY ACCOUNT VALUE IN EXCHANGE FOR MORE INCOME.	❑	❑	❑	❑	❑
I CAN ACCEPT A SMALL RISK OF LOSS AND SOMEWHAT LARGER FLUCTUATIONS IN MY ACCOUNT VALUE IN EXCHANGE FOR CONSERVATIVE GROWTH OPPORTUNITY AND THE POSSIBILITY OF MORE INCOME.	❑	❑	❑	❑	❑
I CAN ACCEPT A GREATER RISK OF LOSS AND GREATER FLUCTUATIONS IN MY ACCOUNT VALUE IN EXCHANGE FOR MORE AGGRESSIVE GROWTH OPPORTUNITIES.	❑	❑	❑	❑	❑
I CAN ACCEPT THE RISK OF SIGNIFICANT LOSSES AND LARGE FLUCTUATIONS IN MY ACCOUNT VALUE IN EXCHANGE FOR VERY AGGRESSIVE, RAPID GROWTH OPPORTUNITIES.	❑	❑	❑	❑	❑

Figure 6.6 (Con'd)

PLEASE ANSWER BOTH PART 1 AND PART 2 BELOW:

PART 1. FOR EACH OF THE TWO INVESTMENT DECISIONS BELOW, CHECK THE OPTION WITH WHICH YOU ARE MOST COMFORTABLE.

DECISION 1 - CHOOSE BETWEEN

- ❑ A. A SURE GAIN OF $25,000
- ❑ B. A 25% CHANCE OF WINNING $100,000 AND A 75% CHANCE OF WINNING NOTHING.

DECISION 2 - CHOOSE BETWEEN

- ❑ A. A SURE LOSS OF $75,000
- ❑ B. A 75% CHANCE OF LOSING $100,000 AND A 25% CHANCE OF LOSING NOTHING.

PART 2. FOR EACH OF THE TWO INVESTMENT DECISIONS BELOW, CHECK THE OPTION WITH WHICH YOU ARE MOST COMFORTABLE.

DECISION 1 - CHOOSE BETWEEN

- ❑ C. A SURE GAIN OF $250
- ❑ D. A 25% CHANCE OF WINNING $1,000 AND A 75% CHANCE OF WINNING NOTHING.

DECISION 2 - CHOOSE BETWEEN

- ❑ C. A SURE LOSS OF $750
- ❑ D. A 75% CHANCE OF LOSING $1,000 AND A 25% CHANCE OF LOSING NOTHING.

Figure 6.6 (Cont'd)

PLEASE ANSWER THE FOLLOWING QUESTIONS:

FOR YOUR CURRENT INVESTMENTS, WHAT HAS BEEN YOUR ANNUAL RATE OF RETURN? __________

HAVE YOU BEEN SATISFIED WITH THAT RETURN? __________

IF NO, WHY NOT? __________

WHAT PERCENTAGE OF YOUR PORTFOLIO CAN YOU AFFORD TO LOSE OR HOW MUCH MONEY CAN YOU AFFORD TO LOSE IN ANY ONE YEAR?

WHAT ACTION WOULD YOU TAKE IF THE MARKET DROPPED 50% FROM ITS PRESENT VALUE? __________

____

REGARDING YOUR FINANCES, WHAT, IF ANYTHING, DO YOU SPEND THE MOST TIME THINKING ABOUT?

____

____

ARE THERE THINGS IN YOUR FINANCIAL LIFE THAT YOU WISH YOU HAD DONE DIFFERENTLY?

____

____

ARE YOU PLEASED WITH YOUR ABILITY TO MANAGE AND SHELTER YOUR INCOME FROM TAXES?

____

ARE YOU PLEASED WITH THE DIVERSIFICATION AND PERFORMANCE OF YOUR PORTFOLIO?

____

WHAT IS THE BEST AND WORST INVESTMENT DECISION YOU HAVE EVER MADE?

BEST: __________

WORST: __________

ARE THERE ANY INVESTMENTS THAT YOU WILL NOT SELL FOR PERSONAL REASONS?

____

ARE THERE ANY INVESTMENTS THAT YOU WILL NOT BUY FOR SOCIAL REASONS?

____

Chapter 7

Cash Flow and Debt Management

Determining Cash Flow

I find that some of the biggest complaints that we hear from prospective clients is in regards to the amount of initial homework required by many financial planners. This can be a real deal breaker. In a recent consumer article comparing various financial planning providers, one practitioner assigned enough homework that it took the client 13 hours to compile the initial data requested. I don't know about you, but that sounds more painful than drinking a gallon of Go Litely in preparation for a colonoscopy.

If we can't develop ways to minimize this burden on our clients and perspective clients, many of them will continue to procrastinate on getting important financial planning work done. I feel that our primary job as financial advisors is to help empower our clients to make smarter financial decisions. Our job is not to force them to go through excruciating pain pulling together details and records that may not be necessary for us to provide the advice needed. We must focus on ways to minimize unnecessary activities or those that produce minimal benefits for the time, energy, and expense involved – ours' and our clients'. This will increase the likelihood that a prospective client will engage our service, a current client will continue working with us, and it will help to improve our profitability on each engagement.

One of the primary time wasters in this area is the process of determining a client's cash flow needs. We have all heard of many different strategies used in determining where the money goes. Some advisors ask their clients to pour over months of check registers, bank and credit card statements, categorize all expenses, throw out the one time expenditures, and then provide the advisor with a historical average monthly budget. Others provide clients with a detailed questionnaire asking the client to reveal how much they are spending in each and every area listed on the questionnaire. The unfortunate thing is very few Americans have any idea where their money is going. So does this exercise actually provide value for the energy expended? This exercise alone could take the client several hours, if not days, and I argue in most situations this activity produces inaccurate results, and does not help achieve the desired outcome.

I have found that determining cash outflow is usually the most time-consuming and agonizing part of the homework we can assign to a new client. To accurately gauge where their money has gone historically, the clients must be extremely committed to the process and have time to fulfill your request. But that only implies that they have the determination and dedication to complete the homework assignment. It does not necessarily imply that the results of this assignment can be used with any degree of confidence in our planning projections. So why put the clients through the agony of this massive homework assignment, if we don't have confidence in the results?

Clients come to us seeking answers, not homework. In fact, if a prospective client determines that the work involved on their part is too significant, they may decide to just, "skip all that" and not proceed with the engagement. We do need to find ways to ascertain a client's cash flow needs without jeopardizing the engagement.

Too often, I have discovered that "budgets" provided to me for my analysis are, in reality, merely best guesstimates of what clients think their cash flow needs are. In their attempt to be thorough and conservative, we may discover that our clients "say" they plan to spend more in a given month than they actually bring in. People cannot spend more then they take in unless they are depleting assets or going into debt.

Clients have also provided me with "budgets" which implied that they had regular surplus income, only to discover during the presentation of my final analysis, that they did not have any surplus at all. Most Americans, by nature, spend whatever they have. If we have no debts to pay or investments we know we must make, all of our net income goes toward basic living expenses and things we want or think we need.

I do not use the traditional or conventional ways of arriving at current cash flow needs. I do not care where clients have spent their money historically. I do care whether they can afford to continue to spend at the current rate, and how that will affect their financial objectives that they have asked me to help them achieve.

I determine the cash flow needs much more quickly and easily - and I feel, more accurately, than by using the conventional techniques. If I am working with a salaried wage earner, I start with the net income illustrated on their paycheck stub. I also need to know their liability payments, current investment contributions, insurance premiums, and itemized deductions. This information can be readily obtained from my Confidential Questionnaire, the client's paycheck stubs, tax returns, investment account statements, and insurance declaration pages. This is data we generally request for all new client engagements anyway. I then subtract the current liability payments, insurance premiums, and regularly occurring investment contributions from the client's net pay to determine their basic living expenses. I presume that the clients are spending all of their net paychecks unless they can prove otherwise.

A client's net worth will reflect what is actually occurring. If clients are not spending 100% of their net income, they must be paying down debt or accumulating savings or assets, or depleting saving or assets and accumulating debt. If their net worth statement is not affected, the clients are spending 100% of their net income. This approach eliminates a significant amount of the client's homework and increases our likelihood of getting the engagement and receiving requested data in a timely manner.

Managing Cash Flow

I then run my financial planning projections to determine whether the client can afford to continue to spend at their current level and achieve their other financial objectives. If they cannot afford to continue to spend 100% of their net income, which most cannot, we develop a plan and begin automatically saving the required funds. If the savings required are substantial, compared to the client's net income, we may begin this automatic savings program slowly and overtime increase the savings contributions to where they need to be.

At this time, it may be appropriate for clients to begin tracking their cash flow - going forward. I am only interested in their cash flow once I begin working with them. Now that we have a plan and know how much needs to be saved, the clients have the understanding and motivation to do what they need to do to accomplish their objectives. Prior to having their financial plan, they didn't know how much they needed to save, how to best save it, or how failing to save this money would negatively impact their financial lives. They need the clarity and motivation which a financial plan provides to work within a budget. And we can be the catalyst to help our clients get on track and stay accountable to what matters most in their financial lives.

For clients with variable income, we approach the questions of cash flow needs in a similar fashion. Unfortunately, this process is not quite as straightforward as that with our salaried wage earners. How much income have they netted this year? Have they increased or decreased net worth over this time period? If they earned it and it did not affect their net worth statement, then they spent it. If their net worth statement reveals that they increased liabilities or decreased assets, then they actually spent more than they made.

With our salaried clients, I find it very simple and practical to determine a monthly budget. However, with clients with variable income, frequently the best that we can do is determine an annual budget. However, determining the annual cash flow requirement is the information that we need to base our long-term projections and determine whether they are on target to meet their retirement projections and whether they have enough life insurance and disability insurance.

I want to know the agonizing details of how and why debt was accumulated. If we determine from the above exercise that the clients are simply spending more than they bring in, the common first step required to remedy the problem is recognition and acknowledgement. Clients must become very thoughtful of their spending decisions and allow us to help them employ strategies to avoid unconscious spending.

Figure 7.1

Cash Flow Questionnaire

Item	Monthly	Annual
Housing		
House payment	______	______
Rent payment	______	______
Lease payment (not mortgage)	______	______
Property improvements	______	______
Home association dues	______	______
Household incidentals (supplies)	______	______
Household furnishings	______	______
Other: ______	______	______
Other: ______	______	______
Subtotal:	______	______
Food		
Groceries	______	______
Dining out	______	______
Other: ______	______	______
Other: ______	______	______
Subtotal:	______	______
Clothing		
Clothing	______	______
Dry cleaning	______	______
Other: ______	______	______
Other: ______	______	______
Subtotal:	______	______
Personal Care		
(Hair styling, etc.)	______	______
Other: ______	______	______
Subtotal:	______	______

Figure 7.1 (Cont'd)

Item	Monthly	Annual
Automobile		
Monthly payment	________	________
Operating expenses (gas, oil, etc.)	________	________
Maintenance	________	________
Lease payment	________	________
Other: ________	________	________
Subtotal:	________	________
Property Tax		
Automobile	________	________
House	________	________
Boat	________	________
Trailer	________	________
Other: ________	________	________
Subtotal:	________	________
Utilities		
Telephone	________	________
Cellular Phone	________	________
Water	________	________
Electric	________	________
Gas	________	________
Trash removal	________	________
Cable	________	________
Other: ________	________	________
Other: ________	________	________
Subtotal:	________	________
Entertainment		
Books	________	________
Newspaper	________	________
Movies (theatre, video, plays, etc.)	________	________
Club dues (golf, music, etc.)	________	________
Other: ________	________	________
Other: ________	________	________
Subtotal:	________	________
Professional Expenses		
Travel	________	________
Vehicle rental	________	________
Parking	________	________
Lodging	________	________
Meals	________	________
Entertainment	________	________
Other: ________	________	________
Other: ________	________	________
Subtotal:	________	________

Figure 7.1 (Cont'd)

Item		Monthly	Annual
Alimony (paid)		________	________
	Subtotal:	________	________
Child Support (paid)		________	________
	Subtotal:	________	________
Child Care			
Daycare		________	________
Domestic help (babysitter)		________	________
Other: ________		________	________
	Subtotal:	________	________
Gifts			
Birthdays		________	________
Christmas		________	________
Anniversaries		________	________
Other: ________		________	________
Other: ________		________	________
	Subtotal:	________	________
Charitable Contributions			
(Churches, schools, etc.)		________	________
Other: ________		________	________
Other: ________		________	________
	Subtotal:	________	________
Medical Expenses			
Doctor visit co-pay		________	________
Prescription co-pay		________	________
Dental care		________	________
Vision care		________	________
Other: ________		________	________
	Subtotal:	________	________
Insurance			
Health		________	________
Automobile		________	________
Homeowners		________	________
Renters		________	________
Life		________	________
Umbrella liability		________	________
Professional liability		________	________
Other: ________		________	________
Other: ________		________	________
	Subtotal:	________	________

Figure 7.1 (Cont'd)

ITEM	MONTHLY	ANNUAL
CREDIT CARDS		
Credit card #1: ______	______	______
Credit card #2: ______	______	______
Credit card #3: ______	______	______
Credit card #4: ______	______	______
Credit card #5: ______	______	______
Credit card #6: ______	______	______
Other: ______	______	______
Other: ______	______	______
Subtotal:	______	______

NOTES: ______

Clients engage our services to answer the question, "when can I retire" or "how much do I need to save now so that I can to retire when I want to?" Presuming that clients are spending all of their income that is not being saved, we "solve for" whether they can afford to continue their same spending patterns. This is a quick and easy way to answer the question, "how much can I afford to spend?"

Americans generally spend whatever we think we can afford. As financial planners, one of our primary responsibilities is to empower and motivate our clients to do what they have asked us to help them do. Clients want to retire someday, take care of their loved ones, and enjoy their lives. Therefore, we must tell them how much they can spend and still achieve their objectives, now and in the future. When a client knows how much they *can* spend, and they *know* the ramifications should they go overboard, then they will determine that this is how much they *need* to spend.

Effective money management takes a significant amount of discipline. However, budgeting is a very simple concept. Rather than burden your clients with having them determine how much they are spending, tell them how much they can afford to spend.

Of course, if I am working with a couple who diligently tracks their expenditures, I will start with their numbers. Frequently, however, the result is the same – it appears that they are spending more then they make or, most commonly, they have surplus cash flow. When asked about surplus cash flow, we discover that this money never shows up on the balance sheet. It is not used to pay down debt or saved for the long-term. Instead, it is spent.

Preparing for Cash Flow Shortfalls

I am often asked, "How much should I keep in cash reserves?" There is no single answer that is appropriate for everyone. I do not like most of the general guidelines that are espoused. The concept of having on hand "X" months' of basic living expenses is undeniably essential, but how one funds those living expenses, and how many months of expenses are funded varies according to the individual. A client who has been employed by the federal government for the past 20 years may need significantly less reserves than an individual who is new to a job and who is paid 100% commissions. Regardless of whether the individual *needs* a certain amount of cash reserves, they may not be *comfortable* with that amount.

Also, many avenues may exist to help fund this cash flow need in the event of an emergency. Many middle Americans receive gifts or loans from family members, borrow money on a home equity line of credit or from their 401(k) plan, or liquidate investments when an emergency or unplanned opportunity arises. How much money can your client access in these events? How much are they willing to prepare for? They must have cash reserves to cover those potential emergencies or unforeseen opportunities if they do not have access to other resources.

I recommend that all clients with at least 20% equity in their homes secure a home equity line of credit (if they don't have one already) because there is generally no time to apply for a line of credit in the event of an emergency or an unplanned opportunity. Many emergencies are caused by temporary lapses in employment, and obtaining credit without an income can be difficult, if not impossible, to do.

To limit the number of unplanned expenditures, planners must explore the cash flow needs and desires of our clients during the financial planning process. Certain events can, and will occur; therefore, money should be allocated for these predictable expenses. We must account for periodic maintenance and repairs to houses, cars, and other personal property. In addition, we must consider and plan for health care costs for clients and their families. If clients want to fulfill certain financial objectives (e.g., paying for a wedding or a family vacation), we should plan for those expenditures as well. Since we can estimate the costs and timing of these predictable expenditures, clients can begin an automatic savings plan to accumulate sufficient resources for each type of expense.

For example, clients in the accumulation stage typically replace their vehicles every seven years at a net trade-in cost of $25,000. Therefore, we would build into their budget an "auto escrow" amount. The client should set aside $250.00 per month, assuming they get a 5% return on their money, to fund the replacement of vehicles at this cost and frequency (see the Auto Escrow worksheet in Figure 7.2 and on the CD-ROM).

Figure 7.2

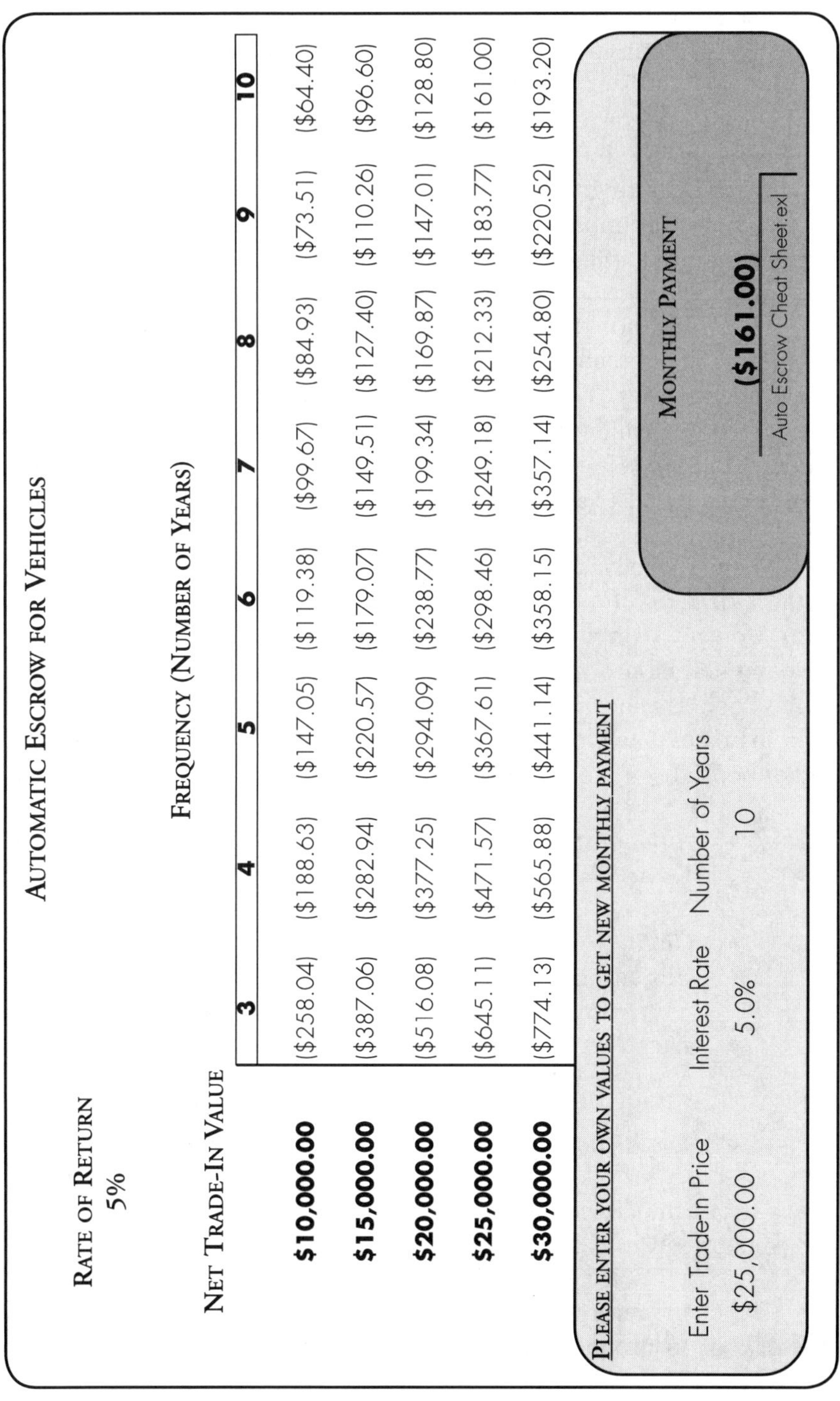

AUTOMATIC ESCROW FOR VEHICLES

RATE OF RETURN
5%

FREQUENCY (NUMBER OF YEARS)

NET TRADE-IN VALUE	3	4	5	6	7	8	9	10
$10,000.00	($258.04)	($188.63)	($147.05)	($119.38)	($99.67)	($84.93)	($73.51)	($64.40)
$15,000.00	($387.06)	($282.94)	($220.57)	($179.07)	($149.51)	($127.40)	($110.26)	($96.60)
$20,000.00	($516.08)	($377.25)	($294.09)	($238.77)	($199.34)	($169.87)	($147.01)	($128.80)
$25,000.00	($645.11)	($471.57)	($367.61)	($298.46)	($249.18)	($212.33)	($183.77)	($161.00)
$30,000.00	($774.13)	($565.88)	($441.14)	($358.15)	($357.14)	($254.80)	($220.52)	($193.20)

PLEASE ENTER YOUR OWN VALUES TO GET NEW MONTHLY PAYMENT

Enter Trade-In Price	Interest Rate	Number of Years
$25,000.00	5.0%	10

MONTHLY PAYMENT

($161.00)

Auto Escrow Cheat Sheet.exl

Costs related to the maintenance, repair, or replacement of a vehicle continue as long as a car is driven; thus, we must include a projection of these costs in our cash flow analyses. Regardless of whether the "auto escrow" amount is used to repair a vehicle, save for the purchase of the next automobile, or make a current lease or loan payment, this monthly expense should be built into our budgets. When we plan for the ongoing expense of operating, maintaining, and replacing vehicles, we minimize or eliminate the impact of one of the primary "unplanned" cash flow emergencies that affect many Americans.

These are the strategies I follow to help clients resolve spending problems. First, I begin by determining liability payments and other required expenses. Then, I subtract this amount from the clients' net income to determine discretionary income. From there, I talk clients through the process of allocating their remaining funds where they can provide the highest value.

Then, I briefly talk them through the principles espoused by the authors of *Your Money or Your Life: Transforming Your Relationship with Money.*[1] I provide them with a one page written copy of these fundamental money management principles. I also keep several copies of this book on hand and give a copy to any client with cash flow problems who indicates a willingness to try the money management principles. Other books I sometimes recommend include:

- *Affluenza: The All-Consuming Epidemic*, by John De Graaf, David Wann and Thomas H. Naylor.[2]
- *Getting a Life: Strategies for Simple Living*, by Jacqueline Blix and David Heitmiller.[3]
- *The Overspent American: Why We Want What We Don't Need*, by Juliet B. Schor.[4]
- *The Richest Man in Babylon*, by George S. Clason.[5]

For a list of my "Recommended Personal Finance Books for Clients," see Appendix B.

The client and I then schedule our next meeting, which I generally set for four to six weeks into the future. I want clients to have enough time to work through the basic principles we discussed at our first meeting, while keeping them accountable for what they say they want to accomplish between meetings. I do not do any work behind the scenes. All of my work for these clients is done interactively with them. Our meetings usually lasted one hour. We booked the next appointment, clarify their assignment(s), and they paid on their way out.

We would continue to meet every few weeks until the client(s) begins to consistently achieve their objectives for each session. Over time, clients will have either gained control over their cash flow, or they stop coming in for appointments. Unfortunately, the success rate I have experienced is less than satisfying. It takes people a long time to change old habits and belief systems. Many clients will not invest the time and energy necessary to change. However, those that do make these changes make it all worthwhile.

Debt Management

The credit industry has evolved dramatically over the last few years. Credit is easy to obtain, regardless of who you are, and we can now obtain credit reports and credit scores over the Internet. There are resources available to help individuals interpret this information and determine how credit scores can hurt or help them. I like www.Nolo.com, www.Myvesta.org and Liz Pulliam Weston's books on debt management. They are great resources on debt management, and establishing, improving, and repairing credit.

Now more than ever, adults must maintain good credit because credit ratings affect so many areas of our lives. Frequently, you cannot rent a car or book a hotel room without a credit card. Insurance companies, lenders, and many employers use credit scores in making their underwriting, lending, and hiring decisions. People who have poor credit will pay higher insurance premiums and loan rates (presuming they can get insurance coverage or borrow money in the first place). These additional costs further impair their abilities to maintain good credit. If we have poor credit, we may miss out on a job promotion or not get the job in the first place. Having bad credit can cost clients in more ways than they realize. It takes only one moment of compulsive spending in front of a timeshare salesman, or one missing paycheck, to negatively impact someone's credit and financial plans. However, it can take months or years to recover.

When counseling clients on debt management issues, I stress that paying off debts and improving our credit takes time and discipline, but the rewards are worth it. For a period of time, they must be brutally honest with themselves, and with me, about how they spend their money. They must track where every penny is spent for the near future. Planners must raise their clients' consciousness about their spending habits.

I also provide the following types of informational sheets, which we at my firm call "One-Sheets" to help explain certain topics and assist in the implementation of our recommendations. Figures 7.3 through 7.6 are quick resource sheets that we place behind the Appendix tab in the client's plan binder. I will share other examples of our "One-Sheets" on the accompanying CD.

Once the clients have had the opportunity to receive a copy of their credit report and file a letter with the credit bureau disputing any inaccuracies, we meet again to establish a debt reduction plan.

I use Quicken's Debt Reduction Planner to produce a suggested repayment schedule. We require that clients bring current copies of all liability statements and their credit report to the meeting. During the meeting, we review the repayment schedule and mutually determine a plan of action that the clients themselves will implement prior to our next meeting. We schedule the next meeting two to three months in advance. Clients are asked to bring their most current liability statements and any documents used to track expenditures. We continue to meet on this frequency until period objectives are met. We then schedule a follow-up "accountability meeting" for six months in the future. These accountability meetings may continue for quite a while. My role is to serve as accountability coach and see that clients stay on task. The clients do all the work. My only billable time is that spent directly in front of the client.

Figure 7.3

How can I get a copy of my credit report?

Free annual credit reports are now available in every state. To order your free report, go to www.annualcreditreport.com, and either order your report online or download a form to mail in your request. You can also call 877-322-8228.

Also, you are entitled to one free copy of your credit report each year under the following circumstances:

- you have been denied credit because of information in your credit report and you request a copy within 60 days of being denied credit;
- you are unemployed and looking for work;
- you receive public assistance; or
- you believe your file contains errors due to fraud or you are (or you think you are) a victim of identity theft
- you have been denied employment (or another adverse employment decision has been made) based in whole or in part on information contained in the report, or
- your report has been revised based upon an investigation you requested.

http://www.nolo.com/article.cfm/ObjectID/CA15D662-EABF-409F-8758FC7E8655EB65/catID/8f8c3c1a-2347-419a-9c65b0b8c7762e3b/213/FAQ/

Figure 7.4

What should I do if I find mistakes in my credit report?

As you read through your report, make a list of everything out-of-date. The credit bureaus should remove this information from your credit report:

- Lawsuits, paid tax liens, accounts sent out for collection, criminal records (except criminal convictions, which may be reported indefinitely), late payments, and any other adverse information older than seven years.
- Bankruptcies older than ten years from the discharge or dismissal. Credit bureaus often list Chapter 13 bankruptcies for only seven years, but they can stay for ten.
- Credit inquiries (requests by companies for a copy of your report) older than two years.

Next, look for incorrect or misleading information, such as:

- Incorrect or incomplete name, address, phone number, Social Security number, or employment information
- Bankruptcies not identified by their specific chapter number
- Accounts not yours or lawsuits in which you were not involved
- Incorrect account histories – such as late payments when you paid on time
- Closed accounts listed as open – it may look as if you have too much open credit, and
- Any account you closed that does not say "closed by consumer."

After reviewing your report, complete the "request for reinvestigation" form the credit bureau sent you or send a letter listing each incorrect item and explain exactly what is wrong. Once the credit bureau receives your request, it must investigate the items you dispute and contact you within 30 days. Some states require bureaus to complete reinvestigations more quickly. If you do not hear back within 30 days, send a follow-up letter. If you let them know that you are trying to obtain a mortgage or car loan, they can do a rush investigation.

If you are right, or if the creditor who provided the information can no longer verify it, the credit bureau must remove the information from your report. Often credit bureaus will remove an item on request without an investigation if rechecking the item is more bother than it's worth.

If the credit bureau insists that the information is correct, call the bureau to discuss the problem:

- Experian: 888-397-3742
- Trans Union: 800-888-4213
- Equifax: 800-685-1111

If you don't get anywhere with the credit bureau, directly contact the creditor and ask that the information be removed. Write to the customer service department, vice president of marketing, and president or CEO. If the information was reported by a collection agency, send the agency a copy of your letter, too. Creditors are forbidden by law to report information they know is incorrect.

If you feel a credit bureau is wrongfully including information in your report, or you want to explain a particular entry, you have the right to put a brief statement in your report. The credit bureau must give a copy of your statement – or a summary – to anyone who requests your report. Be clear and concise; use the fewest words possible.

Figure 7.5

WHAT CAN I DO TO REBUILD MY CREDIT?

After you've cleaned up your credit report, the key to rebuilding credit is to get positive information into your record. Here are two suggestions:

- If your credit report is missing accounts you pay on time, send the credit bureaus a recent account statement and copies of canceled checks showing your payment history. Ask that these be added to your report. The credit bureau doesn't have to, but often will.

- Creditors like to see evidence of stability, so if any of the following information is not in your report, send it to the bureaus and ask that it be added: your current employment, your previous employment (especially if you've been at your current job fewer than two years), your current residence, your telephone number (especially if it's unlisted), your date of birth and your checking account number. Again, the credit bureau doesn't have to add these, but often will.

Figure 7.6

I'VE BEEN TOLD THAT I NEED TO USE CREDIT TO REBUILD MY CREDIT. IS THIS TRUE?

Yes. The one type of positive information creditors like to see in credit reports is credit payment history. If you have a credit card, use it every month. Make small purchases and pay them off to avoid interest charges. If you don't have a credit card, apply for one. If your application is rejected, try to find a cosigner or apply for a secured card – where you deposit some money into a savings account and then get a credit card with a line of credit around the amount you deposited.

But a word of caution: It won't do you any good in the long-run to apply for credit before you're back on your feet financially. You'll just end up with high cost credit that will put you back in the hole again. Even if you can get a card earlier, wait until you are ready to start using credit again.

Strategies for Handling Credit Problems

There are many community and private credit counseling providers available today. Occasionally, I receive inquiries from people who would be better served by groups such as Consumer Credit Counseling Services (CCCS) or www.Myvesta.org. If I don't feel that I can effectively and affordably assist prospective clients, I refer them to our local CCCS office or to www.Myvesta.org.

When I first re-directed my practice to work on an hourly, as-needed basis with clients, I anticipated a lot of cash flow problems. Fortunately, the overwhelming majority of my clients have positive cash flow, and I am not doing much debt management planning. Nevertheless, effective debt management is a common problem for Middle Americans. Practitioners who decide to offer these services will find it frustrating, yet very rewarding. It is a much-needed service and, when successful, literally changes people's lives.

Endnotes

1. Joe Dominguez and Vicki Robin, *Your Money or Your Life: Transforming Your Relationship With Money and Achieving Financial Independence* (Penguin, September 1999).
2. John De Graaf, David Wann and Thomas H. Naylor, *Affluenza: The All-Consuming Epidemic* (Berrett-Koehler, June 9, 2001).
3. Jacqueline Blix and David Heitmiller, *Getting a Life: Strategies for Simple Living* (Penguin, January 1999).
4. Juliet B. Schor, *The Overspent American: Why We Want What We Don't Need* (Harper Collins, May 1999).
5. George S. Clason, *The Richest Man in Babylon* (Signet, January 2002).

Chapter 8

Risk Management

Protecting or Replacing Income

Life Insurance

Virtually all Middle Americans do not have enough life insurance and they do not have much surplus cash flow either. Therefore, I continue to recommend low-cost, high-quality term life insurance for most people because (1) they need a lot of pure life insurance protection, and (2) they have tax advantaged investment strategies available to them that are not fully being utilized; i.e. so they don't need another option to shelter taxes.

SRI Consulting released a survey in 1999 revealing that some 73% of U.S. households have life insurance coverage, but most of this coverage is provided through their employer or another group plan.[1] Most Americans are also drastically under insured. The survey went on to reveal a decline in the number of cash value life insurance policies in force. Americans are dropping their cash-value policies or replacing them with term insurance. These people need many times the amount of life insurance they have. They are finding the most cost effective way to obtain the coverage they need is through the direct purchase of term life insurance. These policies are extremely competitive. The Internet has leveled the playing field and now anyone can comparison shop, gather information, and even apply for a policy online or by calling an insurance company directly. The Internet and direct sales of term life insurance has played a major role in driving down the price of coverage. However, clients still need our objective view of just what type and amount of life insurance is right for them.

When reviewing Middle Americans' financial objectives, I find that they almost always need to: (1) save more for retirement and (2) buy more life insurance. But the fact that they have limited resources (and lots of other requirements for their money) cannot be overlooked either. While preparing the retirement capital needs analysis, with just a few extra key strokes, we can also determine the appropriate amount of life insurance coverage needed.

During the Presentation Meeting with the clients (more on Presentation Meetings in Chapter 13) I discuss the assumptions that went into the calculation of additional life insurance needs with the clients. The default assumption is that nothing changes the current plan. If the couple is planning to retire at a certain age and lifestyle, provide a college education for their kids, and build their dream home in five years, we assume nothing would change if one of them were to die prematurely. We also assume that nothing changes regarding the employment status or earning potential of the survivor.

But, are these things likely to change? When working with young couples, we discuss what life might be like if one of them were not around. Other possible questions include: Would they like the surviving parent to have time at home with a young child for a period of time? What would be the likelihood of a "stay-at-home" parent continuing to have no earned income? Would the survivor stay in their current home? Would they want the mortgage paid off at the death of either party? Can the survivor afford to save or pay for the children's college education on their salary alone?

If the clients can afford it, we suggest that they obtain sufficient insurance to provide for the life they are planning together, even if one dies prematurely. However, in the event that clients must weigh the options and choose between fully insuring their surviving family and providing for their future should they live, a compromise must be reached.

Some couples I've worked with have determined that they are comfortable taking certain risks and have elected to provide just enough life insurance to support the survivor for twenty years and provide for their kids' college educations.

However, a lot of things can happen in twenty years. What if the clients live to a ripe old age? We must plan for the possibility of premature death, but balance that consideration with our plans for living. Middle Americans need our help in determining and achieving the appropriate balance.

I use MoneyTree Software's EasyMoney module for the life insurance needs analysis. Once the coverage requirement is determined, we consider the appropriate type of coverage, and then have the client either contact the company directly, or have one of a select group of insurance specialists implement our recommendations.

Another standard assumption that I make for all stay-at-home parents is that it will take no less than $250,000 to replace their services should they no longer be able to care for the family's young children. This is my minimum number. And it really doesn't matter much whether we are talking about one child or four. The ages of the children and their need for constant supervision are critical.

Many of the stay-at-home parents' services could be replaced with a full-time nanny. In many parts of the country, such as Kansas City, it would cost at least $25,000 per year to obtain the services of a qualified, full-time nanny. In other parts of the country, it may cost twice that much. For my planning purposes, I want to ensure that the surviving family does not endure any more hardship then they already have with the loss of a parent. If affordable – and it really needs to be – the family should purchase life insurance on the stay-at-home parent's life for the number of years until the youngest child is self-sufficient times the annual cost of a full-time nanny.

Example
Stay-at-home mom
5 year old child
Cost of full-time nanny = $25,000

Mom dies, child is 5 years old. Need to immediately hire a nanny at $25,000 per year and continue their employment until the child goes off to college in 13 years. Ah heck, let's play it safe and say 15 years. $25,000 x 15 years is a present value life insurance need of $375,000. For this 40 year old stay-at-home parent, the annual cost to protect the family from this additional risk is about $400 to $600.

Tip: Many good consumer publications on all types of insurance can be found at www.insurance.wa.gov/readonline.htm.

Disability Income Protection

In addition to not having enough life insurance, most middle Americans also have limited or no income protection in the event of long-term disability. The majority of the clients I saw had some long-term disability coverage through their employers; however, this coverage rarely exceeds 67 percent of pre-tax earnings. Considering that most families feel they need at least 100 percent of their current net income to maintain their lifestyle, how are they going to cope with loosing 1/3 of a wage earner's income? Most Middle Americans cannot comfortably absorb that drastic a change in their lifestyles, but unfortunately that is what most would have to do – being uninsured or underinsured.

A long-term disability could not only affect the client's current situation, it most likely will also dramatically affect their lifestyle when their disability income benefits expire at age 65. They no longer have this income and they also do not have the savings that their extra income would have enabled them to accumulate to help cover the costs of retirement, if they had never become disabled.

Obtaining additional coverage by purchasing a personal policy may not eliminate the long-term cash flow problem either. Thus, regardless of how much insurance clients may have, a long-term disability can severely impact their financial plans.

Planners must discuss the risks clients face currently, the options of self-insuring all or a portion of this risk or purchasing additional coverage, and the impact each may have on their lifestyle. Disability insurance is not cheap, but the impact of the lack of adequate coverage may not be tolerable.

Figure 8.1

DISABILITY INSURANCE POLICY CHECKLIST

Date:__________________

		YES	NO
1.	Does my company have a Comdex rating of at least 80?	____	____
2.	Is my policy non-cancelable?	____	____
3.	Are the premiums guaranteed?	____	____
4.	Does the definition of total disability protect me in my occupation?	____	____
5.	Are part-time and full-time return-to-work income replacement benefits included and payable to age 65?	____	____
6.	Can I receive benefits without being totally disabled first?	____	____
7.	Does my policy use the "earned and received" method of accounting during my residual (partial) disability?	____	____
8.	Can my earnings loss be averaged to generate a greater benefit?	____	____
9.	When I am on claim, are my policy benefits adjusted for inflation?	____	____
10.	Can I increase my monthly benefits even if I am uninsurable?	____	____
11.	Can these increases be made (and are they payable) during an existing claim?	____	____
12.	Does my policy pay benefits for my lifetime if totally disabled?	____	____
13.	Do I have a policy (Business Overhead Expense Disability Plan) to cover my business expenses if I am disabled?	____	____
14.	Do I have a policy (Reducing Term Disability Plan) to cover my business loan payments?	____	____
15.	Do I have maximum benefits based on my current income and fixed business expenses?	____	____

Note: It is advisable to review your disability insurance policies once a year with a qualified specialist.

Figure 8.1 (Cont'd)

DISABILITY INSURANCE ANNUAL PREMIUMS
(Per $1,000 of Monthly Benefit)

PLAN DESIGN:
90-Day Elimination Period
$1,000 per month benefit
Benefit Period "To Age 65"
Benefit Update Rider
Cost of Living Adjustment Rider
Residual Benefit Rider

5A OCCUPATION CLASS

This class includes persons in professional, managerial, and technical occupations within select business and professional sectors of the economy. These occupations require extensive education, training, and experience. All work is performed in an office setting with less than 20% of the person's time spent out of the office and no direct supervision of persons with manual duties.

Age	Male	Female
30	$370	$540
35	$420	$640
40	$550	$780
45	$670	$900
50	$840	$1,070

4A OCCUPATION CLASS

This class consists primarily of those professional, managerial, and technical occupations which are not generally eligible for our most favorable classes. Work may involve more than 20% of the person's time being spent outside of the establishment. Occupational duties involve no direct supervision of persons with manual duties.

Age	Male	Female
30	$390	$620
35	$450	$670
40	$580	$820
45	$710	$950
50	$900	$1,120

Figure 8.1 (Cont'd)

3A Occupation Class

This class is made up of social service, clerical, medical support, and select commissioned sales occupations in which stability and potential high earnings qualify individuals for long-term benefits. It also includes those medical and dental occupations that have demonstrated less favorable experience than class 4. Work is performed in a hospital, office, or retail setting and involves only light manual duties. Occupations that meet the criteria of class 3 may be rated as class 4 if the individual has had personal earned income of at least $50,000 in each of the three years prior to application.

Age	Male	Female
30	$450	$750
35	$500	$800
40	$650	$970
45	$780	$1,100
50	$1,000	$1,300

Females can receive up to a 30% premium discount if insurance is employer-sponsored. Premiums shown are not discounted.

Reprinted with permission of John Ryan, Ryan Insurance Strategy Consultants, 8301 E. Prentice Ave., Suite 310, Greenwood Village, CO 80111.

Medical Insurance and Long-Term Care Insurance

The 2001 U.S. Census revealed that the majority of middle Americans have health insurance.[2]

Citizens Covered by Health Insurance

Household Income	Total	Private	Medicaid	Not Covered
$50,000 - $74,999	88.2%	83.1%	3.6%	11.8%
$75,000 and higher	91.7%	88.4%	2.1%	8.3%

In many cases, employers pay all or the majority of the cost of a full-time employee's health insurance. Employees may also be able to obtain health insurance for their spouses and children through their employer's plan, however due to the raising costs of health insurance, many employers are no longer subsidizing the family's health insurance premiums. Frequently, with married couples both spouses have employer-provided health insurance available. We must then consider which spouse's plan is best for the family's coverage, from a quality, flexibility, and cost standpoint.

Ineligible employees and individuals without employer-sponsored health insurance may be able to obtain group coverage through a professional organization, alumni association, or labor union. High-risk individuals may have access to a high-risk pool available through their state.

Individual policies are more expensive than group coverage, but the coverage can be tailored to fit specific needs. Most individual plans offer options including Health Maintenance Organizations (HMOs), Preferred Provider Organizations (PPOs), point-of-service plans, and traditional fee-for-service plans. Individual policies must be compared carefully because premiums and benefits can vary widely.

Clients engage us to provide advice regarding employer-provided health insurance plans. If individual coverage is needed, planners must coach clients on the benefits to look for in a policy and refer them directly to a qualified, independent insurance specialist to secure coverage.

Some employers provide health insurance benefits to their retirees. However, these benefits are rare and generally not guaranteed. Care must be exercised when planning for long-term retirement income needs; health insurance for senior citizens can easily run $200 per month or more.

The USAA Educational Foundation provides an informational piece on comparing health insurance plans (see www.usaaedfoundation.org.) and useful health insurance shopping tips. It discusses employer-sponsored group plans and individual plans.

Long-Term Care Insurance

Long-term care insurance provides coverage for medical care and assistance in a nursing facility or in the home or a community environment. Determining whether long-term care insurance should be purchased depends on many factors, primarily age, health status, income and assets, and need for security.

It is difficult to know if, when, and for how long a person may need long-term care. USAA Educational Foundation provides guidelines regarding who should, and should not, purchase long-term care insurance. See www.usedfoundation.org.

The majority of Americans should consider obtaining long-term care insurance at some point. The USAA Education Foundation guidelines illustrate that if you do not have enough income and assets to purchase the insurance, you should not. At the time assets are nearly depleted Medicaid will provide assistance. But there are also occasions when clients are self-insured or choose to take on the risk of paying for long-term health care and assistance. Often, clients are reluctant to seriously discuss long-term care needs. They are convinced that they and their loved ones will not end up in a nursing home. Clients may actually avoid or limit the amount of time they spend in a nursing home if they have insurance with home health care benefits. Thus, education can be key to making a proper decision.

I strongly encourage people to read the National Association of Insurance Commissioner's *Shopper's Guide to Long-Term Care Insurance.*[3] The Guide thoroughly covers all the major issues a client should consider when shopping for long-term care insurance. We provided this booklet to any client who might be a prospect for or know someone who should purchase long term care insurance. We would also provide clients with contact information on long-term care insurance specialists to assist with selection and implementation.

Remember, I received no compensation for the implementation of insurance products for my clients. But I was a fiduciary, and as a fiduciary I felt it was my responsibility to become and remain educated on the subject of risk management and serve as a catalyst to help my clients do what they hired me to help them do – in this case, minimize and manage intolerable risks.

I believe clients should consider buying long-term care insurance especially if there is a family history of chronic illness or need for long-term health care. We also must consider who could provide care in the event of a long-term need. I have asked the petite spouse of a husky client, "if he broke his hip, you'd be able to care for him, but could you lift him?"

Once clients conclude that long-term care insurance may be appropriate for them, they ask, "when should we buy it?" "The day before you actually need it," I respond. I then explain the trade-offs we must make. At one time I recommended that clients who should own long-term care insurance purchase it between 60 and 65 years of age. However, now I would consider purchasing coverage between 45 and 65. Of course there were times when I recommended coverage for much younger clients. Most clients I worked with chose to take the risk of waiting a few years before buying coverage, so they can continue to save aggressively for retirement.

I strongly encourage clients to get quotes on policies with 4 or 5 years and lifetime coverage, cost of living adjustments, sufficient home health care benefits, and a waiting period of usually nine months. The daily benefit and the benefit period are adjusted until the clients and the insurance specialist arrive at the type of insurance protection the client is comfortable with and is willing to pay for. Occasionally clients will discuss the policy quotes they receive with me before they buy a policy. But for the most part, my job in the area of long term care needs was to identify risks, communicate those risks to the clients, discuss optional strategies, and motivate the client to take action that we mutually agree upon.

Property and Casualty Insurance

We provide advice to clients regarding their auto, homeowners and liability insurance coverages. The most important thing I concern myself with is whether the coverage is appropriate, adequate, and reasonably competitive. We frequently find that liability coverages should be increased, deductibles should be increased, and riders need to be added to policies.

We ask clients to provide us with a copy of their most current insurance declaration pages. These reports provide us with the majority of the information needed to determine whether the coverage is appropriate and adequate, and assess its competitiveness.

Early in my hourly practice I established relationships with property and casualty insurance specialists. Some of these specialists represent many of the top property-casualty companies in the country. Others represent only one company, which happens to be extremely competitive in the areas of auto and homeowners insurance.

Clients should periodically obtain quotes from other insurance companies to make certain that they have appropriate and competitive insurance protection. However, many consumers do not know what they should be looking for in a policy and what they should be prepared to pay. Frequently Middle Market consumers can save $100 to $300 a year simply by shopping around. I do not advocate that a consumer with an established history with their property and casualty insurance providers change companies merely to save a few dollars. I feel that obtaining appropriate and adequate protection with one insurance company and staying with that insurance company for many years much better serves consumers. Claims paying ability and customer service are the most important considerations.

There have been dramatic changes in the property and casualty insurance industry in recent years. For example, a few years ago I purchased a 73-year-old home and went shopping for homeowner's insurance as well as replacement coverage for my car. In my search I learned that State Farm discontinued writing coverage on homes in my area. I also discovered that Allstate only insures homes up to 30 years old. I talked with another carrier who would not provide coverage because I did not have homeowner's coverage immediately before I purchased my new home. Another company whom I really wanted to use turned me down because my home still had some original nob and tube wiring. They are an outstanding company, with the best premium rates and coverages around, and their underwriting requirements reflect why that they are able to offer such competitive rates. They only take preferred risks.

We live in a part of the country that is known for hailstorms. I know, you probably think of Kansas as Tornado Alley. But hail, wind, and ice storms damage significantly more property each year then do tornados. In working with my property and casualty insurance specialists, I learned that most companies depreciate roofs. However a few companies still offer full replacement coverage. In an area such as ours, having full replacement coverage for the roof can mean the difference between being adequately insured and opening yourself up to a cash flow emergency.

When helping our clients shop for proper coverage, we fax the declarations pages to a couple of our insurance specialists. Generally within 48 hours we receive suggestions for improvements, as well as quotes from their top providers. It is not at all uncommon for our P & C specialists to recommend that clients not change their current coverage, or change their coverage, but stay with their current carrier.

The specialists continue to receive opportunities to replace or add coverages for our clients, if they continue to provide us with objective feedback regarding the client's current coverage. It takes time to develop a trusting relationship with the various specialists with whom we work. However, once these relationships have been developed, these specialists can serve an extremely valuable role to the general practitioner serving the Middle Market consumer, and the consumers themselves.

As general practitioners we cannot be specialists in all areas of the financial planning process. Middle Market consumers cannot afford to hire experts in every area. Nor can they afford to go without competent advice. By strategically aligning ourselves with allied professionals as we do, our clients receive quality, affordable advice in all areas important to their financial situation, even those outside of our scope of expertise.

Occasionally clients have other types of property and casualty insurance or insurance needs. We refer these clients directly to their property and casualty insurance specialist, or one of the specialists we work with, to review and update these coverages.

Tips for purchasing homeowners insurance and auto insurance are listed in Figure 8.2.

Figure 8.2

Homeowners Insurance Buying Tips

Basic Coverages:

Coverage for the Structure of your Home – pays to repair or rebuild your home if it is damaged or destroyed by fire, hurricane, wind, hail, lightning or other disaster listed in your policy. Separate coverage must be obtained for flood and earthquake protection.

Be sure to obtain "full replacement cost" coverage for your home. Note: you do not need to insure the land, only the physical structures and contents.

Most policies also cover "detached" structures, (i.e., garage or shed) up to 10% of the coverage on the structure. Additional coverage can be purchased.

Coverage for your Personal Property – pays to replace the contents of your home if items are stolen, damaged or destroyed by a covered risk. Most policies cover up to 70% of the amount of your coverage on the structure.

If you have specialty items (jewelry, electronics, antiques) or collectibles (stamps, coins, figurines) you may need a separate "Rider" for those items. Consult with your homeowners' insurance agent to confirm that your coverage is adequate.

Consider videotaping and/or completing a detailed inventory listing of the contents of your home. Keep this documentation off premises, such as in a safe deposit box.

Liability Protection – covers you against lawsuits for bodily injury or property damage that you, family members or your pets cause to other people.

Liability limits generally start at $100,000. We recommend at least $300,000 of liability protection.

You can purchase an umbrella liability policy, which provides coverage above and beyond your auto and homeowners liability protection. This coverage costs about $150 to $250 per year for a $1,000,000 policy.

Used with permission from The Insurance Information Institute (www.iii.org.).

Figure 8.2 (Cont'd)

Ways to Reduce Costs of Homeowners Insurance:

Shop Around for competitive quotes.

www.insure.com
www.quicken.com/insurance
www.esurance.com

Check the financial health of insurance companies with rating companies such as A.M. Best (www.ambest.com) and Standard & Poor's (http://www.standardandpoors.com.)

Increase your Deductibles – We recommend deductibles of at least $500. If you can afford to raise it to $1,000, you may save as much as 25% according to the Insurance Information Institute.

Purchase Auto, Homeowners and Umbrella Liability Coverages through same Company

Inquire About Discounts

Used with permission from The Insurance Information Institute (www.iii.org.).

Figure 8.2 (Cont'd)

Auto Insurance Buying Tips

Basic Coverages:

Collision – pays for damage to your car resulting from a collision or accident.

Comprehensive – coverage for most everything other than collision or accident, such as wind or hail damage, broken windshield, and theft.

Bodily Injury Liability – covers you and any other designated driver if you cause injury to another person.

The Insurance Information Institute recommends that you have $100,000 of bodily injury protection per person and $300,000 per accident.

Property Damage Liability – covers damages that you may cause to someone else's property, i.e., vehicle, fence, landscape, etc.

Medical Payments or Personal Injury Protection (PIP) – pays for medical payments and possibly lost wages of someone injured in an auto accident.

Uninsured and Underinsured Motorist Coverage – reimburses you if accident is caused by an uninsured or underinsured driver.

Ways to Reduce Costs of Auto Insurance:

Shop Around for competitive quotes.

www.insure.com
www.quicken.com/insurance
www.esurance.com

Increase Your Deductibles for Collision and Comprehensive coverages.

According to the Insurance Information Institute increasing your deductible from $200 to $500 could reduce your collision and comprehensive coverage cost by 15% to 30%. Going to a $1,000 deductible can save you 40% or more.

Maintain a Clean Driving Record

Purchase Auto and Home Owners Coverage through same Company

Inquire About Discounts

Used with permission from The Insurance Information Institute (www.iii.org.).

Figure 8.3

TIP 13 STEPS TO PREVENT IDENTITY THEFT – DON'T LET IT HAPPEN TO YOU

Q. Identity theft is in the news. How common is it, and what can I do to prevent this form happening to me?

A. Identity theft – stealing someone's personal identifying information, then fraudulently using it to establish credit or to take over existing accounts – is the #1 white-collar crime in America today. MasterCard® and Visa® losses due to identity theft approach $1 billion a year, according to the General Accounting Office. Some 250,000 to 750,000 Americans are victims of identity theft each year, and this number is growing rapidly.

Could it Happen to You?

Many people naively believe fraud occurs only when a wallet is stolen or private information is given to unscrupulous parties over the Internet. But a confidential statement in the trash, stolen mail, or a photocopied ID card is a first step to identity theft and a point of vulnerability for almost all of us. With this information, an identity thief could open the door to your bank and investment accounts, order new credit cards, and maybe even get a mortgage in you name.

If you think it can't happen to you, think again. Consider one identity theft victim's all-too-common story.

> I was alerted to more the $35,000 in credit card transactions when a collections agency called my house. This involved different companies in less than a 60-day period. Interestingly enough, no driver's license, Social Security card, or mother's maiden name had ever left my possession. However, when I saw the applications at several department stores, it was all there – but with a different lady's picture. It took many months and much effort to resolve the matter properly.

Using the most basic personal information, almost anyone can put their picture on a counterfeit driver's license and pretend to be you to open credit card accounts. Only when you apply for credit or you need a current copy of your credit report, do you find out your record is filled with late payments, collections and delinquencies.

Figure 8.3 (Cont'd)

While phony credit cards are frightening, identity theft can get worse. Once a crook has a counterfeit driver's license with our name on it, they can visit any branch of your bank and clean out your account.

How to Protect Yourself

Caution and protection are key, and so is a healthy paranoia. Beyond the obvious recommendations such as shredding your sensitive trash and guarding your Social Security number, be aware of your exposure through corporations and organizations, For starters, identity fraud rings can exist at your bank, department store, or financial institution or in the back office of an Internet service provider. Too many employee, not all of whom may be ethical, have access to your records. Be wary of ever disclosing more private information than necessary, avoid any unnecessary credit lines, and deal only with well-known providers.

Other preventive measures include the following:

- *Watch the incoming mail for your regular bills.* If one is missing, track it down immediately. Filled-out checks can be acid-washed and filled back in with new payees or amounts due.
- *Shred your documents.* How much information can be found in your trash? Experian, the credit reporting agency, went dumpster diving in 400 household garbage bins. If found that 72 percent contained an individual's full name and address, 40 percent provided a full credit or debit card number, 32 percent divulged the card's expiration date, 20 percent held bank account numbers and sort codes, and one trash can even had a signed blank check.
- *Lock your mailbox.* Better yet, call 888-567-8688 to opt out of credit card solicitations altogether.
- *Guard your passwords and care for your cards.* Sign any new credit cards immediately. Don't attach your pin numbers to bankcards, and never carry Social Security card. Carry only the cards you really need.
- *Consider using distinct passwords for various bank and brokerage accounts and any Internet site where personal information is communicated or stored.*
- *Know your bank's policy on fraud.* Is there a policy for reviewing fraudulent activities? If you can prove it wasn't you, will they work toward a consumer-friendly resolution? Conditional or provisional credit should be given in all fraud cases.
- *Monitor your credit report and consider subscribing to an alert service.* By the time identity theft is discovered – an average of 14 months after the first crime, according to

Figure 8.3 (Cont'd)

Equifax – a thief can wreak havoc on your credit standing. Monitoring your credit report annually is a good start, but it gives scam artists months between your reviews to open new accounts. So choose an online credit monitoring service to notify you instantly when someone tries to open an account in your name or when one of your credit cards gets hit with a surprisingly large purchase. Choose a service that monitors all three credit reporting agencies and that alerts you in real time – not quarterly or monthly.

- *Be aware.* Stay alert to the information that you release, be aware of changes to accounts or credit, and guard all your transactions as if they were personal and confidential – and maybe they'll stay that way.

End Note$

A leading source of information on identity theft is the Federal Trade Commission's Web site (www.consumer.gov/idtheft). It includes tips on how to minimize your risk, what to do if you're a victim, and how to file a complaint, among other useful information.

EILEEN S. FREIBURGER, CFP® (El Segundo, California)

Source: Sheryl Garrett, CFP®, Just Give Me the Answers, pp. 35-37 (Dearborn Trade Publishing, 2004).

ENDNOTES

1. SRI Consulting Business Intelligence, "More Households Have Inadequate Life Insurance," (March 12, 1999).
2. U.S. Census Bureau, Current Population Survey, March 2000 and 2001. See also Charles T. Nelson and Robert J. Mills, "The March CPS Health Insurance Verification Question and Its Effect on Estimates of the Uninsured," (U.S. Census Bureau, August 2001); www.census.giv/hhes/hlthins/verify/html.
3. This document can be viewed at www.ltcfeds.com/documents/files/NAIC_Shoppers_Guide.pdf.

CHAPTER 9

AMERICANS' FUNDAMENTAL FINANCIAL OBJECTIVES

HOME OWNERSHIP

Owning a home is truly part of the American dream. According to the U.S. Census Bureau, over 70% of married couples age 30 or older own their own home.[1] As ages increase, the percentage of home ownership increases. These statistics have increased over the years as more liberal lending policies have been introduced. It is now possible to purchase a home with as little as 3% down, and sometimes even zero down.

There are many advantages and disadvantages to owning one's own home. Advantages include: pride of ownership; building equity; the ability to deduct mortgage interest and real estate taxes on federal and state income tax returns; and building long-term security.

There are also disadvantages that must be acknowledged. Owning a home is a big responsibility. When the furnace goes out or the lawn needs mowing, the homeowner either has to take care of it or hire someone and pay that person to do things the homeowner can't or won't do. Some middle Americans are actually better off renting. Yes, their rents can go up year after year, but so can real estate taxes and maintenance expenses. Renting has its benefits—it is simple and the renter won't get whacked with unexpected expenses relating to the maintenance of the property.

One major disadvantage of renting, however, is that the renter will never stop paying rent. On the other hand, with home ownership the mortgage will eventually be paid off and the homeowner's only expenses that will continue indefinitely will be real estate taxes, homeowner's insurance, and maintenance. Generally, these expenses are significantly less then rent. Plus, the homeowner has a fully paid for, appreciating (hopefully) asset.

At some point, homeowners may decide to sell their homes and seek out low maintenance housing alternatives. We are seeing more and more clients these days who want to purchase a newer home with only minor maintenance needed, one they can stay in throughout retirement (or at least for the foreseeable future).Generally, these clients desire a ranch-style or patio home with all of the essential services on the main floor, and a small yard (or one with outside maintenance provided). Many of these clients who downsize their current residence for one that is more appropriate for their retirement needs assume that their total housing cost will decrease. However, the total cost of the new residence is often many times equal to or greater than the home in which they currently live. Although the costs for maintenance and utilities may go down, the additional cost of higher real estate taxes and homeowner's association dues may not and, therefore, must be factored into our planning discussions.

Helping clients achieve their financial planning dreams is extremely fulfilling. The purchase of a home for many middle Americans is their single biggest financial decision and, often times, their most significant near-term goal. In a relatively short period of time, we can help clients determine: the right price range; how they should fund the down payment; the type of mortgage that is right for them, and where they can find competitive interest rates.

If this project is part of a more comprehensive financial plan, the answer to "*what* is affordable?" will be more scientifically derived. As planners working with Middle Market clients we may be asked to address this issue in relative isolation. In that event, we must start with the client's current budget, including housing costs. We must then make adjustments for the income tax benefits of owning a home and the additional costs that come with home ownership to determine the affordable price range. With the information provided on our Confidential Questionnaire (see

Figure 6.1 in Chapter 6) and additional data gathering, we are able to provide input as to where the clients should obtain the down payment and what type of mortgage is appropriate. We can check www.BankRate.com for indications of current interest rates and then call local, competitive mortgage companies to get current rate quotes for the client. Or use www.BankRate.com's feature, which provides an option to get quotes from lenders in your area. Check out this service and compare it with the quotes you obtain from lenders who are known for being very competitive in your area.

Occasionally, clients or lenders fax us copies of "Good Faith Estimate" forms for our review and feedback. The interest rate is a critical factor and many lenders will quote the same rate. The "Good Faith Estimate" provides the advisor with the details of the other costs involved. Lenders can vary greatly on their costs.

Doing due diligence thoroughly and updating that information periodically will help the advisor arrive at a good list of competitive lenders to call or send clients to for first or second mortgages. These lenders can also provide the advisor with information on any available "First Time" homebuyers programs. Try using www.Ask.com. Type in "first time home buyers programs" and you'll find a lot of information about state sponsored programs as well as other tips.

As mentioned before, there are tax advantages to owning one's own home. However, I too frequently hear "I think we should buy a bigger house because we need the tax breaks." Clients need our guidance to help them determine how many of these "tax breaks" they can really afford. Remember, just because interest on a mortgage is tax deductible, doesn't mean that one still doesn't have to pay the mortgage. The mortgage may cost only 5% after adjusting for the tax benefits, but it still costs 5% a year on the total amount borrowed.

One of the other things planners often fail to consider is the actual value of the mortgage deduction. To truly evaluate the tax benefits, we also must consider the automatic standard deduction we would receive if we didn't itemize. For many Middle Americans, the total of their itemized deductions is not significantly greater than their standard deduction. Therefore, we may be overestimating the value of the tax benefits of owning a home.

Consider the simple comparison in the following example. Suppose the clients pay $700 per month now on rent and want to find out how much house is "affordable" for them. An $80,000 mortgage at 7% for 30 years would result in a principal and interest payment of $532 per month. The total payment, including real estate taxes and insurance would be approximately, $690 per month (at least in the Kansas City market). This is before factoring in the tax savings. On the surface, it looks like an $80,000 mortgage, with the additional maintenance expenses associated with home ownership, may come out pretty even to the client's current rent.

I use www.Leadfusion.com/products/calculators for these types of calculations. They have an incredible variety of calculators on this site and the reports and graphs are very well done.

Clients often ask me whether they should accelerate the repayment schedule on their mortgage, or pay off their mortgage entirely. In the past, I nearly always recommended that they do the "right" thing financially. However, over time I've come to realize that the psychological reasons clients may have for wanting to pay off their mortgage are far more important. So now I tell them that there are two answers to that question. One is financial and the other is psychological—and sometimes the two don't always agree. We must keep in mind that security is one of the primary motivators of our clients. Owning one's home, free and clear, provides clients with possibly the greatest feeling of financial security they will ever have.

Other clients may want to accelerate their mortgage payments so they can eliminate the need for private mortgage insurance (PMI). Typically, if a borrower has less then a 20% down payment they must pay PMI. This additional expense might be about $60/month on an $80,000 mortgage. However, the borrower may now request that their mortgage company remove the PMI once they have at least 20% equity. This equity can be obtained by appreciation and/or by paying down the mortgage. We provide clients with a "One-Sheet" on how to eliminate the PMI (see below) and coach them on the process.

Cancellation of Private Mortgage Insurance (PMI)

Only the lender knows for sure if the borrower can cancel the PMI. Many lenders have specific requirements for canceling. If the borrower's loan closed on or after July 29, 1999, the Homeowners Protection Act (HPA) requires the lender to cancel PMI at the borrower's request when the mortgage balance reaches 80% of the home's original value. Or, the mortgage insurance will cancel automatically by the lender when it reaches 78%. The borrower should contact the lender directly for details.

As I mentioned in Chapter 7 on Cash Flow and Debt Management, I strongly encourage all clients with at least 20% equity to have a home equity line of credit for emergency purposes. Even if a client doesn't have a first mortgage any longer, having a line of credit already in place is a good idea because it may become necessary for them to access the equity in their home on very short notice.

Over the last few years I've worked with a lot of clients who needed to refinance their mortgages. General guidelines previously stated that if a homeowner could reduce his or her interest rate by 2%, one should probably refinance. More often than not, however, it makes sense to refinance when there is a much smaller deferential in rates. For instance, if the homeowner plans on staying in the house forever, a small reduction in interest rates (presuming the upfront costs are reasonable) may be worthwhile. However, in my experience, clients generally need to stay in their home for at least three years to come out ahead on a refinancing. There is a calculator at www.Leadfusion.com/products/calculators that can assist in determining how long it takes to be "in the money" after refinancing. You'll need the information from the "Good Faith Estimate" to complete this calculation.

The equity buildup in one's home may also be accessed for retirement income. In some circumstances, using a reverse mortgage can be a very appropriate financial planning strategy. However, it is still only theoretical for me. Personally, I haven't yet advised someone to take out a reverse mortgage, but, I do see that there could be optimal circumstances where such a strategy might help.

The clients must be at least 62 years of age and typically have a least 70% equity in their home. For more information visit AARP's guide to reverse mortgages at www.aarp.org/revmort. Consider providing a copy of this guide to clients who may benefit from a reverse mortgage.

College Funding

The most important financial goals to middle Americans tend to be:

- owning their own home;
- educating their kids; and
- retiring comfortably.

College funding is almost always a priority for people with children. Although most parents had to pay part or all of their own way through college, today many want to pay the lion's share of the costs to send their children to the colleges of their choice. They usually don't realize that tuition is five to ten times the amount it was when these people were in college! (Fortunately, required room and board has not increased that dramatically.) Quicken (www.quicken.com) has a wonderful tool that allows the advisor to quickly find the current tuition rates and room and board for any college in the country. Many online financial planning software applications also have this information built into their system. I find it valuable to have current costs for our local colleges and universities readily available.

The standard of living for college students is also much greater today than it was when the current generation's parents were in school. Their parent's generation (i.e., my generation) drove old, fully paid for cars—if we had one at all. Two pairs of good jeans was a wardrobe. We didn't have cell phones, computers, Palm Pilots, and three pairs of Nikes. We didn't eat out much, and when we did it was on the cheap. Cooking to a college student meant "mac and cheese" out of a box, 3 for $1.

But the generation heading off to college today has had it pretty good as young, middle Americans. Their standard of living may drop dramatically when they move away from home unless mom and dad support them. Parents today usually don't want to see their kids have to struggle. They often desire to provide more financial support to their college students than they can afford. Helping our clients to balance priorities is one of our most important jobs as financial planners. Remember parents of college students: there is no such thing as financial aid for retirement!

Most clients that have hired me for college funding advice have also engaged me to provide retirement projections. Thus, we knew what assets and discretionary income they have to accomplish both goals. Generally, some compromise must be achieved. Clients will either have to tighten their budget, or make other adjustments, such as working longer. They may have to forgo their plan to retire at 60 if they want to send junior to the art institute.

Most clients are willing to adjust their retirement objectives—but only so far. If they can retire at 65 and still be able to send junior to the art institute, they want our help to make that happen. However, if our analysis reveals that the parents would have to work 15 years longer than they had hoped, the shortfall will probably be coming out of the kid's college education fund.

I rarely meet parents that are willing to forego their retirement to make sure they pay for their kids' college educations. But it does happen occasionally. I have worked with families who would do *anything* to make sure they could send their children to any institution they wanted to go. The education of their children is the primary goal of these clients. It is my belief that if a person wants to go to college, they can and should go. There are lots of options to help them achieve that goal. Parents need to realize that they may not have the option of working forever. And they should take reality into account when deciding how much they can realistically afford to contribute toward their child's college education.

The cost of a college education varies greatly depending on the institution selected, the financial assistance available, and the student's lifestyle. The tuition for a community junior college is often a fraction of the price to attend a state university. And in-state tuition is significantly cheaper than out-of-state tuition.

If the student attends his first two years at junior college, then transfers to the university of his choice, mom and dad could save a lot of money and the diploma would still say "My-Choice-U." What negative impact would attending junior college for two years and then graduating from the state/private university have on the child's career or life ambitions? We need to help our clients determine the financial impact of these decisions.

This is the art of what we do. We must help the clients achieve appropriate balance for themselves without letting our personal judgments interfere. We are advisors, and there is a fine line between providing advice and making judgments. It's the client's lives, not ours, and we are hired to help *them* plan for their life financially.

At the rate technology and distance learning programs are advancing, and traditional college tuitions increasing, in the future we may be seeing a lot of students attend "virtual" college classes.

The cost of sending a child to college can be a difficult thing to estimate. We must project the type of institution they will attend, how many years they should plan for, how much college costs may inflate, and the cost of room and board. Unless parents can easily fund both their retirement and education objectives—which makes trying to achieve a balance a moot point—we generally run two scenarios. We start by getting input from the clients regarding (1) the minimum goals they want to accomplish, and (2) their optimum goals. The first projection will show how their retirement plans will be impacted if they are funding for the minimal level of college support. The second scenario will reveal the impact of the full funding objective. With that information, we can assist the client in making the best decisions for them.

There are many excellent college-funding calculators on the web. I recommend www.Quicken.com/calculators and www.LeadFusion.com/products/calculators. As I mentioned earlier, we use MoneyTree's EasyMoney as our primary financial planning software. EasyMoney has a quality education-funding module. It provides more flexibility than any of the online college funding calculators with which I have worked.

Once we determine the appropriate funding level, we then must consider the most effective funding strategy. Over the last few years, Congress has given us some new and wonderful education funding programs (see Figure 9.1).

Figure 9.1

Education Incentives

Incentive	Tax Benefit	Higher Education Expenses Covered	Phaseouts
Qualified Tuition Plans	Up to $100,000 or more can be contributed to a tax-deferred account per beneficiary. If not used for education, then earnings subject to 10% penalty. Can be rolled over to other beneficiaries.	Tuition, fees, books, supplies, equipment, room, and board.	Not Applicable.
HOPE Scholarship Credit	Credit of $1,650 per student for each of the first two years of postsecondary education. Credit is 100% of first $1,100 of expenses and 50% of second $1,100 of expenses. These amounts could be indexed annually for inflation in future years.	Tuition and related expenses of taxpayer, taxpayer's spouse, or taxpayer's dependent. Not room, board, books, student activity fees, athletic fees, insurance expenses, or transportation expenses.	For 2007, phased out for single taxpayers from $47,000 to $57,000 ($94,000 to $114,000 for joint filers).
Lifetime Learning Credit	Credit of 20% of up to $10,000 of higher education expenses paid by the taxpayer. Cannot be used in year HOPE Credit is claimed.	Same as HOPE Credit.	Same as HOPE Credit.
Coverdell Education Savings Account	Up to $2,000 per year can be contributed to a tax-free account. Limited to $2,000 per beneficiary (child). Not taxable when used for beneficiary's education expenses. If not, then subject to additional 10% penalty. Can be rolled over to other beneficiaries.	Tuition, fees, books, supplies, equipment, room, and board. Also, qualified elementary and secondary education expenses, such as tuition, fees, academic tutoring, and special needs services, and computers or Internet access fees during any school years of the beneficiary.	Phased out for single taxpayers from $95,000 to $110,000 of AGI and for joint filers from $190,000 to $220,000 of AGI.
Interest on Education Loans	Above the line deduction for interest on student loans. $2,500.	Tuition, fees, books, supplies, equipment, room, and board.	Phased out for single taxpayers from $55,000 to $70,000 of AGI and for joint filers from $110,000 to $140,000 of AGI.
Educational Savings Bonds	Interest earnings can be withdrawn tax-free if used for education.	Same as HOPE credit, but taxpayer must be at least age 24.	For 2007, phased out for single taxpayers from $65,600 to $80,600 of AGI and for joint filers from $98,400 to $128,400 of AGI.

Reprinted with permission from *101 Tax Saving Ideas* (Wealth Builders Press, 8th edition, 2006), by Randy Gardner, LL.M., CPA, CFP®, and Julie Welch, CPA, CFP®.

Coverdell Education Savings Account (ESA)

The first great option is the Coverdell Education Savings Account (ESA), previously called an Education IRA. When ESAs were first introduced, individuals were allowed to contribute $500 per year, per child, in a tax deferred investment account. Subsequently, the laws were greatly improved by increasing the allowable contribution to $2,000 per child, per year.[10] Before, it was difficult to invest $500 conveniently, but investment options are greatly enhanced now that the maximum annual-per-child contribution has been increased to $2,000.

The primary features and benefits of the Coverdell Education Savings account are very similar to those of Roth IRAs:

- The client doesn't get a deduction at the time of contribution. But, the earnings grow tax-free and if the funds are used to pay qualified education expenses, they are not taxed upon withdrawal.
- The child is the owner of the account.
- The maximum contribution is $2,000 per year, per child.
- Contributions can be made until the child/owner reaches age 18.
- Contributions may be made until April 15 of the following year.
- Anyone with income of less than $110,000 ($220,000 if married filing jointly) may contribute on behalf of the child.
    - A full contribution is allowed if income is less than $95,000 for single taxpayers and $190,000 if married filing jointly.
    - Phase-out occurs between $190,000 and $220,000 for those who are married filing jointly. For all other taxpayers, phase-out occurs between $95,000 and $110,000.
    - Parents who are ineligible to make an ESA contribution due to income levels may gift funds to another family

member, such as a grandparent, who meets the income requirement who can, in turn, make the annual contributions.

- Money contributed to an ESA can qualify for the gift tax annual exclusion.

- The balance of the account generally must be distributed by the time the child reaches age 30.

    - Distributions are tax-free and penalty-free if used to pay for qualified education expenses. (Qualified education expenses include any qualified elementary, secondary, and post-secondary school tuition, fees, books, and supplies. Room and board for a full-time college student may also be considered qualified education expenses.)
    - The child may transfer the account tax-free and penalty-free to an ESA of a family member or their own child.
    - Distributions for any other purpose are subject to tax and penalty.

- A parent may claim the Hope Scholarship Credit or the Lifetime Learning Credit for part of the educational expenses and use tax-free ESA distributions for the expenses over and above the credit taken.

Section 529 Plans

Qualified tuition savings plans (Section 529 plans) have evolved into one of the most attractive college savings programs available to Middle Americans. Contributions grow tax-free until distribution. Distributions are also tax-free if used to pay for qualified education expenses.

Contributions to a Section 529 plan can be significantly greater than those allowed in an Education Savings Account. Contributors may also be able to take a tax deduction on their state income tax return for the year in which the contribution is made if they are residents of the state sponsoring the plan and the state allows a deduction. One can make contributions to any state's qualified tuition savings plan; however, no state income tax deduction is granted unless the contributor resides in that state.

The amount contributed into a qualified tuition plan is considered a gift, unlike contributions to ESAs. The maximum allowable contribution to a plan is set by the state sponsoring the plan.

An excellent resource on 529 plans is the web site www.SavingforCollege.com. It provides proprietary "5-Cap Ratings" on all 529 plans offered. This site also allows one to conduct a side-by-side comparison of all 529 plans based on criteria that is important to your client. It is an extremely valuable comparison tool.

UTMA/UGMA

With the other education savings plans available today, we find no use for UTMA/UGMA (Uniform Transfer to Minors/Uniform Gift to Minors) accounts. With the 1986 tax law changes, the advantages of these accounts became extremely minimal—too minimal, in my opinion, for parents to give up control of assets. However, a lot of our clients still have them. Most were set up prior to 1986.

We must be aware that taxable income and capital gains distributions come from UTMA/UGMA accounts. They may have to be reported on the parent's tax return if the child is under age 18. These accounts are not tax-deferred or tax-free education savings plans and pale in comparison to the Section 529 and Coverdell Education Savings accounts now available.

Many clients have asked if they can take money out of over-funded UTMA/UGMA accounts to keep it away from a child nearing age of majority. The answer is no, they can't. These funds are already the children's assets. As guardians of minor children, parents must protect these assets. Parents have a legal obligation to provide for the care of their children. Unfortunately, I know of no court case that has defined just exactly for what reasons a custodian can remove assets from a child's ownership.

Financial Aid

Financial aid planning is an important subspecialty of college planning. Regardless of whether our clients have the assets to pay for their child's college expenses, it is generally advisable for them to apply for financial assistance with federal and state governments, and institutional assistance as well.

I do not consider myself to be a financial aid specialist, so I would usually outsource this service to a college funding specialist firm, such as, *Fox College Funding*. I can efficiently provide an extremely useful service. Most Middle Americans can greatly benefit from implementing the basic strategies revealed in a "Solutions Plan." These simple, but often-overlooked, techniques will enhance the amount and possibility of receiving financial aid for the student.

Practitioners serving the Middle Market should know the deadlines and processes involved in applying for financial aid. With appropriate lead time, we may be able to lower the "Expected Family Contribution." Simple income and asset transfer techniques can result in hundreds of dollars saved for the client.

Education funding is one of the top three financial objectives of Middle Americans. Financial aid is a significant factor for most clients being able to achieve their dream. Practitioners who elect to specialize in college funding must dedicate themselves to continual education in the area of financial aid, or outsource this part of their service.

As we discussed earlier, parents must often compromise their retirement objectives in order to accomplish their desire to pay for their children's college education. Generally, when we are talking about this type of compromise, college is many years away. But, unfortunately, many parents don't have a lot of time to plan and save. They have three children ranging in age from 12 to 16. Their compromise may have to come from their children. They may have to pay for these costs out of cash flow, somehow, or they may have to borrow money personally.

When borrowing money to pay for college expenses, I first want to see the student take out Stafford (federal unsubsidized) loans. These student loans are *not* need-based. The student can receive this loan regardless of whether the family qualifies for financial aid. The current interest rate on these loans is 6.8%. Repayment of the principal of Stafford loans begins six months after the student graduates.

The next best option for college financing is generally Federal PLUS (Parents' Loans for Undergraduate Students) loans. These are unsecured loans and the current interest rate is 8.5%. Interest on student loans is also tax deductible in many cases. If additional borrowing is necessary, we consider a home equity line of credit and then a 401(k) plan loan, while remaining conscious of the need for balance between the education and retirement funding objectives.

Financial Independence / Retirement

Performing a retirement capital needs analysis will answer the question "how much is enough?" But first we must know what the client's retirement lifestyle might be like. Will the client stay in their current home or will they downsize at or during retirement? Do they plan to travel or take up an expensive hobby once they have more leisure time? Some costs may go down at retirement, but very few retirees actually spend less than they did before they retired—unless they have to.

For most clients, we project that they will need a least 100% of what they currently spend for basic living expenses. We allow debt service payments to continue on their current amortization schedule. The cost of other periodic expenses such as home repairs, vacations, and the replacement of vehicles are added to the projection. Do we need to add the cost of health insurance or long-term care insurance? Which expenses will cease in the latter years of retirement? Elderly adults tend to spend much less on basic living expenses and entertainment than younger retirees. However, I am reluctant to project that living expenses will go down in the future. The cost of health care has increased significantly faster than most other expense items. The reductions experienced in some areas may be offset by increased health care costs.

It is estimated that seniors spend approximately ⅓ of their monthly income on health care expenses. I once ran a retirement scenario that illustrates this potential inevitability. My client spent $5,500 per month on basic living expenses, including her health insurance, prescriptions and other related medical costs. I inflated living expenses at 3%. However, as a very knowledgeable consultant to the health care industry, she was uncomfortable with that assumption for medical expenses. As a result, my client asked me to separate the health care costs from her other expenses, and inflate just those costs (health care) by 10% per year instead of the 3% per year I had been using for all living expenses. It was shocking how much this impacted her total living expense needs later in life. Heath care costs made up half of her income need at mortality.

Retirement Capital Needs Computation

When I was actively serving clients we utilized MoneyTree's EasyMoney module for most of our financial planning analysis and projections and I would continue to do so. We also owned MoneyTree's Golden Years and Silver Planner retirement projection modules, which are integrated with EasyMoney. Each module serves a different planning purpose. For quick projections and to graphically illustrate the impact of a change to basic assumptions (e.g., savings rate or inflation), Silver Planner is used. For clients with detailed cash flow planning needs, or for those who are nearing or in retirement, Golden Years is a very powerful tool. However, for most retirement projections we used EasyMoney.

MoneyTree also has a Monte Carlo simulation program. I find this analysis very informative. It helps us to remain ever conscious of the errors of averages. Remember, when we use averages, actual annual returns will be higher or lower then the average. We must be very conservative when we use static averages in our long-term projections. Unfortunately, some clients don't want to "buy-in" to assumptions they feel are too conservative. Our initial retirement capital needs computation may indicate that the client will meet their retirement income objectives if they receive an annual rate of return of 7%, year-in and year-out. Sounds simple enough, doesn't it?

Monte Carlo simulation reveals the impact of volatility on the assumed rate of return. One may be able to achieve a long-term average return of 7% with limited or substantial volatility. These ranges of returns over time provide us with the "average" rate of return. Monte Carlo takes into account the assumed volatility of returns and plots out potential outcomes. If a series of bad results happen in the early years of retirement, the client may run out of money decades too soon. If the best results happen in the early years of retirement, the client may die with millions of dollars. However, the average result may show that they might narrowly achieve their objective.

Advisors and clients must understand the limits of static averages in financial planning projections. Monte Carlo simulation helps illustrate the probabilities of achieving financial independence based on certain assumptions. We lower the static average assumption until the probability of success is fairly certain.

There are numerous software programs and retirement calculators on the Web that consumers can use. Many of these programs are excellent tools. However, most are very simplistic and cannot handle the huge number of potential variables and planning options a professional advisor is trained to recognize and project.

The basic assumptions a professional advisor uses will generally be significantly more reliable than what a novice consumer might think is appropriate. My default assumptions are as follows:

- Clients will need at least 100% of their current income in retirement, and possibly more, in the early years of retirement.

- Cost of living increases at projected at no less than 3% per year.

- Long-term rates of return on retirement assets are no more than 4% above the inflation rate.

- Social Security projections:

    - I do not project that clients under 40 will receive any Social Security retirement benefits.
    - I discount the projected amount of Social Security benefits for clients between 40 and 50 by 50%.
    - For clients over 50, we illustrate the client's projected retirement benefit. However, if clients can handsomely meet their retirement objectives without including Social Security, I will run a scenario without it. There are so many variables that can change long-term projections. I do not want to give clients the illusion that they have all this surplus wealth now. I don't want them to change the wonderful habits that will make their goals possible.

  - I use an inflation assumption on Social Security income of 1% per year.
- I do not assume tax rates will go down in the future. However, I may very likely increase tax rates in the future if I feel that would be most prudent.
- I project life expectancy to at least age 100.

As I discussed earlier in this chapter, most clients have to achieve some compromise in their financial objectives. Virtually no one can have everything they might want, no matter how much money they have. We all must decide what is most important to us.

Earlier in this century, average life expectancy was *much* shorter then it is now. When the Social Security program was introduced, recipients were only expected to receive benefits for a couple of years. Now many Americans will live longer in retirement than they spent in the workforce.

However, most Americans still hope to retire by age 65. This objective may be unrealistic because the capital needed to fund retirement income for 35 years is staggering. Most middle Americans will not be able to maintain their standard of living for such a long period of time. They must work longer, have additional income after "traditional" retirement, reduce their living expenses or save a substantially larger asset base than they might be able to accumulate. A professional advisor must help clients balance their objectives with reality.

I am seeing a trend with clients who want to "retire" from their current careers in their 50's and 60's, but continue to earn an income doing something they really love. Most of the time this means that they will have much less income. But balance and quality of life are most important to them. Consequently, they are willing to work much longer than traditional retirement ages if they can do what they truly love.

I once had the pleasure of working with a couple in their mid-40's who had achieved enough success to enable them to leave their fulltime professional careers and live the life they dreamed. They had both become successful part-time artists and they planned to enjoy this work indefinitely. In our retirement planning projections we determined that they would need to cover their basic living expenses with income earned from their artwork until at least age 75. This part-time income, along with their inherent frugality, made it possible for them to leave the hectic pace of their former careers and still have a high probability of achieving financial independence.

Qualified Retirement Plans

Virtually every Middle American that I've worked with needs to save more to achieve their retirement objectives. Many also have access to a qualified retirement plan through their employer, or could establish a qualified retirement plan as self-employed individuals. Generally, Middle Americans are not fully utilizing these vehicles and I believe the underutilization of qualified retirement plans is a result of:

- ignorance regarding how the plans work;
- underestimating the benefits of utilizing these plans; and
- lack of understanding of just how much must be saved in order to achieve our retirement objectives.

Throughout the planning process, we calculate the savings requirement and help educate people on the mechanics and value of their qualified retirement plan. Retirement plans are the best tax shelter around. Many employer-sponsored retirement plans also provide a matching contribution (or a percentage-based contribution, based on the employee's contributions) to participants. This is like finding "free money" and clients who are not fully taking advantage of a retirement plan with an employer match need to be educated that they are walking away from free money. That just doesn't make sense for most people to ignore. How else can they get a guaranteed 25 to 50% or more return on their money? There are very few good excuses for not participating in an employer sponsored retirement plan. These plans usually have hardship withdrawal provisions; they may also have loan provisions. In the event of many emergencies, the money or a portion of it could be accessible, so why not contribute?

Generally, consumers are uncomfortable investing in something they do not understand, or something they feel they are locked into.

As professional advisors, we can help eliminate the mystery of qualified retirement plans and illustrate the substantial benefits of tax-advantaged retirement savings vehicles for our clients.

I use "One-Sheets" to illustrate the value of investing through a 401(k) versus a non-tax deferred retirement vehicle (see below).

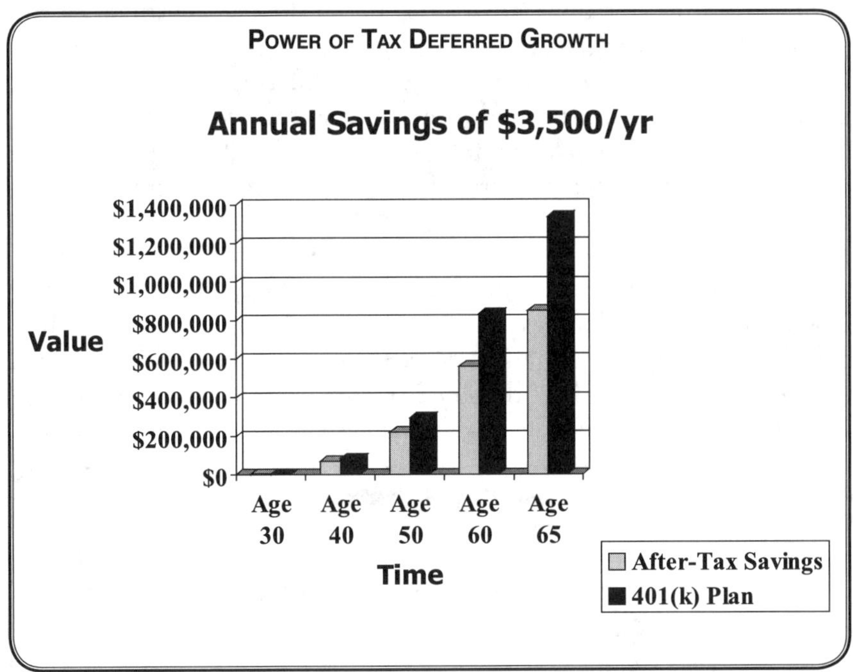

Two common types of qualified retirement plans available to average Americans are the 401(k) and 403(b) plans. I'll just focus my discussion on 401(k) plans because 403(b) plans function very much like 401(k) plans.

The maximum percentage of salary that can be deferred into a 401(k) plan (according to the government) is now 100%, however, each employer plan may have a lower limit. The maximum dollar amount of salary you can defer into a 401(k) plan for 2007 is $15,500 if you're under 50 years of age, and $20,500 if you're over 50 and over.

Many consumers are unaware that all of the money that they defer into a 401(k) plan is *theirs* if they leave the company. Many employers will also match a portion of the amount the employee contributes to the plan. Commonly, an employer will provide a matching contribution of 25% to 50% of the first 5% or 6% of salary contributed by the employee. Only employer contributions are subject to a vesting schedule.

It's hard for an employee to go wrong participating in a company's 401(k) plan when the employer provides a matching contribution. Even if the investment options are paltry, the matching contribution can provide a substantial return on investment. If the participant invests his or her contributions into a stable value subaccount and receives a minimal return of 4 to 5% per year and also receive a 25% matching contribution, the employee's total return is nearly 30% per year. There are no other vehicles that can provide this type of investment return with such minimal risk.

Once we convince clients that they should participate in their employer's 401(k) plan, we then have to help them increase their contributions from the minimum percentage to at least the level at which the employer matches. I use the simple techniques outlined below ("Save That Raise") to coach clients on increasing their 401(k) contributions.

SAVE THAT RAISE!

- Consider increasing your 401(k) contribution each time you receive an increase in your salary.

  Example: You receive a 2% cost-of-living increase. Subsequently, you increase your 401(k) contribution by 3%.

  After factoring in your tax savings, your net take home pay hardly changes. But you are saving an additional 3% of your salary to help meet your long-term goals.

- Another strategy is to make a deal with yourself to spend one-half of any salary increase and invest the other half in your 401(k) plan.

Once clients have increased their 401(k) plan contributions to the amount of the matching contribution, we then encourage them to make Roth IRA contributions, presuming (1) they need to save more for retirement (which is usually the case), and (2) they're eligible to contribute to a Roth IRA. If they're not eligible to make a Roth IRA contribution, we generally recommend that they increase their 401(k) and traditional IRA (nondeductible) to the maximum allowed by law, or their retirement funding requirement, whichever comes first.

In some circumstances, clients have minimal investments outside of qualified retirement plans. In these cases, we recommend that clients first contribute to their 401(k) plan in the amount the company will match, then make Roth IRA contributions, and then invest any additional savings for retirement in their personal ownership. This is not the most tax-effective investment strategy, but it does provide considerably more flexibility and, therefore, may be more palatable to the client.

There are ways to minimize current taxation on personal investment assets. We'll discuss ways to manage the tax effects in the chapter on investments. The most important factor is that the clients save the required amount needed to achieve their retirement objectives.

If you're self-employed, you can establish a retirement plan for yourself and make tax-deductible contributions. Self-employed people can set up a Keogh plan or a Simplified Employee Pension Plan (SEP) or a SIMPLE plan. The chart in Figure 9.4 compares the basic features of these plans.

Figure 9.2

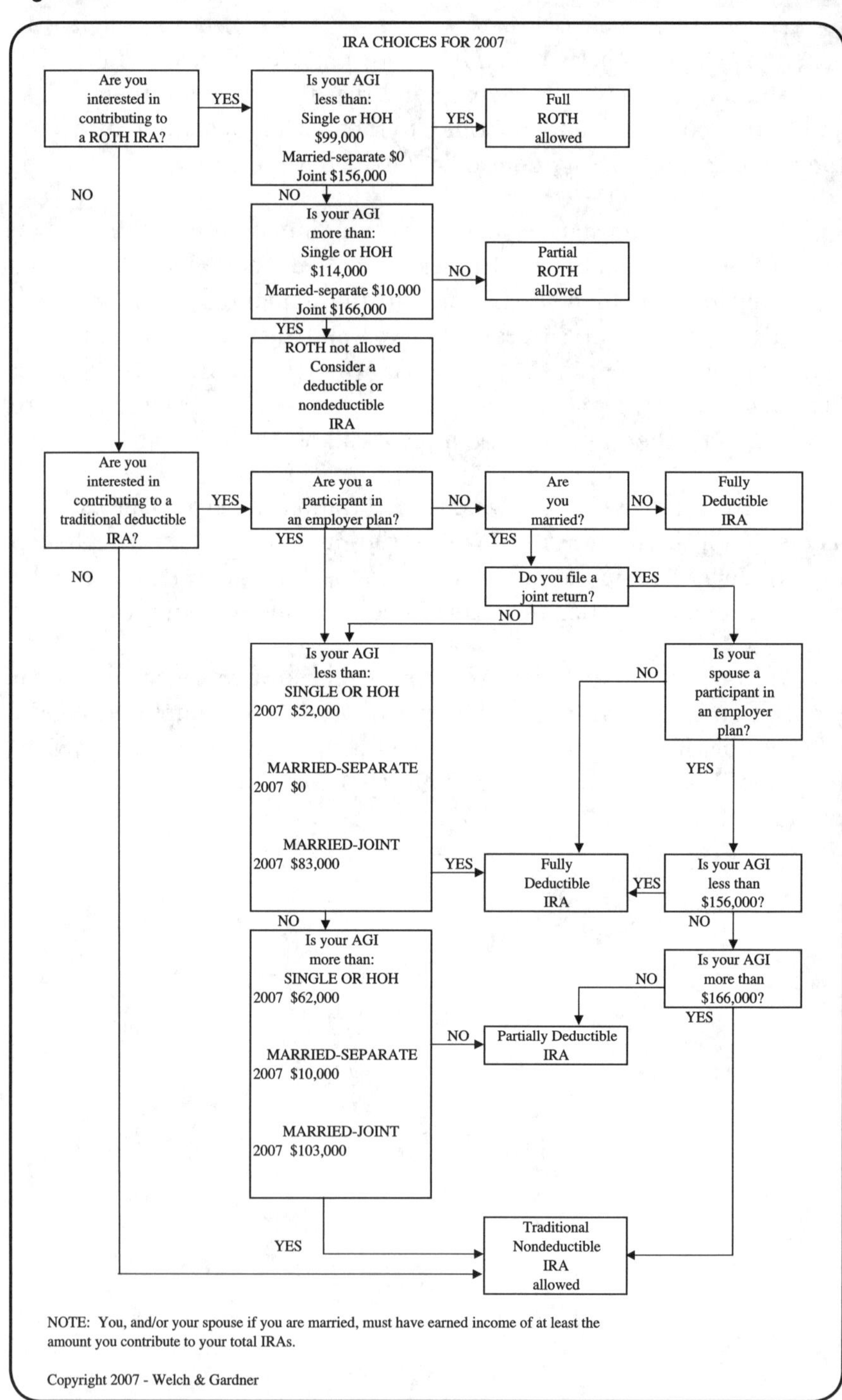
IRA CHOICES FOR 2007
Are you interested in contributing to a ROTH IRA?
YES
Is your AGI less than: Single or HOH $99,000 Married-separate $0 Joint $156,000
YES
Full ROTH allowed
NO
NO
Is your AGI more than: Single or HOH $114,000 Married-separate $10,000 Joint $166,000
NO
Partial ROTH allowed
YES
ROTH not allowed Consider a deductible or nondeductible IRA
Are you interested in contributing to a traditional deductible IRA?
YES
Are you a participant in an employer plan?
NO
Are you married?
NO
Fully Deductible IRA
YES
YES
Do you file a joint return?
YES
NO
NO
Is your AGI less than: SINGLE OR HOH 2007 $52,000 MARRIED-SEPARATE 2007 $0 MARRIED-JOINT 2007 $83,000
Is your spouse a participant in an employer plan?
NO
YES
YES
Fully Deductible IRA
YES
Is your AGI less than $156,000?
NO
NO
Is your AGI more than: SINGLE OR HOH 2007 $62,000 MARRIED-SEPARATE 2007 $10,000 MARRIED-JOINT 2007 $103,000
Is your AGI more than $166,000?
NO
YES
NO
Partially Deductible IRA
YES
Traditional Nondeductible IRA allowed
NOTE: You, and/or your spouse if you are married, must have earned income of at least the amount you contribute to your total IRAs.
Copyright 2007 - Welch & Gardner

Figure 9.3

IRA vs. Taxable Account

You are in the 34% (28% Federal and 6% state) tax rate bracket. You earn 10% (6.6% after tax) (10% x (1 - 34%)) on your investments. You make $4,000 contributions at the beginning of the year for 20 years to the following accounts:

	Roth IRA	Traditional Deductible IRA	Traditional Nondeductible IRA	Taxable Account
Annual contribution	$ 4,000	$ 4,000	$ 4,000	$ 4,000
Tax savings				
($4,000 x 34%)		1,360		
Cumulative contributions	80,000	80,000	80,000	80,000
Account value – Year 20	252,010	252,010	252,010	167,356
Tax on distribution				
($252,010 x 34%)		(85,683)		
(($252,010 - 80,000) x 34%)			(58,483)	
Net cash from tax savings including interest earned		56,901		
Net cash	$252,010	$223,228	$193,527	$167,356

Thus, if your tax rate stays the same for all 20 years, and if you have a choice between the above accounts (based on your income level and your participation in a retirement plan), your first choice would be to make your contributions to a Roth IRA.

However, if your tax rate decreases after you retire, a traditional deductible IRA may be better. Assume your Federal tax rate drops to 15% (21% including the 6% state tax rate) in year 20 when you withdraw the money.

	Roth IRA	Traditional Deductible IRA	Traditional Nondeductible IRA	Taxable Account
Annual contribution	$ 4,000	$ 4,000	$ 4,000	$ 4,000
Tax savings				
($4,000 x 34%)		1,360		
Cumulative contributions	80,000	80,000	80,000	80,000
Account value – Year 20	252,010	252,010	252,010	167,356
Tax on distribution				
($252,010 x 21%)		(52,922)		
(($252,010 - 80,000) x 21%)			(36,122)	
Net cash from tax savings including interest earned		56,901		
Net cash	$252,010	$255,989	$215,888	$167,356

In this case, your first choice would be to make your contributions to a traditional deductible IRA.

Reprinted with permission from *101 Tax Saving Ideas,* (Wealth Builders Press, 8th edition, 2006), by Randy Gardner, LL.M., CPA, CFP®, and Julie Welch, CPA, CFP®.

Figure 9.4

RETIREMENT PLAN ALTERNATIVES FOR 2007

PLAN TYPE	CONTRIBUTIONS	DISTRIBUTIONS	PHASEOUTS
Individual Retirement Accounts (IRA)	Limited to $4,000 ($5,000 if age 50+) per person or rollover amount. Deductible if not active participant in qualified plan or if under phase-out levels.	Taxable unless contributions were not deductible. May be subject to 10% penalty tax unless taxpayer is 59½, dead, disabled, first-time homebuyer, receiving over life expectancy, using for higher education expenses, or using for deductible medical expenses.	If active participant, $52,000 of AGI if single ($83,000 if married). If spouse only is active participant, $156,000 - 166,000 of AGI.
Roth IRA	Limited to $4,000 ($5,000 if age 50+) for IRAs and Roth IRAs, or rollover. Not deductible. May be made after age 70½. Conversion opportunity.	Not taxable. May be subject to 10% penalty if made early.	Phased out for single taxpayers from $99,000 to $114,000 of AGI and for joint filers from $156,000 to $166,000 of AGI.
Simplified Employee Pension Plan (SEP).	Deductible up to the lesser of $45,000 or about 20% of earnings/compensation. Discrimination rules apply.	Taxable. May be subject to 10% penalty if made early.	Not Applicable.
Keogh Plans	Deductible up to the lesser of $45,000 or about 20% of earnings. Discrimination rules apply.	Taxable. May be subject to 10% penalty if made early.	Not Applicable.
401(k) Plans	Exclusion from wages up to lesser of 15% of wages or $15,500 ($20,500 if age 50+).	Taxable. May be subject to 10% penalty if made early.	Not applicable, but special rules apply for highly compensated employees.
SIMPLE Plans	Deductible up to $10,500 ($13,000 if age 50+). Requires employer match for most employees.	Taxable. May be subject to 10% penalty if made early.	Not Applicable.

Reprinted with permission from *101 Tax Saving Ideas*, (Wealth Builders Press, 8th edition, 2006), by Randy Gardner, LL.M., CPA, CFP®, and Julie Welch, CPA, CFP®.

Only after all of the above retirement funding options have been maximized and the clients have developed a fairly substantial, tax-efficient personal portfolio will we consider annuities as a retirement funding vehicle.

PLANNING FOR LIFE'S TRANSITIONS

Many clients initially contacted me because they were going through some type of life transition. They may have been starting their first job, changing careers, newly married, starting a family, preparing for a divorce, reacting to a divorce, or preparing for retirement. Possibly current market events may have prompted them to seek out the advice of a financial planner. In any case, people sometimes assume that because I allow clients to engage me for a very limited scope of services that I don't discuss the key details of the client's overall financial situation with them. Regardless of the event that motivated a prospective client to call, I recommend always going through the thorough "get acquainted" meeting as a conversation and data gathering process centered on our Confidential Questionnaire (see Figure 6.1 in Chapter 6) at each initial meeting.

The objectives for the initial "Get Acquainted" meeting are to:

- determine the scope of services that should be provided at this time;

- provide a fee quote;

- request additional data needed to complete the project; and

- schedule the presentation meeting.

Prospective clients may have contacted me for input on their 401(k) plan allocation. However, by the time we have discussed the information provided on the Confidential Questionnaire we generally determine that there are several other areas that need to be addressed at this time as well.

Clients rarely balked at the services I recommended or my fee quote. I presume this was due to the fact that I am very conscientious of their needs, priorities, and resources. I try to put myself in their shoes. If I only had $4,000 in the bank and $200 dollars a month discretionary income, how much would I be willing to spend on a financial advisor's services at this time? What services are really essential? What can the client do to keep the cost down?

As I've mentioned before, I would much rather help a client with one or a few areas of their financial situation, than miss out on the opportunity to help them at all.

The client who is changing careers or just starting a new job may need advice on completing their W-2 form, taking full advantage of the employee benefits plan, and allocating 401(k) contributions.

If a client is leaving a current salaried position to start a business of their own, we must consider additional issues. We strongly recommend that a home-equity line of credit be established before leaving current employment, if one is not already in place. The options available for medical and disability insurance must also be considered. Can this individual be covered under their spouse or domestic partner's group plan? Can the employer-sponsored medical or disability insurance be converted to individual policies? If these options are not available, approximately how much will it cost to adequately replace this insurance protection? Eventually, we will need to consider establishing a qualified retirement plan to maximize the self-employed individual's retirement funding options.

For those clients who are newly married or just starting a family, our primary focus will be on current and near-term cash flow needs. How has the merger of two individual's financial lives set the stage for their financial planning together? Many of these issues need to get out in the open. My role is to help clients recognize how their financial lives have changed and what steps we need to be taking now to help them fulfill their long-term financial objectives.

Unfortunately, many clients came to me for the first time immediately after divorce. I say unfortunately because often times they may have been much better served seeking out the advice of a financial planner *prior* to negotiating their divorce settlement. I did not hold myself out as a divorce-planning specialist. In the event that a prospective client needing specific divorce planning expertise contacted me, I referred this individual to a colleague who specializes in this area. Once the divorce is final, however, I would have been more than happy to have entered into a traditional financial planning relationship with the client.

For clients who've already divorced, we generally need to focus their attention on redefining themselves as an individual financially. What are their expenses? What income sources do they have? What are the most immediate and pressing needs of this client? What are his or her financial and life goals? We must spend a considerable amount of time working out the current cash flow needs before we can start planning seriously for the future.

These types of engagements often involve several meetings spread over many months. Occasionally, people come to me looking for a miracle. I had an initial meeting with a prospective client who had retired from teaching three years earlier. She was receiving her full teacher's retirement benefit, but that only provided her with about one-half of the income she needed. So she went back to teaching full-time, with another school district, and continued to draw her pension. She spent all of her income. She hoped that I could invest her IRA assets ($56,000) so that she could afford to quit working in three years when she turns 65. I could tell that she would likely run out of money within 5 years if she didn't work longer, save more, *and* spend less. That was not the news she wanted. She wanted an investment miracle.

I gave the prospective client a copy of *Your Money or Your Life* and encouraged her to start making reductions to her budget now and save more for retirement. I also told her that she needed to consider working longer if she couldn't greatly reduce her expenditures. In other words, there would have to be an adjustment in lifestyle. It would come either when she ultimately retired, or could begin immediately. I stressed that it would be easier to tolerate if these adjustments were gradually implemented over time.

Unfortunately, too many Americans go into retirement with a warped perspective regarding how much money they will *really* need to maintain their standard of living. Without the assistance of a qualified financial advisor, these retirees may have a very rude awakening. They fail to appreciate the devastating effects inflation can have on their standard of living over time. They expect the current interest rate environment to remain unchanged. Their retirement plans may work out okay—if they don't experience any market downturns.

At one point, I saw a lot of clients who had adequate cash flow when interest rates on fixed income investments were higher, but subsequently were receiving less than two-thirds of the income they received just a few years ago. If they had any money in the stock market, it had also lost ground. These retirees are facing the hard realities that too many Americans have faced in the past. Without the guidance of a personal financial advisor, many people retire before they are financially able to do so, and/or they invest their retirement nest egg inappropriately.

Early in my hourly practice I allowed myself to get into a debate with a prospective client who, with some limited knowledge, had convinced himself and his wife that they could retire in 10 years and maintain their current standard of living. They had about $500,000 in investment assets when we met. The gentleman concluded that in 10 years, when they were age 60, they should have about $1,400,000. This was based on his assumption that he could earn 10% per year, year-in and year-out, on these investments. He knew that the stock market has averaged about 10% per year over time, and that is what he was basing his calculation on.

The couple's objective was to receive $100,000 per year in after-tax income. So the gentleman determined that they needed $1,400,000 at retirement to provide $140,000 (10%) gross earnings, which would yield about $100,000 after-tax.

I tried to explain why this strategy had little hope of success. Primarily, the prospective clients couldn't count on 10% rates of return, year-in and year-out, and they had not factored in the effects of inflation. The gentleman felt that if they received $100,000 per year in after-tax income, they should be able to handle whatever inflation comes their way. He felt that "a good financial advisor" could make certain that they received a "measly" 10% per year return (this was in 1999). Needless to say, I told them I couldn't deliver those results with any degree of certainty and anyone who said they could, shouldn't be trusted. We parted company and I haven't heard from them since.

Financial planning is all about setting goals and plotting a course that will help clients to achieve their goals with a high probability of success. However, events may crop up that abruptly change the course of our clients' lives. The death of a family member, the loss of a job, or long-term illness can all have a major impact on one's life, but they don't necessarily have to have a major impact on one's financial plan. We must do our best to prepare for these events physically and mentally by adequately insuring our families, having an appropriate level of cash reserves, and not overextending ourselves.

Chapter 10

Investment Portfolio Design, Implementation and Maitenance

Investment Portfolio Design

As financial planners we are often involved with reviewing clients' exsisting investment portfolios and making recommendations for improvement. We may also take on the role of providing periodic or ongoing montioring and management of clients' portfolios. However, as we know, investments are only one aspect of financial planning.

A financial planner has the unique role of "quarterback" of the financial services team. We may help clients by providing guidance and advice regarding specific issues, or prepare and assist in implementing a comprehensive financial plan. Unfortnately, too many people, including some within our industry, view investment advice as the primary or sole function of a financial planner. As we know, investment advice is an important component of financial planning, but it is only one component. I would like to see financial planners focus on financial planning, and let specialists focus on their areas of specialty.

In recent years, we have seen numerious developments in the investment arena. The Internet has made investment research and portfolio management accessible to everyone. Brokerage commissions have plummeted. The popularity of passive investment strategies, the use of index funds and the advent of Exchange Traded Funds has changed the landscape dramactically. Investors and advisors are implementing asset allocation strategies designed to minimize fees, taxes and the need for continual and ongoing portfolio supervision.

Possibly, the financial planner is not the most appropriate professional to be providing continual and ongoing portfolio supervision to the client. Firms like Portfolio Solutions, Inc. out of Troy, Michigan work directly with investors, and now many financial planners, to provide any continual and ongoing portfolio management needed.

As an independently registered investment advisor I was licensed to provide investment advice to my clients and I felt competent in doing so. And to a certain degree, with most clients, I did provide investment advice. But there were occasions when clients would be best served by having a full-time professional portfolio manager. As a hourly advisor, I made the business decision not to "manage money". As a fiduciary, I have great difficulty justifying what I would have to charge to provide continual and on-going portfolio supervision services, when I could outscorce this service to a team of professionals, CFAs and traders, to firms like Portfolio Solutions, Inc. They charge 0.25% or less per year. I can't compete with that price, and that is presuming I could do as well (or better) for my clients than these full-time professional money managers. As fiduciaries we are obligated to always put our clients' best interests first. I challenge financial planners to seriously consider if they are breaching their fiduciary responsibiliities by taking on the specialist role of money manager for their clients.

I also recognized that the overwhelming majority of clients who came to me were validators and do-it-yourselfers. They were not interested in, or didn't need full-time, ongoing portfolio management services. But most did need and requested investment advice. This chapter outlines my approach to investment portfolio design and implementation for these clients.

The first step in designing an investment portfolio is determining the objectives for the assets. For what purposes are the funds being accumulated? When will the funds be needed? Some objectives must be funded immediately (i.e., *needs*). Other objectives are *desires* that the client hopes to accomplish in the future; these can be funded over time.

There may be many objectives and time horizons that apply to a client's investment portfolio. Clients will probably have assets that need to be available in a few years to replace a car, pay for college expenses or pay for a wedding. Other assets may be earmarked for longer-term objectives (e.g., buying a retirement home), and still other assets must be available to fund retirement living expenses.

As mentioned previously, we all must prioritize our objectives and determine what we are willing to sacrifice in order to achieve our most important objectives. We can't have everything we may want. The greatest value a professional advisor may provide to their clients is in prioritizing goals, developing strategies that most effectively achieve these goals and helping clients stay on track to see their goals fulfilled.

Determining Risk Tolerance

In my opinion, determining a client's tolerance for risk is a very subjective art. Human beings tend to be overly confident when their most recent investment experiences have been very positive. Conversely, investors often become overly pessimistic when their recent experiences have been very negative.

My firm utilized a Risk Tolerance Questionnaire (see Figure 10.1). We had an industrial psychologist (one who specializes in developing questionnaires for the financial services industry) create our Risk Tolerance Questionnaire. The goal of the questionnaire was to make it short enough that a client would complete it, but thorough enough to provide meaningful information.

There are newer and really good options available now to assist us in determining clients' preferrences and attitudes toward risk. Please check out FinaMetrica and Financial DNA. They both have powerful tools that could be very useful.

We then provided this questionnaire to hundreds of clients, anticipating that we'd be able to draw some conclusions about the responses provided on the questionnaires and the clients' tolerance for risk. Early on, I'd hoped we would be able to generate a workable scoring system. Unfortunately, the only scoring that can be automated is on pages one and two of the questionnaire. Page three consists of essay questions, and this is where I generally get the most valuable information.

Figure 10.1

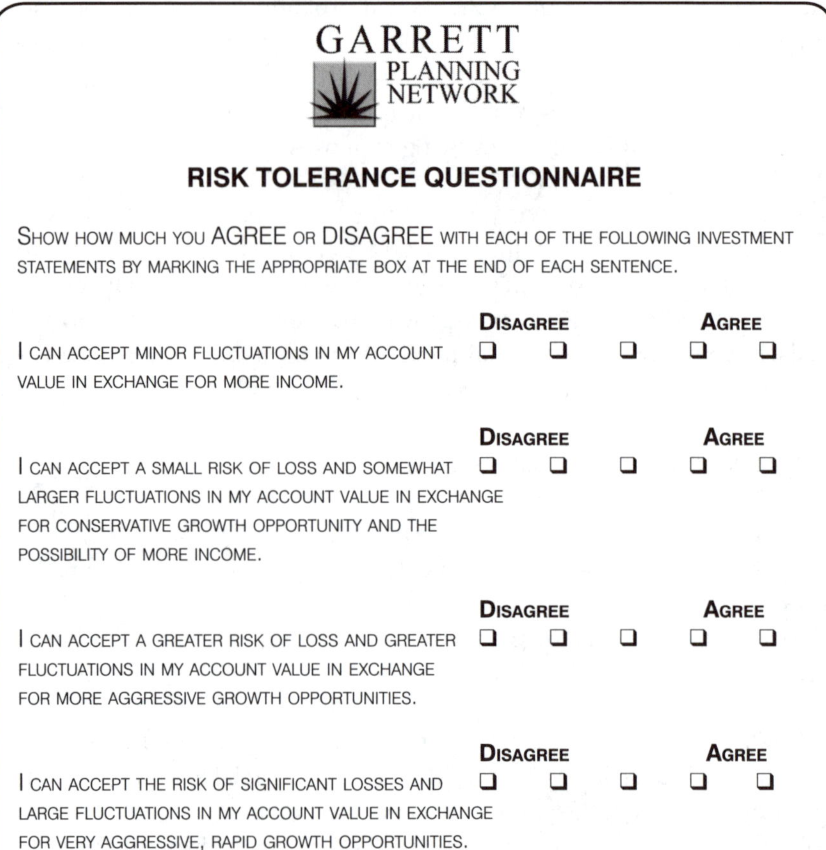

GARRETT PLANNING NETWORK

RISK TOLERANCE QUESTIONNAIRE

SHOW HOW MUCH YOU AGREE OR DISAGREE WITH EACH OF THE FOLLOWING INVESTMENT STATEMENTS BY MARKING THE APPROPRIATE BOX AT THE END OF EACH SENTENCE.

	DISAGREE				AGREE
I CAN ACCEPT MINOR FLUCTUATIONS IN MY ACCOUNT VALUE IN EXCHANGE FOR MORE INCOME.	❑	❑	❑	❑	❑
I CAN ACCEPT A SMALL RISK OF LOSS AND SOMEWHAT LARGER FLUCTUATIONS IN MY ACCOUNT VALUE IN EXCHANGE FOR CONSERVATIVE GROWTH OPPORTUNITY AND THE POSSIBILITY OF MORE INCOME.	❑	❑	❑	❑	❑
I CAN ACCEPT A GREATER RISK OF LOSS AND GREATER FLUCTUATIONS IN MY ACCOUNT VALUE IN EXCHANGE FOR MORE AGGRESSIVE GROWTH OPPORTUNITIES.	❑	❑	❑	❑	❑
I CAN ACCEPT THE RISK OF SIGNIFICANT LOSSES AND LARGE FLUCTUATIONS IN MY ACCOUNT VALUE IN EXCHANGE FOR VERY AGGRESSIVE, RAPID GROWTH OPPORTUNITIES.	❑	❑	❑	❑	❑

The survey revealed that investors' attitudes toward risk are much more subjective than we wish they were. We might like to have clients complete a questionnaire that would allow them to respond to each question simply by checking a box. Scoring becomes much less subjective when clients have to choose "True" or "False," or (A), (B), (C) or (D). However, the validity of the result becomes suspect if clients must choose their response from a limited number of options. The accurate response might be "sometimes," "it depends," or "possibly" rather than an absolute "always" or "never."

Figure 10.1 (Cont'd)

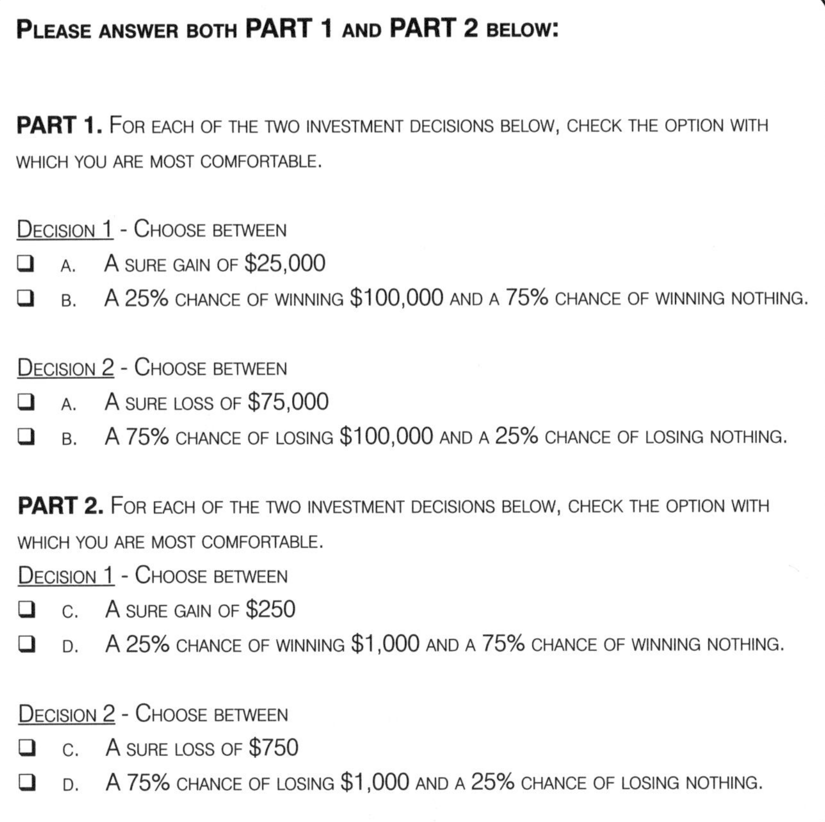

PLEASE ANSWER BOTH PART 1 AND PART 2 BELOW:

PART 1. FOR EACH OF THE TWO INVESTMENT DECISIONS BELOW, CHECK THE OPTION WITH WHICH YOU ARE MOST COMFORTABLE.

DECISION 1 - CHOOSE BETWEEN

- ❑ A. A SURE GAIN OF $25,000
- ❑ B. A 25% CHANCE OF WINNING $100,000 AND A 75% CHANCE OF WINNING NOTHING.

DECISION 2 - CHOOSE BETWEEN

- ❑ A. A SURE LOSS OF $75,000
- ❑ B. A 75% CHANCE OF LOSING $100,000 AND A 25% CHANCE OF LOSING NOTHING.

PART 2. FOR EACH OF THE TWO INVESTMENT DECISIONS BELOW, CHECK THE OPTION WITH WHICH YOU ARE MOST COMFORTABLE.

DECISION 1 - CHOOSE BETWEEN

- ❑ C. A SURE GAIN OF $250
- ❑ D. A 25% CHANCE OF WINNING $1,000 AND A 75% CHANCE OF WINNING NOTHING.

DECISION 2 - CHOOSE BETWEEN

- ❑ C. A SURE LOSS OF $750
- ❑ D. A 75% CHANCE OF LOSING $1,000 AND A 25% CHANCE OF LOSING NOTHING.

I found that I had to blend a lot of subjective and objective information together to form a conclusion about someone's risk tolerance. I relied not only on my Risk Tolerance Questionnaire, but also on comments the client(s) may have made during our initial meeting, the structure of their current portfolio, and their motivation for contacting me.

Behavioral finance teaches that human beings are most highly motivated by recent events. Consequently, I want to hear from the client(s) and see in their own handwriting how they feel about certain events and issues. I extrapolate from all possible sources: current portfolio allocation, recent trading activity, dialogues about priorities and the need for security, and the formal Risk Tolerance Questionnaire.

Figure 10.1 (Cont'd)

PLEASE ANSWER THE FOLLOWING QUESTIONS:

For your current investments, what has been your annual rate of return? ________

Have you been satisfied with that return? ________

If no, why not? ________

What percentage of your portfolio can you afford to lose or how much money can you afford to lose in any one year? ________

What action would you take if the market dropped 50% from its present value? ________

____

Regarding your finances, what, if anything, do you spend the most time thinking about?

____

____

Are there things in your financial life that you wish you had done differently?

____

____

Are you pleased with your ability to manage and shelter your income from taxes?

____

Are you pleased with the diversification and performance of your portfolio?

____

What is the best and worst investment decision you have ever made?

Best: ________

Worst: ________

Are there any investments that you will NOT sell for personal reasons?

____

Are there any investments that you will NOT buy for social reasons?

____

ASSET ALLOCATION

I then classified the client(s) according to one of five model allocations, ranging from conservative to aggressive. I found that most of this determination is subjective, but I relied heavily on the responses to their Risk Tolerance Questionnaire (primarily page 3) and their comfort level with their current portfolio allocation.

Our model portfolios (see Figure 10.2) began with broad allocations between fixed-income and equities, and between foreign and domestic securities. We then further allocated between large and small cap, and growth versus value. For our model portfolios, the allocations were fairly generic. We didn't make global allocation decisions on how much we might direct funds toward international fixed income, emerging markets, real estate, etc. But that doesn't mean that these asset classes were excluded from all client portfolios. For the models specifically, we limited the allocations to very traditional, broad-based asset classes.

With the type of relationship I had with clients (i.e., providing advice on an as-needed basis), I tried to do my best to provide them with an asset allocation that would *serve them well over time*. We never know, for certain, how often or when we'll see them again for a review. We *want* our broad allocation decisions to stand the test of time (the key word here is *want*). They were based on my judgment about the future and my interpretations of the client's risk tolerance level. Needless to say, it is very subjective.

I was not acting as a money manager – I was a financial planner who also gave investment advice. My objective was to achieve consistent, predictable returns over time on the entire portfolio to help the client achieve his or her financial objectives. Consequently, I strived to use assumptions in my long-term projections that have a very high probability of achieving the desired outcome.

I'm a true believer in asset allocation, but I'm not comfortable with the way many advisors use optimizer software programs. I've subscribed to the top optimizer programs over the years. I appreciated having that kind of resource available – not to design recommended portfolios, but to test how different portfolio allocations would have performed over various periods of time. To make the optimizer a predictive tool, however, I'd have to know what historical time period most resembles the period

Figure 10.2

Model Portfolios

For Illustration Purposes Only

Equity

Portfolio		Value	Blend	Growth
Conservative	Large	20	5	
	Med.			
	Small			
Moderately Conservative	Large	20	10	5
	Med.			
	Small			
Moderate	Large	20	15	15
	Med.			
	Small			
Moderately Aggressive	Large	25	20	10
	Med.	10		
	Small	5		5
Aggressive	Large	30	25	20
	Med.	10		5
	Small	5		5

Fixed

Portfolio		Short	Intermediate	Long
Conservative	High	50	25	
	Med.			
	Low			
Moderately Conservative	High	40	25	
	Med.			
	Low			
Moderate	High	30	20	
	Med.			
	Low			
Moderately Aggressive	High	15	10	
	Med.			
	Low			
Aggressive	High			
	Med.			
	Low			

	Conservative	Moderately Conservative	Moderate	Moderately Aggressive	Aggressive
US/ FOREIGN SPLIT	95/5	90/10	85/15	80/20	70/30

we're moving into now. I can't predict the future – and neither can you. (I still haven't learned how to use the crystal ball on my conference table!)

I have found Roger Gibson's book, *Asset Allocation: Balancing Financial Risk* (McGraw-Hill Trade, 2000), to be an excellent resource for advisors. Many of the graphics he provides in this book can be useful in helping clients understand and appreciate the value of a *truly* diversified portfolio.

I now recommend Richard Ferri's book, *All About Asset Allocation* (McGraw-Hill, 2006), and another great resource, William Bernstein's book, *The Intelligent Asset Allocator* (McGraw-Hill, 2000). Berstein also has a great web site at www.efficientfrontier.com.

Refer to Figure 10.3 for examples of illustrations of individual asset classes versus more diversified portfolios over time (These graphics were reprinted with permission from the *Tools & Techniques of Financial Planning*, The National Underwriter Company, 6th edition, 2002, pp. 48, 55.)

Figure 10.3

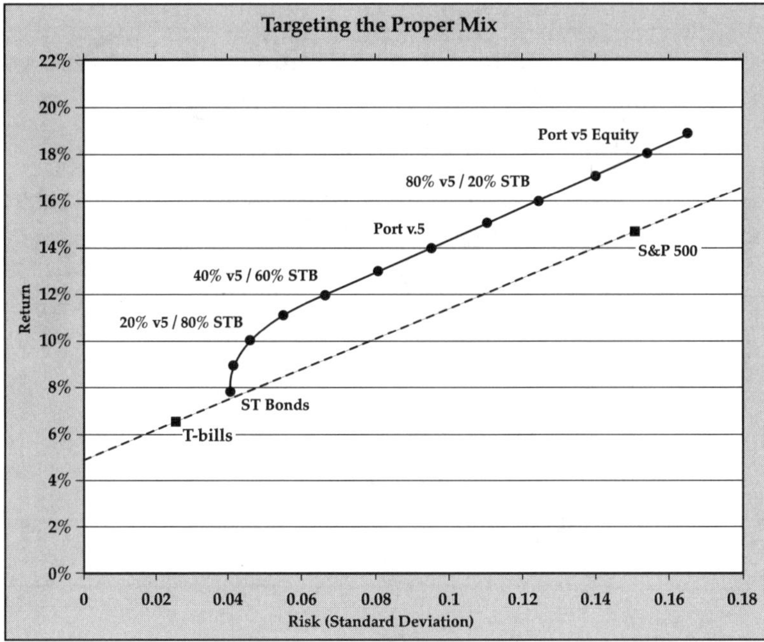

"The reference portfolio (v.5) has been diversified into eight equity segments. Seven of those segments have outperformed the S&P 500 Index on a historical basis, and one is the S&P 500 itself." (See *Tools & Techniques of Financial Planning*, p. 46.)

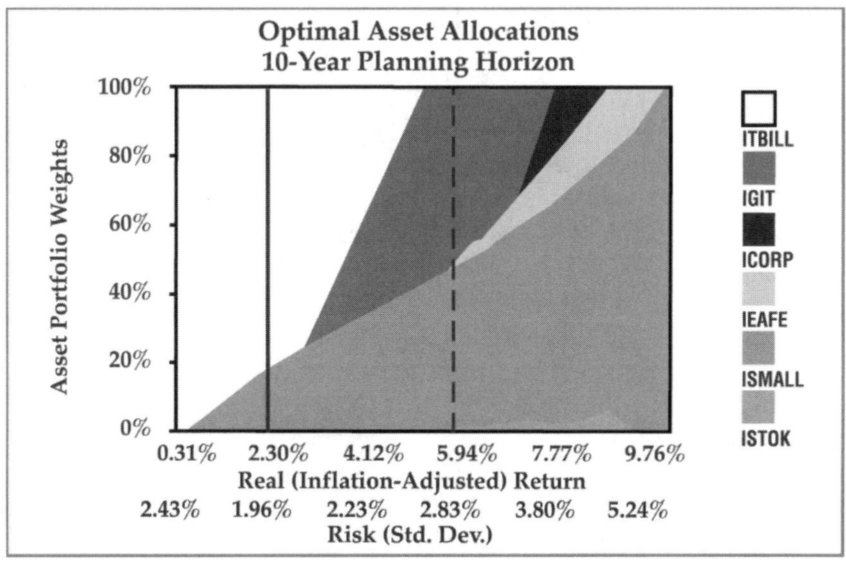

Figure 10.3 (Cont'd)

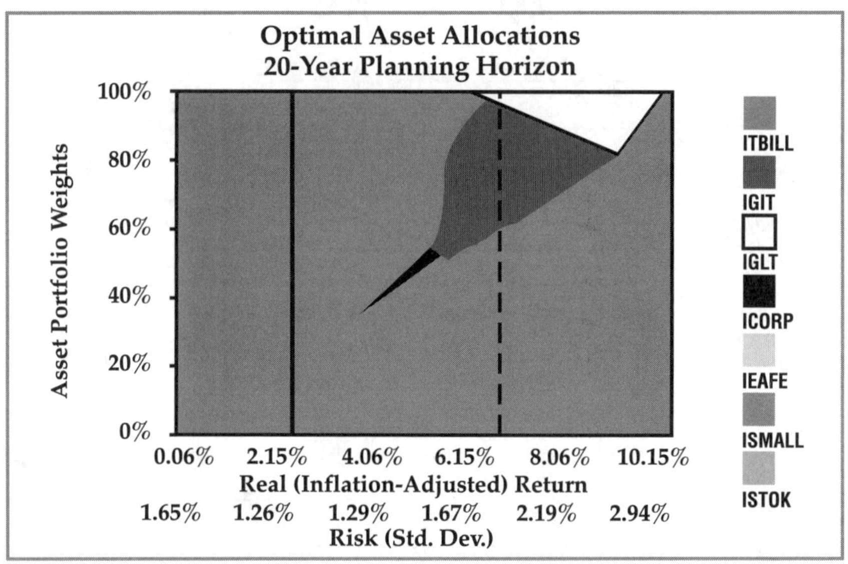

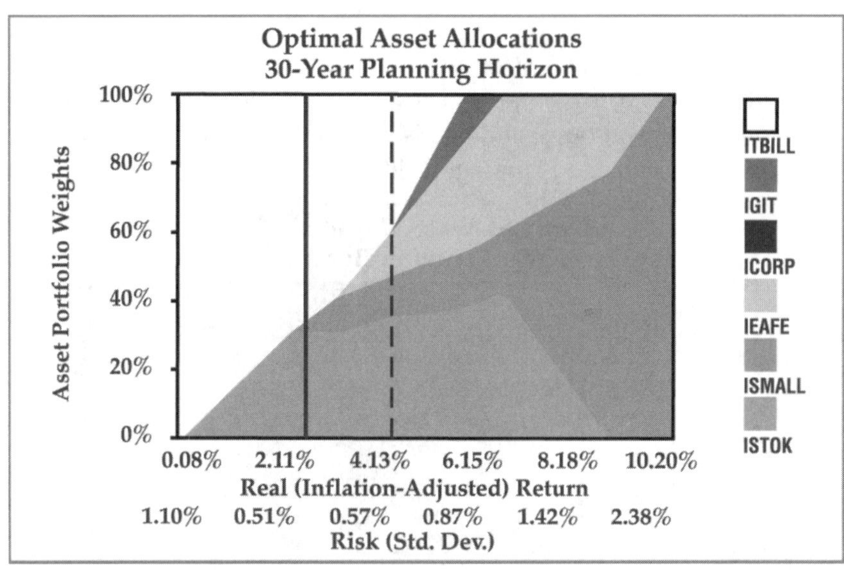

Figure 10.3 (Cont'd)

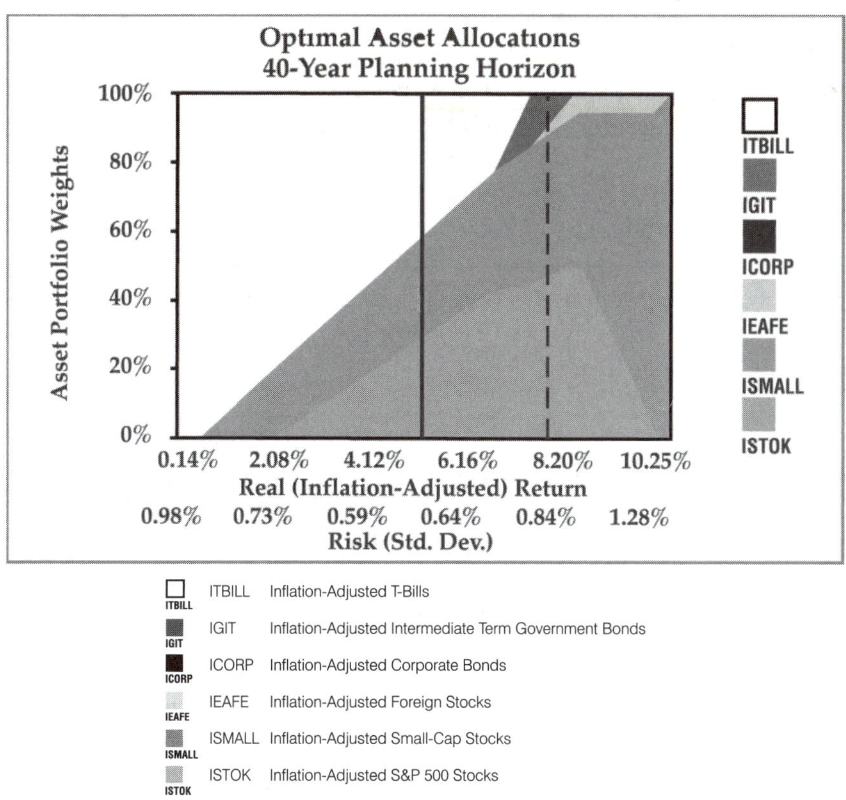

As stated earlier, I strived to provide clients with a portfolio allocation that will serve them well over time, because I never knew for sure how often, or when, I'd see them again, since I didn't require long term contracts or provide ongoing portfolio management. Given the service model under which I served clients, I didn't feel that an "active" investment strategy was appropriate. Active investment strategies should be continually monitored, therefore I feel these strategies are appropriate only for clients who engage their advisors for continual and ongoing investment supervision.

Accordingly, I would use passive investment strategies in the implementation of clients' portfolio allocations. For equity exposure, I utilized low cost, consistant performing mutual funds or Exchange Traded Funds exclusively. For the fixed-income component of the portfolio I usually recommended individual securities (if the portfolio is large enough to warrant individual securities). FIS Securities is a fixed income manager – not dissimilar to Portfolio Solutions – which I would recommend for the evaluation, selection, and implementation of individual bond portfolios. For smaller allocations to fixed-income, or to provide specific exposure to convertible bonds, high-yield, or foreign fixed income securities, I recommended mutual funds.

Index funds (e.g., the Vanguard 500 Index and the Vanguard Total Stock Market Index) or similarily exposed Exchange Traded Funds (ETFs) are my vehicle of choice for core U.S. large-cap or broad market exposure. In my opinion, it is very difficult for an actively managed large-cap blend U.S. stock fund to compete over time against a low-priced index or Exchange Traded Funds.

But to tailor the portfolio in the manner I felt appropriate, I'd complement the core exposure with "actively" managed mutual funds. These funds are technically considered "actively" managed, however, they tend to be extremely inactive – utilizing long-term, buy and hold philosophies. For example, over the last several years my firm maintained a bias toward value funds. I use vehicles such as Thornburg Value, Ameristock, Dodge & Cox Stock, Clipper, T. Rowe Price Equity Income, Third Ave Value, Bridgeway Small Cap Value, and Weitz Value Funds for this type of exposure.

I feel that the large-cap U.S. stock market is extremely efficient, yet one may be able to capitalize on inefficiencies in the small-cap market and foreign markets. Therefore, for international and small-cap exposure, I prefer actively managed mutual funds over index funds.

There is ample academic research illustrating the benefits and simplicity of passive investment strategies. I'm a firm believer that once the appropriate asset allocation has been determined, the best method of implementation for the portfolio is to use a long-term, buy and hold approach. This is especially true for clients whom we serve on a periodic or as-needed basis. We need to help clients determine their risk tolerance level, the appropriate asset allocation, and the specific vehicles with which to implement the recommended allocation.

When designing specific implementation recommendations for a client's investment portfolio I began with the investment plans and accounts with the most limited or restrictive options. The "best" choices available within variable contracts and qualified plans are identified first. Next, we selected cash reserve vehicles and tax-efficient investments for the client's personal portfolio. Finally, we utilized IRA assets to fill out the balance of the allocation as shown below.

- Variable annuities and life insurance
- Employer-sponsored retirement plans
    - 401(k)
    - 403(b)
    - Deferred compensation plans
- Taxable portfolios
- IRAs

Tracking Performance

At the beginning of each year, we underwent an intensive, methodical mutual fund screening process utilizing Morningstar's® Principia Pro™. We screened for the top performing mutual funds on a risk-adjusted basis in each category of Morningstar's® 9-Box Style Grid™. Once we had narrowed the available options from hundreds of funds to a few dozen, we did further research, including cross-referencing with Litman/Gregory's investment consulting service, *Advisor Intelligence* (www.AdvisorIntelligence.com), to select the funds that would go on our recommended list.

I maintained at least four different recommended mutual fund grids: (1) domestic equity; (2) foreign equity; (3) taxable bonds; and (4) tax-exempt bond.

My recommended fund lists are much longer than those of most traditional finanical planners and definitely much longer than that of a money manager. I find it most efficient to pre-screen select funds from the major fund companies providing 401(k) plans because so many of my clients participated in 401(k) plans. Consider adding your select funds from each of the 401(k) plans you review on a grid of its own, labeled "Top 401(k) Plan Picks." The next time you work with a client who has those same investment options, you will already be aware of the funds you like. Most of your time will be spent on the allocation decision, rather then the specific investment decisions regarding the 401(k) plan assets.

You can keep track of your recommended/watch list funds' performance relative to their peers with any of the online portfolio tracking tools. I used the Mutual Fund Education Alliance's web site (www.MFEA.com) to track funds, but there are dozens of quality, free portfolio tracking tools on the web now. I'd label the portfolio "Large Value" and enter one share of each mutual fund on my recommended/ watch lists for that Morningstar® category into the portfolio. I also added "Most Popular" funds and benchmarks to each portfolio. With this information I could quickly determine how my fund selections were competing against a peer group and benchmark on any given day, during the last month, and year-to-date. I had a quarterly subscription to Morningstar's® Principia Pro™ (mutual funds, stocks and variable annuities). I found it very valuable to have instant access to peer group comparisons through my online portfolio tracking tools.

I've also assisted clients in setting up online tracking portfolios for themselves. We've used the Mutual Fund Education Alliance (wwwMFEA.com), Quicken (www.Quicken.com), and Morningstar® (www.Morningstar.com). We've also coached clients on using their discount broker's website and portfolio tracking tools. This coaching would be provided in my office or I would go to their computer "virtually" through our subscription with WebEx, a virtual conferencing service (www.webex.com). There are many similar, yet much less expensive options now available, such as GoToMeeting.com.

How to Work Effectively With a Discount Broker

I've found that clients who are interested in saving money are more than willing to set up an investment account directly with a mutual fund company or discount broker. Clients can easily consolidate and implement a diverse portfolio of securities through a discount broker. We have worked primarily with Schwab, Vanguard, TD Ameritrade, Scottrade, and Fidelity. I have my personal preferences, but the main objective is to find a discount broker who can most effectively and affordably fulfill the client's needs.

For example, if we'll be using a lot of Vanguard funds, we recommend that the clients establish an account with Vanguard Brokerage Services. Not only can the clients purchase Vanguard funds at no fee, but within the same account they can also hold positions in virtually any other no-load fund. It's a simple, yet diversified approach – that's why I love mutual fund marketplaces with discount brokerage firms.

Unfortunately, Vanguard doesn't have any local reps in our area, so a client must be comfortable completing all the paperwork (i.e., to establish new accounts and transfer assets) themselves through the mail or online, or they could hire my firm to complete these applications and transfer forms for them. I tried to empower and support my clients so that they would be able to do much or all of this implementation work themselves. It helped to keep their costs down and allowed me to focus on what I feel was my highest and greatest good as their financial planner – analyzing their current situation and providing advice and empowerment.

My firm's retail discount broker of choice was Schwab. We developed a wonderful working relationship with our local retail branch office. Our primary contact, Dominick Lopez (at the Kansas City Country Club Plaza branch), worked directly with many of our clients. Clients provided Dominick with detailed, written instructions from our firm, and he prepared all of the paperwork, processed the transfers, and placed the trades. If he had any questions, he called me. My clients had someone who would gladly take on the responsibility of the logistics of portfolio implementation and they didn't have to pay extra for this service. Clients commented favorably on this personalized, attentive service. In order for clients to hire me to provide those same services, they would have had to pay an additional fee of several hundred dollars. This is yet another way I could provide just what the client needed from me at an affordable price. Again, the frugal planner mindset comes into play.

Creating an alliance with a discount brokerage house – especially when you can establish an alliance with a professional, branch office representatives who offer affortable, personalized service – is a winning situation for all parties involved. I no longer had to fill out forms, follow-up on transfers, or place trades – and I did not miss those activities. Far too often I underestimated the amount of time it actually took to implement portfolio recommendations. As a result, when I provided fee quotes, I also underestimated the fees. The only thing I disliked more than filling out forms and resolving transfer problems is not getting paid for it.

The client also avoids the majority of the headaches involved with investment implementation when working with a representative from a retail discount broker's branch office.

And finally, the branch office representative and the brokerage company also benefit by bringing additional assets to their firm. If a client already has an account with a discount broker and it's working well for them, I attempted to use that brokerage firm to implement my recommendations. It doesn't matter to me with whom a client consolidates his assets. The only thing that matters is whether the client will be able to implement the recommended portfolio easily and cost effectively.

When I worked at various wealth management firms, I dealt primarily with the institutional side of discount brokerage firms. However, once I started working with clients exclusively on an hourly, as-needed basis I found working with retail branches to be much more effective for my clientele and business model.

CHAPTER 11

OTHER PRIMARY FINANCIAL PLANNING TOPICS

TAX PLANNING

I don't hold myself out as a tax specialist. Fortunately, most of my clients have had pretty basic tax situations. When I have run into an individual needing higher-level tax expertise, I have gladly referred them to a specialist. I find that I generally have access to all the tax information and expertise I need by using: (1) a quick reference chart provided to me annually by Julie Welch,[1] one of the CPAs on my list: (2) the current editions of *Tax Facts on Investments* and *Tax Facts on Insurance and Employee Benefits* (published annually by the National Underwriter Company[2]): and (3) my network of tax advisors. (Federal income tax rates can be found on the CD-ROM.)

When working with a client for the first time, or upon an annual review, it is beneficial to have a copy of their most current tax returns for various reasons. One of those reasons is to arrive at current cash flow as discussed in Chapter 7 on Cash Flow and Debt Management. I most commonly derive basic living expenses by going through the following steps:

Start with: • Net paycheck (paycheck stub, year-to-date numbers)

Subtract:
- Itemized deductions (Form 1040, Schedule A)
- Insurance premiums (insurance declaration pages)
- Investment commitments (paycheck stub, investment, and retirement account statements)
- Liability payments (mortgage, loan, and credit card statements)

When it comes to tax planning, we don't have too many options for reducing income taxes for most middle Americans. These individuals are generally employed homeowners. They may be able to take better advantage of their employer's retirement plan or flexible spending plan. We may even be able to improve on the tax efficiency of their investment portfolio. Aside from these issues, however, missed tax deductions and tax credits are the most common tax planning opportunities that I've encountered (see Figure 11.1).

Figure 11.1

ITEMIZED DEDUCTIONS AND COMMONLY MISSED OPPORTUNITIES

- Medical Expenses
  - Medical and dental expenses over 7.5% of AGI are deductible from adjusted gross income, unless the expenses are reimbursed.
  - In 2007, self-employed individuals may deduct up to 100% of their health-insurance costs on the federal return.
- State and Local Income Tax Payments
  - Pay state 4th quarter estimated taxes by December 31st.
- Real Estate and Personal Property Taxes
  - Not only can you deduct the real estate tax on your home on your federal income tax return, you can also deduct taxes paid on vacation homes, time-shares, and raw land.
  - Personal property taxes paid on vehicles, motorcycles, boats, and motor homes are deductible as well.
- First and Second Home Mortgage Interest
  - Motor homes, vacation homes and some boats may qualify as a second home.
  - Home equity loans may also be deductible up to $100,000.

Figure 11.1 (Contd)

- Points Paid in the Year Home was Purchased
    - If points are paid when refinancing, these points may be deducted over the life of the loan, and any remaining balance may be deductible if the home is sold or the mortgage is refinanced again.
- Investment Interest Paid
    - Investment interest is deductible up to the amount of net investment income earned; the balance can be carried forward.
    - One can elect to treat capital gains as ordinary income to increase net investment income earned.
- Charitable Contributions
    - Cash contributions are deductible – taxpayer must keep records.
    - All contributions require a receipt from the charity.
    - Donations of professional services or labor are not deductible.
    - Non-cash contributions are also deductible – must keep records.
        - If non-cash contributions are $500 or less, that amount must be recorded on Schedule A. Form 8283 must be completed for larger contributions of property.
        - Obtain a copy of IRS Pub 561 for information on determining the value of donated property.
    - Donate Appreciated Property.
        - Sell *depreciated property* and donate the proceeds.
- Casualty Losses
    - May be deductible. Subject to limitations.
- Misellaneous Deductions
    - Employee Expenses
        - Unreimbursed employee expenses
        - Professional dues and subscriptions
        - Union dues
        - Tools and uniforms
        - Job hunting costs
    - Investment Expenses
        - Tax return preparation fees
        - Investment management / financial planning fees
        - Custodial fees
        - Investment books, subscriptions, and software
        - Online fees for tracking investments
        - Safe deposit box rental fees
    - Maximize by bunching deductions into one year.
- Moving Expenses

Common Income Tax Problems

The most common income tax problems I have seen with employed individuals are inappropriate withholding, not fully taking advantage of tax advantaged employee benefits, and tax inefficient investment portfolios. The most common tax problems I have encountered with self-employed individuals are failure to deposit adequate funds in an escrow account to cover estimated tax payments and failure to file payroll taxes in a timely manner.

I recommend that Schedule C wage earners set aside 33% to 40% of their gross income each time they are paid into a money market account earmarked exclusively for tax payments. I also suggest they add a consistent percentage of their gross wages to their retirement plan each time they get paid. What is left is their "net pay," and can be used to cover the "here and now" living expenses.

Unfortunately, if a client doesn't have the funds, they don't pay their taxes in a timely fashion. Clients occasionally owe back taxes, penalties, and interest totaling thousands of dollars. Sometimes I need to refer these individuals directly to a tax attorney or CPA to resolve these problems with the IRS. Other times we simply need to help the client develop a workable plan to pay their back taxes while progressing toward their other financial goals.

Tax Issues, Opportunities, and Pitfalls for Non-Traditional Couples

From an income tax standpoint, unmarried partners may be better off than married couples due to the "marriage penalty."

Unmarried partners may be able to arrange their tax-deductible expenses so that the higher wage earner pays for the *tax deductible* items and makes the charitable contributions for the couple, while the other partner claims the standard deduction. On the other hand, legally married counterparts can't take an itemized deduction *and* a standard deduction.

When opening a joint investment account, consider *whose Social Security number is listed* as *primary* on the account. If all else is equal, use the Social Security number of the partner in the lowest income tax bracket. That person will receive the Form 1099 and be required to report the income on their tax return.

Older unmarried couples can earn larger amounts of income than married couples before their Social Security retirement benefits become subject to taxation.

When two people marry, or have a similar committed, long-term relationship, it is often their desire to "merge" their finances and own property jointly. But, be aware of the potential for inadvertent gifting. *Transferring assets to another individual is a gift*. Married individuals are allowed to claim *unlimited marital transfers* (which are not subject to gift tax); however, unmarried people are not afforded that luxury.

If one party owns a home individually, and then re-titles the asset to joint ownership, that person has *effectively made a gift* of one-half of the home to the other person. There is no problem if the other person is their legally wedded spouse. However, if the other party is not the spouse, a gift tax return must be filed if the value transferred is over $12,000 (as indexed in 2007) in any one year.

One strategy that's sometimes used when a couple wishes to transfer an asset from individual to joint ownership is to work with an attorney to draft a document that spells out the terms of the ownership transfer. For instance, if an asset valued at $50,000 was to be transferred to another person, the transfer could be set up to legally occur over a period of five years, with $10,000 being transferred to the co-owner each year. The agreement should specify the terms of the transfer in detail and what is to occur in the event of premature death, or separation of either party.

More commonly, employers are offering their unmarried workers health and other benefits for their "domestic partners." Nearly one out of every four large companies (5,000+ employees) provides health benefits to non-traditional partners, and dozens of cities and counties and a few states provide domestic partner benefits to their employees.[3] However, these benefits are *taxable to the employee*.

With domestic partner benefits, employees pay for their portion of the cost of the coverage with *post-tax dollars*, and then must pay taxes on the employer's share of payment for the benefits as *added income*. Married employees, on the other hand, pay no taxes on the traditional benefits they receive.

I've mentioned the primary factors regarding income taxes that one must consider when planning for "non-traditional" clients. For much more on the subject of financial planning for unmarried couples, I recommend the book I co-authored with Debra Neiman, CFP®, MBA, *Money Without Matrimony* (Dearborn Trade, October 2005).[4]

Elder Issues

Retirement Income

In recent years, I've worked with a lot of older clients who are having difficulty maintaining sufficient cash flow. They may have chosen (or been forced) to retire before they were financially able to do so. Sometimes their cash flow shortfall is a result of the drop in interest rates on fixed income investments. For other individuals, the difficulty lies in the fact that the value of their investment portfolios, from which they are taking periodic withdrawals, has dropped significantly as the stock market has declined. Others may have incurred substantially more health related expenses than they anticipated. Whatever the cause, many older Americans do not have the income they need to maintain their standard of living.

It is not uncommon for the majority of an older American's wealth to be tied up in his or her home, bank accounts, or short-term certificates of deposit. When looking for opportunities to maximize cash flow, planners must first examine their investment portfolios. Too often seniors have substantial assets placed in very low-yielding accounts. We can enhance their cash flow simply by reallocating their current assets to fixed-income securities with higher yields. This can be accomplished while exposing the client to extremely minimal, or sometimes no, additional risk to their principal.

I frequently recommend higher-yielding money market mutual funds over checking, savings, and bank money market accounts. I also recommend "ladders" of high quality individual bonds and certificates of deposit for enhanced yield and therefore, cash flow.

Individuals who have had little or no exposure to the stock market may have felt pretty smart and safe in the early part of this decade. However, if they haven't made appropriate changes to their investment allocations since than, they may be exposed to more risk than they are aware. By taking an extremely conservative approach to investing their money, they may not have provided any opportunity for growth in their portfolio. Over time, the effects of inflation can deteriorate one's purchasing power. In less than 25 years, our current cost of living may double. If you're working with a 65 year old retiree who has just enough income now to support his *current* standard of living, how is he going to survive when he needs twice as much income *later* in life?

I believe that almost everyone should have some money invested for growth. Of course, if assets are allocated to growth investments, fewer assets will be available to generate current cash flow. Thus, we must help clients achieve a balance between their need for current cash flow and their need for long-term growth. To achieve this goal, you might consider recommending preferred stocks, income-producing real estate, or natural gas royalty interests. These are vehicles that provide good current income and growth opportunities. Another option worth considering is a reverse mortgage. This strategy provides current cash flow by accessing the equity in one's home. Although I have considered reverse mortgages on a few occasions, I have yet to recommend one personally. Not that I am fundamentally against reverse mortgages; I simply view this option as one of last resort.

Social Security

Social Security usually provides one-third to one-half of the income clients I've worked with need to maintain their standards of living. The rest must be generated from the client's assets.

Clients often ask when they should plan to start drawing their Social Security retirement benefits. This answer will vary depending on whether the client still has earned income, their age, how long they expect to live, and our faith that the Social Security system will remain unchanged.

For long-term projections, we assume that clients begin receiving Social Security benefits at age 62 or upon their retirement, whichever is later. We also project that they will live at least until age 100. If they live beyond average life expectancy, clients would be far better off by deferring receipt of their retirement benefits (based on our current Social Security system). The present value of the higher benefit is by far greater if our life expectancy assumption is accurate. Therefore, it is prudent to illustrate receipt of a lower benefit if projecting life expectancy beyond average mortality assumptions.

For more information regarding the assumptions we use in projecting Social Security retirement benefits please refer back to the Retirement Capital Needs Computation section of this chapter.

Medicare

Americans who have attained the age of 65 have access to Medicare. Medicare Part A provides hospitalization coverage and is premium-free to qualified recipients (i.e., those who have 40 quarters of credit with the Social Security system). Part B covers other medical expenses and recipients pay a premium for this coverage.

Individuals should apply for Medicare benefits during the period beginning three months prior to turning age 65 and ending three months after turning age 65. If an individual has applied for Social Security retirement benefits prior to age 65, they will automatically receive a card acknowledging Medicare coverage in the mail prior to their 65th birthday. Recipients of Social Security retirement benefits will automatically be enrolled in Medicare Parts A and B. However, one can simply indicate on the card if one prefers to postpone receipt of Part B benefits.

If an employee is covered by their employer's health-insurance plan and they are over age 65, it is advisable for them to enroll in premium-free Medicare Part A. The employer group plan will be the primary insurer, and Medicare Part A will become the secondary insurer for hospitalization benefits. The client can wait until after retirement to obtain Medicare Part B coverage.

If a person is *not* covered by an employer's health insurance plan, and they do *not* enroll in Medicare during the initial enrollment period, they may be subject to a 10% penalty.

Most people should also obtain Medicare Supplemental Health Insurance ("Medigap") to adequately insure themselves during retirement. In 1992, federal regulations set uniform standards for all Medigap policies. Except in Massachusetts, Minnesota, and Wisconsin, there are 12 standard plans: Plan A through Plan L. At any time within the first six months after first enrolling in Medicare Part B, a client may purchase any Medicare supplemental policy without medical screening or underwriting based on health or pre-existing conditions.

As I mentioned earlier, most employed clients and their spouses have health insurance through their employer's plan. If the client retires at age 65 and goes on Medicare, will the spouse be able to continue group coverage if she is under age 65? What happens if the employee dies? Will the spouse lose coverage?

Medicare provides very minimal assistance with long-term care costs. Medicare may cover the costs of the first 20 days of skilled nursing care, and a portion of the costs from day 21 through day 100. However, the patient must have first had a *qualifying* hospital stay.

Medicare Part D is a voluntary program of health insurance that covers a portion of prescription drug costs not generally covered by other Medicare programs.[5] Prescription drug coverage is offered through private health plans. Participants may stay with traditional Medicare and enroll in a drug-only plan, or may choose a Medicare Advantage plan with comprehensive benefits. In 2007, Part D offers the following benefits:

Prescription Drug Expenses	**Beneficiary Costs**	**Medicare Pays**
First $265	100% (up to $265)	Nothing
$265-$2,400	25% (up to $533.75)	75% (up to $1,601.25)
$2,400-$5,451.25	100% (up to $3,051.25)	Nothing
Above $5,451.25	Up to 5% (based on income	95% or more

For more information and excellent resources (e.g., booklets), visit www.Medicare.gov.

Medicaid

Medicaid provides health and long-term care insurance to individuals with very limited income and assets. The majority of residents in nursing facilities are either on Medicaid or their expenses are privately paid. Long-term care insurance is still relatively new and that is one reason most nursing home residents do not have private insurance coverage for long-term care costs.

Older Clients and Financial Security Issues

The deterioration of one's physical health, along with loss of control and/or the ability to manage one's personal affairs, are significant concerns for many older Americans. Clients may also experience emotional issues regarding their finances as they grow older. Older clients often fear that they will run out of money. Working with a professional financial advisor can help minimize the sense of financial insecurity for many older clients. With professional guidance from the advisor, older clients will know how much they can afford to spend, and how their assets should be allocated to ensure or enhance long-term financial security.

I once worked with clients who had begun feeling very insecure about their financial future, and in mid-July 2002, they sold all of their equity investments. Three weeks later they called me to ask what to do. A few years before, I had provided a retirement projection and a second opinion regarding their stockbroker's management of their investment assets. At that time, we found that the clients needed to achieve an average long-term rate of return on their investments of 7% to maintain their standard of living. They had also expressed that they could reduce their standard of living if need be. The stockbroker designed an appropriate and quality investment portfolio for the clients. I gave only minor suggestions for improvement. The clients implemented my recommendations through their broker, and continued to visit with him regularly.

Unfortunately, by 2000 and 2001 the clients had grown increasingly uncomfortable with the behavior of the stock market and their declining account values. They called their stockbroker on numerous occasions, and he encouraged them to "sit tight." In July 2002, they called the broker to discuss their options, but he was on vacation. They viewed their broker as their continual and ongoing investment advisor and felt that it was his responsibility to tell them when to get out of the market. But the clients were determined that they could no longer sit by and watch the value of their accounts decline, so they sold all of their equity positions and parked the proceeds in a money market account yielding about one-half of 1%. Unfortunately, they didn't call me before taking this drastic step.

I met with the clients a few weeks after they had already sold their entire equity position. They talked about the financial insecurity they felt. They also wanted a game plan to "know when to get out of the market." I stressed to them the risks that they faced if they did not achieve a 7% average rate of return in retirement. I pointed out that they must have some growth exposure to achieve that objective. The one-half of 1% they were currently receiving on a portion of their assets was not helping their long-term situation.

I tried to put into perspective the risks associated with *not* having one-third of their assets invested in equities by telling them:

> *"Yes, the stocks can, and did, go down significantly in value. However, these assets will not be needed for many, many years and, therefore, must be invested for the long haul. No one can time the market. Not being in the market when it goes up is more dangerous for you than being in it when it goes down. Keep in mind that just missing out on a few 'good' trading days over the course of several years can cause one to miss the largest percentage of the gain."*

In order to achieve long-term financial security, this couple had to have some equity exposure. They also needed assurance as to where their cash flow was to come from for the foreseeable future.

Many advisors suggest holding three to ten years worth of cash flow in fixed-income investments that are scheduled to mature just when the money is needed. Over time, as this fixed income ladder depletes, one must replenish it by selling equities. I find that a minimum of three years needed cash flow should be earmarked in cash reserves and fixed income investments. With at least three years worth of cash flow set aside, we can survive the downturns of most equity markets. Simply making it clear to the client where their income will come from when the equity markets are down can eliminate a great deal of financial insecurity. This strategy helped encourage the clients in the example above to get back into the market.

Planners must find a workable balance between short-term and long-term financial security. The greater danger faced by the couple in the above example was to their long-term security. Because they were only in their late 60's, I reminded them that in 25 years their living expenses could double. If they left all of the money in secure, fixed-income investments, they would not have enough income to support their standard of living. This is long-term financial *insecurity*.

> *SOMETIMES WE MUST GIVE UP ON A LITTLE SHORT-TERM SECURITY TO ENHANCE THE CHANCE OF LONG-TERM SUCCESS.*

I have also become an advocate of some percentage of most people's retirement income structured in a way that they can not outlive. If the client doesn't have a traditional defined benefit pension plan, and they are too young to *rely* on Social Security for any or all of the administrations' projected benefits, I want to explore an immediate annuity.[6]

ESTATE PLANNING ISSUES

Who needs to worry about estate taxes? Well, not many of my clients. But estate planning is so much more than minimizing estate taxes and expenses. Estate planning also involves the efficient transfer of assets to heirs. It is important for families to discuss their desires regarding the disposition of their assets.

Even though most of the clients I work with do not have an estate tax situation, they generally need to update their estate planning documents. At a minimum, clients should have a will, a living will, health care directives, and a power of attorney for financial decision-making. Many clients could also benefit from a living trust, while others could also take advantage of more advanced estate planning techniques. I know enough about estate planning to recognize these planning opportunities and to refer these clients directly to an attorney who specializes in estate planning.

I provide my clients who have engaged me for estate planning guidance with a copy of the *Five Wishes* brochure published by the nonprofit organization Aging with Dignity (www.agingwithdignity.org).

Five Wishes helps clients express how they want to be treated if they are seriously ill and unable to speak for themselves. It is unique among all other living will and health agent forms because it covers all of a person's needs (i.e., medical, personal, emotional, and spiritual). *Five Wishes* also encourages discussing the client's wishes with their family and physician. *Five Wishes* lets the client's family and doctors know:

1. Which person the client wants to make health care decisions for them when they can't make them.

2. The kind of medical treatment the client wants, or doesn't want.

3. How comfortable the client wants to be.

4. How the client wants people to treat him or her.

5. What the client wants their loved ones to know.

I encourage clients to review this brochure, complete it, and share it with their estate planning attorney when they are having their other estate planning documents drafted. This exercise can help clients evaluate their options and feelings about end-of-life issues in the privacy of their own homes.

Americans often procrastinate about getting their estate planning documents drafted and executed. They procrastinate because they don't realize the importance of these documents, or may not want to face the reality that all of us will die someday. I try to make the subject of estate planning simple, while stressing its importance. I describe in lay terms what I feel the estate planning attorney would recommend, and I encourage them to schedule an appointment. I've gone so far as to schedule the appointment for the client during our presentation meeting. If a client requests, and pays me to, I would attend their meeting with the estate planning attorney. But this occurrs very rarely.

The estate planning attorneys to whom I refer clients provide them with detailed instructions on how to re-title assets and change beneficiary designations on their current life insurance policies, IRAs, and qualified retirement plans. Clients may also be advised to add transfer-on-death beneficiary designations to their personal brokerage accounts, their bank accounts, and personal property.

Asset Transfers

The primary purpose of estate planning for most middle Americans, is to effectively and efficiently transfer assets at death. However, traditional estate planning documents generally do not address the "softer" points of the asset transfer process.

I like clients to have the opportunity to write down how they feel about their loved ones, how they want their possessions to be distributed, and how they want their heirs to behave during this process. An estate planning colleague calls this a "Family Love Letter."

The "love letter" is to be opened and read immediately following the individual's death. While these letters are not likely to be legally binding documents, they do provide instructions to family members regarding the deceased person's thoughts and preferences at the time immediately following death.

It is recommended that these "love letters" be shared with family members and heirs *prior to* death. Open and honest communication helps avoid potentially adverse situations. If every family member knows what the client wants, and the client and the other heirs know what each of the heirs want, many uncomfortable situations can be minimized or eliminated.

To encourage families to start talking about the "softer" points of the asset transfer process, I encourage clients to read *Who Gets Grandma's Yellow Pie Plate?* by Marlene S. Stum.[7]

Although I strongly encourage older adults to discuss the distribution of their assets upon their death with their family members, it may also be appropriate for clients to consider transferring some assets to their heirs *before* death. The heirs may benefit more by receiving the gift now, and the client may also enjoy *seeing* heirs benefit from the gifts.

However, I am reluctant to suggest that most people begin transferring assets to their heirs unless it is obvious that they will *never* need these assets themselves; too many unforeseen events could occur. It is our job as planners to minimize these unforeseen events, advise clients on the benefits and disadvantages of gifting assets while they are living, and help them determine if, when, and how much of their estates could comfortably be transferred to heirs now.

Working with "Specialized Participants"

As you can see, I work with and rely on a host of "specialized participants" in the financial services industry. I take pride in being a financial planning "generalist." Middle Americans need financial planning "generalists" to help them make better money management and financial planning decisions.

To effectively and profitably serve this market, a practitioner must develop strong strategic alliances with quality product and service providers. You should surround yourself with a network of qualified, trusted allied professionals. A financial planning "generalist" should know which products and services offered by various "specialists" are appropriate for her clients, and help the clients fill their needs by directing them to qualified "specialists."

To be profitable and effective working in the Middle Market, I have to focus on what I do best, which is:

- Advising, consulting, educating, and coaching clients on the basic aspects of personal finances.

- Motivating clients to take the appropriate actions necessary to fulfill their objectives.

- Serving as "Accountability Coach" for clients, helping them to do what I was hired us to help them with.

I outsource any project or analysis I do not feel competent handling myself to qualified advisors. I find that if we advisors "stick to our knitting," we can profitably provide a much needed, and very valuable, service to our Middle Market clientele.

To effectively serve the Middle Market, we must be very efficient financial planners and business operators. We've got to systematize and streamline everywhere we can. An advisor should develop a systematic way to do *all* things involved in running a practice. As one of my business strategy coaches, Kevin Poland, always reminds me, "a system is not a system, until it's documented." If you're building a business—even if it's only a business of one—you must *systematize and document* all processes so that they can be refined, improved, and repeated. These processes can be performed by you, an appropriate staff person (if someday you choose to expand), or they can be outsourced.

Remember that you must work *on* your business as much as you work *in* it. If you're not skilled or interested in certain tasks, then outsource them. For example, I outsourced the following functions:

- compliance;
- computer hardware and software updates, and maintenance;
- janitorial services;
- marketing communications;
- payroll;
- tax return preparation; and
- website development and maintenance.

We always have the option of *not* doing these things. Yes, it costs money to hire people to provide all of these services, but you've got to decide where *your* time is best spent. My janitorial service providers charge $15.00 an hour. However, when there's this *untapped market* out there full of folks who are willing to pay me $240.00 per hour, I've got to ask myself, "what is *my* job?"

While still actively serving individual clients, I was a financial planner. I charged by the hour. The more hours I charged, the more money I made, and the more people I could serve. I am not a computer wizard, nor am I a great writer. I don't care for the bookkeeping part of the job. I won't even do my own tax returns. (I hate filling out the forms, and you can always learn something when working with a specialist.) I also don't enjoy compliance and I found it very expensive (my time and the penalties I incurred) to do my firm's payroll. Consequently, I outsourced all of these services.

When we first establish our practices, we have to do most or all of these tasks. However, too many seasoned financial planners are swamped because they are still performing too many non-financial planning responsibilities. This is unfortunate because:

> *To effectively serve the Middle Market, we must be very efficient financial planners – and business operators.*

Building a business is much more than building a clientele. It involves building a system of processes that will make it possible to provide great service to our clients, while enjoying balance in our own lives.

In the next chapter I will share with you the key elements of my final work product and the actual presentation of this information to the clients during our Presentation Meeting.

Endnotes

1. Julie Welch, CPA, CFP® and Randy Gardner, LLM, CPA, CFP® write a guide for consumers and their advisors entitled, *101 Tax Saving Ideas* (Wealth Builders Press, February 2006). The quick reference chart is on the CD-ROM.
2. 2007 *Tax Fact on Insurance and Employee Benefits* and *2007 Tax Fact on Investments* (The National Underwriter Company; www.nuco.com.).
3. Lambda Legal, "Details About Domestic Partner Benefits" (September 28, 1997).
4. Garrett and Neiman, *Money Without Matrimony* (Dearborn Trade, October 2005).
5. John H. Fenton, editor, *All About Medicare*, pp. 81, 82 (National Underwriter Company, 2007).
6. John Ameriks, Ph.D., Robert Veres and Mark J. Warshawsky, Ph.D., "Making Retirement Income Last a Lifetime," *Journal of Investment Planning* (December 2001).
7. Marlene Stum, *Who Gets Grandma's Yellow Pie Plate?* (Minnesota Extension Service, February 1, 1999).

Chapter 12

The Presentation Meeting

In Chapter 6 we discussed the Initial Client Meeting, which I refer to as the *Get Acquainted* Meeting. The goals of that initial meeting are to discuss the client's immediate needs and desires, assess the scope of the financial planning services needed, and define the terms of the engagement. At the Presentation Meeting we review and discuss our observations and recommendations to the clients.

At the beginning of the Presentation Meeting the client receives a notebook containing many or all of the following documents and reports:

- Action Plan
    - Figure 12.1 – Example Action Plan
- Summary Report
    - Objectives Covered/Addressed
    - Observations Noted
    - Key Assumptions
    - Recommendations
    - Figure 12.2 – Snapshot of a Summary Report

- Planning Reports
    - Figure 12.3 – 3 key EasyMoney reports
        - Net worth
        - Cash flow
        - 3rd retirement page
- Investment Analysis
- Other
- Implementation
- Monitoring
    - Figure 12.4 – MFEA.com watch list on Large Cap Value Funds
- Appendix
    - Professional Referral Sources
    - National Association of Insurance Commissioners NAIC Long Term Care Shoppers Guide
    - Aging with Dignity's 5 Wishes Brochure

During the Presentation meeting, we spend about 2 hours reviewing and discussing the contents of the plan binder just outlined. This meeting typically takes place about one month after the Initial Client Meeting. When an appointment begins I start the conversation by asking; *Is anything new since I saw you last?* I want to hear about any big news that might affect their finances right then. If there have been no changes that would cause our meeting not to proceed as scheduled, I ask the client if they are *"ready to get started?"* and physically begin recording my time.

> *Remember – all time working for and with a client is billable time. Whether you get to pass that billable amount on to*

YOUR CLIENT IS ENTIRELY DEPENDENT ON HOW WELL YOU DO WITH YOUR INITIAL ESTIMATE AND HOW EFFICIENTLY YOU WORK. BY KEEPING TRACK OF AND STAYING FOCUSED ON BILLABLE TASKS, IN TIME WE BECOME VERY GOOD AT ESTIMATING PROJECTS AND GETTING PAID FOR ALL OF OUR WORK FOR AND WITH CLIENTS.

I also mentioned that the Presentation Meeting typically takes place about 30 days after the Get Acquainted Meeting. This timeframe seems to work well. It provides two weeks for the clients to pull together any additional documents, questionnaires, and data that the planner requested, and it allows the planner two weeks to complete the work. Yet, it is still close enough in timeframe to the initial meeting that many of the details and passions shared at that meeting are still fresh in the advisor's mind. At least my memory has challenges spanning a much greater length of time. Keep in mind that you'll likely be working on 2-5 client engagements at the same time. Too many projects – spanning too much time – lead to inefficiency and waste.

Near the conclusion of the Presentation Meeting the subject of what implementation steps need to be completed and who will take on the responsibility for each step is discussed and agreed upon. The more we allow or encourage our clients to *delegate* the more our businesses change. How do you want to spend your time? Meeting with clients? Doing analytical work? Filling out forms? Dealing with the compliance department?

The implementation steps that can be delegated to an advisor vary greatly by subject. I could determine how much life insurance was needed, identify high quality, low cost insurance companies, and provide explicit instructions on exactly what and how much to buy, and empower the client to make the phone call themselves…or I could call the insurance specialist and join the clients at the meeting to buy insurance.

Action Plan Topics Potentially Requiring Implementation Assistance:

Minimal delegation possible, if any (typically):

- Goal Setting
- Data Gathering

- Cash Flow Monitoring
- Bill Paying
- Credit Improvement
- Debt Management
- Property and Causality Insurance
- Mortgage Financing
- Home Equity Lines of Credit
- Employee Benefits
- Social Welfare Benefits
- Health Insurance
- Tax Return Preparation
- Preparation of Legal Documents

The client has to do these things for themselves or hire financial services specialists to assist them when necessary.

Action plan items frequently recommended by financial advisors that may be fully delegated by the client to the advisor:

- Investment Portfolio management (typically excluding closely held investments and company retirement plans)
- Life, disability, and long term care insurance
- Bill payment

At the conclusion of the Presentation Meeting, all action plan items having been "divvied up," the clients pay in full for the services rendered, and we schedule our next meeting – whether that is for implementation or follow up purposes, or a periodic or annual "Check-Up Meeting."

In the next chapter, my current business coach, long-time colleague and friend, Mary Lacey Gibson, CFP® has contributed to this edition of Garrett's Guide. Mary has worked with small business owners for over twenty years – coaching them through the hard, but extremely important work of developing and working with a business plan.

As financial planners we know the importance of having a financial plan. But, many of us do not even review our own plans with regularity, and often times, we don't practice the good money management principals that we preach. As a truly independent financial planner, I was not only a financial planner, I was a business owner. My business evolved over the years. A business plan can help you guide the inevitable evolution of your business in the way you want it to go.

Figure 12.1

Action Plan

Prepared for:

Joe and Sara Sample

Date Presented: 5/1/2007

Completed	Date Due	Responsible Party	Action Item
❑	Immediately	Joe & Sara	Obtain more life insurance.
❑	Immediately	Joe & Sara	Contact the estate planning attorney.
❑	ASAP	Joe & Sara	Implement portfolio changes as recommended.
❑	Within 1 Month	Joe & Sara	Begin funding the education accounts.
❑	Within 1 Month	Joe & Sara	Make your Roth IRA contributions for the year.
❑	As-Needed	Joe & Sara	Call or email anytime you have questions or concerns.
❑	Within 2 Years	Joe & Sara	Come in for a check-up meeting.

Figure 12.2

RECOMMENDATION SUMMARY FOR: JOE AND SARA SAMPLE

Objectives

Short-Term Objectives

Review life insurance needs.

Review and provide recommendations regarding current investment portfolio.

Long-Term Objectives

Ensure a secure retirement.

Joe and Sara both retire at age 55.

Provide college education funding for both children.

Observations

Garrett Financial Planning, Inc. was not engaged to review or provide recommendations or advice on any issues other than those listed above.

Joe currently contributes $704/month to his 401(k) and Sara contributes a combined total of $500/month to her 403(b) accounts.

Joe's employer provides him with a company car.

We were provided with a detailed listing of monthly living expenses. We further estimated your basic monthly living expenses by subtracting your mortgage and other liability payments, tax deductible items, and personal investments from your net paycheck.

Recommendations

Education Funding

Applications can be obtained at www.Vanguard.com.

Use the excess cash in your money market account to make the minimum initial investment of $3000 into this fund.

According to our calculations you need to save $460/month from now until your youngest child graduates from college to fully fund your objective.

We recommend that you invest funds for college in your personal ownership rather than in the children's names or in a UTMA or UGMA account.

We suggest that you establish an automatic investment program and begin saving $460/month into the Vanguard Total Stock Market index fund.

Figure 12.3

A6

NET WORTH STATEMENT

Retirement Projection

ASSETS	Joe	Sara	Joint /CP	Trust/Oth.	Total
ORDINARY INTEREST ACCOUNTS:					
Checking accounts			$500		$500
Savings accounts			31,074		31,074
Money Market Accounts			15,658		15,658
Insurance Cash Value and Dividends		4,290			4,290
Total		$4,290	$47,232		$51,522
EQUITY (investment) ACCOUNTS:					
Mutual Funds			61,098		61,098
Total			$61,098		$61,098
RETIREMENT ACCOUNTS:					
401(k) accounts	$76,238				76,238
Regular IRA accounts	14,831				14,831
Other (403(b), SEP, etc.)	13,261	45,837			59,098
Total	$104,330	$45,837			$150,167
PERSONAL USE ASSETS:					
Residence			$190,000		$190,000
Personal Property			40,000		40,000
Autos			25,000		25,000
Total			$255,000		$255,000
Total Assets	$104,330	$50,127	$363,330		$517,787

LIABILITIES	Joe	Sara	Joint/CP	Trust/Oth.	Total
Residence mtg			($119,970)		($119,970)
Total liabilities			($119,970)		($119,970)

NET WORTH	$104,330	$50,127	$243,360		$397,817

Figure 12.3 (Cont'd)

A14

CASH FLOW

Retirement Projection

INCOME:	Monthly Amount	Percent of income
Salaries & Wages	$7,583	100.00%
Total income available	$7,583	100.00%

EXPENDITURES:	Amount	Percent of income	
Federal and State income tax	637	8.40%	D1
FICA taxes	580	7.65%	D1
Residence mortgage	841	11.09%	K1
Basic Living Expenses	2,443	32.22%	
Life insurance	131	1.73%	J1
Homeowners & other insurance	56	0.74%	J8
Auto insurance	103	1.35%	J8
Retirement account additions (IRA, 401k, TSA, etc.)	1,204	15.88%	C5
Charitable contributions	129	1.70%	
Property & other taxes	229	3.03%	
New Car Escrow	370	4.88%	
Education Escrow	460	6.07%	
Child Care Expenses	400	5.27%	
Total spending and savings	$7,583	100.00%	
Cash flow shortage (spending in excess of income)	**$0**		

Figure 12.3 (Cont'd)

Retirement Capital Projection Retirement Projection C4

Age Cl	Age Sp	Annual expenses	Income available / Other expenses: Pension & Min dist. (after tax)	Social Security	Education & other goals	Other Income (expense)	**Annual surplus (shortage)**	Savings and investment	Retirement accounts & Roth	**Total acct values (end of year)**
								$92,172	$150,167	**$242,339**
38	38							$98,056	$178,326	$276,382
39	39							104,328	208,816	313,144
40	40							111,015	241,832	352,847
41	41							118,145	277,588	395,733
42	42							125,748	316,312	442,061
43	43							133,857	358,256	492,113
44	44							142,505	403,692	546,197
45	45							151,730	452,913	604,643
46	46							161,571	506,239	667,811
47	47							172,071	564,019	736,090
48	48							183,273	626,628	809,901
49	49							195,227	694,477	889,703
50	50							207,983	768,008	975,992
51	51							221,598	847,706	1,069,304
52	52							236,130	934,093	1,170,224
53	53							251,642	1,027,739	1,279,382
54	54							268,202	1,129,262	1,397,464
55	55	(77.713)	30,612			(24,793)	(71,894)	207,344	1,208,310	1,415,654
56	56	(79,695)	30,807				(48,887)	167,365	1,292,892	1,460,257
57	57	(81,735)	31,005				(50,731)	123,192	1,383,394	1,506,586
58	58	(83,837)	31,204				(52,633)	74,525	1,480,232	1,554,757
59	59	(86,003)	31,406				(54.597)	21,049	1,583,848	1,604,897
60	60	(88,233)	31,609				(56,623)		1,641,850	1,641,850
61	61	(90,530)	31,815				(58,715)		1,669,523	1,669,523
62	62	(92,895)	32,023				(60.873)		1,695,925	1,695,925
63	63	(95,332)	32,232				(63,100)		1,720,867	1,720,867
64	64	(97,842)	32,444				(65,398)		1,744,138	1,744,138
65	65	(100,427)	32,658			(33,319)	(101,089)		1,715,999	1,715,999
66	66	(95,904)	32,874				(63,030)		1,742,450	1,742,450
67	67	(95,741)	33,092				(62.649)		1,771,318	1,771,318
68	68	(98.566)	33,313				(65,253)		1,798,337	1,798,337
69	69	(101,476)	33,535				(67,940)		1,823,254	1,823,254
70	70	(104,473)	59,334				(45.139)		1,845,795	1,845,795
71	71	(107.560)	86,516				(21,044)		1,865,664	1,865,664
72	72	(110,739)	89,269				(21.470)		1,882,539	1,882,539
73	73	(114.014)	92,126				(21.888)		1,896,074	1,896,074
74	74	(117,387)	94,822				(22,565)		1,905,890	1,905,890
75	75	(120,862)	97,865			(44,778)	(67.775)		1,845,036	1,845,036
76	76	(124.440)	98,718				(25,722)		1,841,504	1,841,504
77	77	(128,126)	101,363				(26,764)		1,832,605	1,832,605
78	78	(131,923)	104,365				(27,558)		1,817,804	1,817,804
79	79	(135.833)	107,019				(28,814)		1,796,520	1,796,520
80	80	(139,861)	109,630				(30.230)		1,768,131	1,768,131
81	81	(144.010)	112,164				(31,845)		1,731,962	1,731,962
82	82	(148,283)	114,579				(33,702)		1,687,290	1,687,290
83	83	(152,684)	116,298				(36.382)		1,633,333	1,633,333
84	84	(157.217)	118,258				(38,951)		1,569,252	1,569,252
85	85	(161,886)	119,290				(42,582)		1,494,145	1,494,145
86	86	(166,696)	119,800				(46.869)		1,407,043	1,407,043
87	87	(171,649)	119,645				(51,958)		1,306,907	1,306,907
88	88	(176,752)	117,958				(58.714)		1,192,626	1,192,626
89	89	(182,007)	115,846				(66,029)		1,072,620	1,072,620
90	90	(187,420)	112,312				(75,108)		926,780	926,780
91	91	(192,995)	106,440				(86.480)		762,968	762,968
92	92	(198.738)	97,758				(100,747)		579,805	579,805
93	93	(204,653)	87,039				(117,114)		375,848	375,848
94	94	(210,745)	72,489				(137.338)		149,605	149,605
95	95	(217.020)	53,984				(161,484)			
96	96	(223,483)	40,465				(183.018)			
97	97	(230,141)	40,760				(189,381)			
98	98	(236,998)	41,057				(195,941)			
99	99	(244,060)	41,357				(202.704)			
100	100	(249.760)	41,660				(208,100)			
101	101									
102	102									
103	103									
104	104									
105	105									
106	106									
107	107									
108	108									
		G1	G2	G2	G4	G4		C5	C5	

8.05

Figure 12.4

Garrett Garrett's Personal Portfolio

As of 5/1/2007†

Fund Name	Ticker	Price	Net Chg.	YTD % Return	1yr.	3yr.	5yr.	Star Rating	Delete?
American Century Equity Income Inv	TWEIX	8.95	0.03	4.58	18.35%	12.4%	10.75%	★★★★	
		Daily Change: 0.03			Shares: 1			Value: 8.95	
Clipper	CFIMX	92.96	-0.02	1.07	14.63%	8.25%	5.62%	★★★★	
		Daily Change: -0.02			Shares: 1			Value: 92.96	
Dodge & Cox Stock *	DODGX	159.73	0.18	5.3	15.84%	16.59%	13.49%	★★★★★	
		Daily Change: 0.18			Shares: 1			Value: 159.73	
Masters' Select Value	MSVFX	17.3	0	5.88	16%	13.35%	10.28%	★★★★★	
		Daily Change: 0			Shares: 1			Value: 17.3	
Oakmark Select I	OAKLX	34.73	0.25	3.73	13.13%	10.63%	8.37%	★★★★	
		Daily Change: 0.25			Shares: 1			Value: 34.73	
Sound Shore	SSHFX	40.51	0.15	3.37	14.51%	13.57%	10.19%	★★★★	
		Daily Change: 0.15			Shares: 1			Value: 40.51	
T. Rowe Price Equity Income	PRFDX	31.05	0.23	6.76	18.75%	14.59%	10.19%	★★★★	
		Daily Change: 0.23			Shares: 1			Value: 31.05	
Vanguard Windsor II	VWNFX	37.1	0.12	6.76	19.02%	15.67%	11.09%	★★★★	
		Daily Change: 0.12			Shares: 1			Value: 37.1	
			Total Daily Change: 0.94			Total Portfolio Value: 422.33			

Mutual Fund Education Alliance — Reprinted with permission ©2007.

Chapter 13

Starting and Planning Your Business

Chapter contributed and copyrighted by Mary Lacey Gibson, CFP® and Small Business Consultant. Reprinted with permission.

Starting your new financial planning business—how exciting it is! But, be forewarned, success belongs to those who go into business with eyes wide open, understanding all aspects of owning and running a financial planning firm. Too often financial advisers open their doors to clients only to find that being a truly independent business owner is much more involved than seeing clients and producing financial plans. Your view of business from the position of being the boss needs to be markedly different from the viewpoint of an employee. You will need to think of yourself not so much as a financial planner, but as the owner of a financial planning *business*.

Making the mental and emotional shift from being an employee to being a business owner can be a difficult undertaking. Until now your entire frame of reference may have been that of an employee. Your responsibilities, decision making authority, and perhaps the time you could work each week has been limited to your job description and by your supervisor. Someone else sets the rules of your work life. Your new role as business owner presents a whole new set of circumstances. Decision making, authority, and the time you need to spend in your business are now only limited by you, the owner. You make the rules, which is often one of the primary motivators for starting a new business.

To further delve into your new role as an owner, you must first understand that there are four basic parts to any business: management, accounting, marketing, and operations. Simply put, accounting keeps track of money coming in and going out; marketing lets the world know you have something to sell; operations involves everything that accomplishes the delivery of your services or products to clients; and management oversees all the actions and information generated by marketing, accounting and operations, analyzes this information and then decides how resources should be reallocated to each department. Employees function at the level of accounting, marketing and operations while owners function at the management level. Employees work *in* the business; owners work *on* the business. For a small business owner, who most likely does all or most of the jobs within the company, knowing when you are working as an employee and when you are the owner is critical. It is when you neglect your role in management, in favor of the familiar role as an employee that your business will run into trouble. Michael Gerber has written a classic business book, *The E-Myth Revisited*, which elegantly addresses this topic.

I know, having helped hundreds of entrepreneurs open new small businesses, that success is greatly enhanced when a new business owner:

(1) has a great deal of experience and/or knowledge about the business;

(2) writes and follows a detailed business plan; and

(3) has enough money to keep the business going until it becomes profitable.

Of these three keys to success, number two, writing a detailed business plan, is probably the most important. Having said that, a business plan without experience and knowledge and the capital to stay in business long enough to become successful won't work either. A business plan will, however, point out where your knowledge, experience and capital may be lacking.

Are You Ready to Start a Business?

All would be entrepreneurs, before taking the leap into a new business, should spend time doing some self analysis. This self assessment involves defining personal goals, determining your risk tolerance for loss of any start-up capital, and identifying your personal business strengths and weaknesses. What resources, within yourself and from your family, social and business network, and community are available to you? Why is it important for you to be in charge?

If you are married or in a committed relationship, it's very important, each step along the way of building your financial planning business, to keep spouses or partners in the loop. Everything you do affects them also. Opening a new business can be exciting but completely stressful at times because it involves so many changes. Your finances and the time you have available for your relationship will be different. Letting your spouse or partner be a part of your venture, by communicating what is going on, will make the transition to business ownership easier for all involved.

Another way to smooth out the start up process is to create a support system of family, friends, and business acquaintances. Utilize this network of experience and talent as a sounding board to gain access to other knowledgeable people with marketing and in decision-making. These folks will be there to help you celebrate your triumphs and to encourage you on those days when you wonder why you ever got started in business. During the start-up phase of your financial planning business you may experience a rollercoaster of emotions. Activity, income and clients will come in fits and starts until the business matures and tends to even out. But in the beginning you will have up and down days. It is very helpful to have a supportive group of people you can rely upon.

Start your personal assessment by writing your personal goals. Our personal goals are our heart's desires. For the purposes of this assessment, do not include any goals that have to do with your financial planning business. Business goals will come later as you write your business plan. A number of businesses I've worked with have not been successful, right from the start, because this important step was not done well. They discovered that the nature of the business they started, the income it could generate, or the time it took each day, did not support their personal or their family's goals. Writing personal goals is something that should be done by you and your spouse or partner. Write your goals for several years if not for the rest of your lives. Include family, educational, fun, travel, spiritual, volunteering, retirement, legacy, and all other aspects of your personal life. Accomplishing a goal takes time and/or money. So, by understanding your personal goals, you can identify: when time, energy and money will be needed; the amount of time needed to accomplish your personal and your family's goals; and the amount of money which will need to be generated by your business. This gives you the first indication whether an independent financial adviser firm is right for you at the present time. Can your new business provide you with the money and time you need to achieve your personal and family goals?

The next area to address is where you will find the money to start your new business. This money will be at risk. Here again, it is very important to have your spouse or partner in agreement. Entrepreneurs by definition are risk takers. So, if you're contemplating starting your own business that automatically puts you into it into that category. This level of risk might not be your spouse or partner's comfort zone. It is important to be clear about what amount of money will be at risk and where it is going to come from. There are no guarantees your new business will succeed even with your hard work and planning. You need to be prepared if you do fail. Choose what you put at risk carefully. Listen to what's being said by people important to you. Listen to your own fears about potential financial loss. Use what you hear to help you make your decision. Many of the ideas and arguments for and against starting your business which come out of discussing the potential loss of income through the failure of a business can be used as you develop your business plan. One way of easing the fear of a more risk adverse spouse or partner is to have them help you write your business plan. As they see your plans unfold and can see how you can become profitable, their fears may ease.

Another important money issue to address is in the recognition that it can take up to five years for a service business such as a financial planning firm to become truly stable and profitable. Is everyone ready to stay the course during this time? Where will the money for your personal needs come from as your business ramps up to profitability? This discussion will help you decide if you are financially ready at the present to start your new business. The third important part of self-assessment in preparing for opening your new business is to create a personal strengths and weakness list itemizing all of the tasks and skills needed to run your business.

Start with a list of all the skills and tasks that are necessary to run your business. Use separate headings for management, marketing, operations and accounting. Make it as complete as possible. For example, under accounting the list might include bookkeeping, invoicing, accounts receivable, accounts payable, payroll, writing checks, banking, [reconciling] and generating monthly, quarterly and annual financials. In my experience I find that most people can immediately identify tasks for the operational part of the business but are a bit more limited when it comes to management, accounting, and marketing tasks. So, once you have completed your list, give it another look and ask yourself: Would my business run smoothly if these were the only things I did? If not, what's missing?

Now, go through the list and state whether you consider yourself strong or weak in each task. Create a picture of what you have to support the business through your ability to do everything that needs to be done. Be brutally honest with yourself. No one does everything well. As you are writing your business plan, you will be using this information to make decisions about such things as when or if to hire employees, outsource functions, what type of marketing you should do, and even if you can eliminate some tasks where you are weak and still have a complete business.

When you've completed all three parts of this self-assessment you should have a pretty good idea of whether you should move forward with the next step, preparing your business plan for your new firm.

Preparing to Write Your Business Plan

It should be intuitive for financial planners to understand the necessity of writing a business plan before starting in business and for ongoing business success. Remarkably, this isn't the case. In the headlong desire to get started, business planning often gets bypassed in favor of other start-up activities. I often hear "I have a business plan but it is all in my head. I haven't written it down." Can you imagine what your financial planning clients would say to you if you told them that their plan was "all in my head?" Unless it is written down, it is difficult to call it a plan. Some ideas, some wishes and some dreams, but not a plan.

Your plan is a decision making tool. It forces you to become intimately involved in all parts of your business and to understand how they integrate together. Your plan allows you to communicate with others about where you are taking your company in the future. It provides benchmarks and ways to measure results. It gets you thinking beyond today so that you can prepare for the tomorrow you desire. A business plan provides you with a process that enables you to envision, plan for, and achieve the business of your goals. Most of all a business plan brings you clarity.

Before you do the hard work of writing a business plan, answer the following questions:

1. What do I hope to accomplish by writing a business plan?
2. Will I commit the time necessary to write and complete a business plan?
3. Will I really use and follow this business plan once written?

Answering these questions will help you stay motivated. Writing a business plan is challenging, hard work and takes time. You will love completing some parts of your plan, but in other sections you may be tempted to skimp on time or effort. Your answers to the questions above can take the form of a personal commitment contract. Be prepared to spend consistent time for several weeks or possibly months to complete your first business plan. On average I've found three to six months is usually required. It works best to aside specific time during the week to do plan writing and to commit to completing your plan by a certain date. Include when you will complete your plan and the hours per week you will do planning. This works well to keep you motivated in your contract. A real motivator is to give your commitment contract to someone who will hold you accountable.

Determining who will be involved in writing your plan is essential. Even if you're a single owner financial planning firm with no employees, you may wish to enlist the help of, as mentioned before, a spouse, a friend or business acquaintance. I highly recommend that you find an accountability partner (look for another business owner who needs to create a plan or a mentor willing to work with you) or hire a small business coach to keep you on track. Rare is the person that can start this task and complete it without seeking someone to help. It's useful to have several eyes, ears, and minds reading and listening to your plans in order to give you reality checks, add additional information, and help you clarify your thoughts.

There are substantial new business, small business and business plan writing resources available to you at the Small Business Administration website, www.sba.gov. SBA also offers local business consulting programs such as SCORE, Senior Core of Retired Executives, and Small Business Development Centers.

Preparing to get into business must also include crafting a detailed vision of a successful business. Planning without a vision simply won't work. What will your business look like two or three years from now? Describe it completely. It is helpful to imagine going to work and telling the story of your business.

Consider everything, for example

What does the outside of the business look like as you walk up to the front door?

What signage do you have?

As you enter your office, what do you see?

Is anyone working for you?

What are their job descriptions?

How many clients do you have and how would you describe what they need and what services they purchase?

How many hours do you work in your business per week?

What money does your business generate?

What marketing is being done and when?

Where do you bank?

How often do you analyze your financials?

If someone asked you to give a detailed description of your ideal, but realistic financial planning firm two years from today, what story would you tell?

Business Plan Writing Tips

Because we usually personally identify with our business, when writing your business plan it is helpful to write in the third person. This helps with objectivity and also helps to separate yourself from your business. Think of your business as a stand-alone entity. Use the royal "we" instead of using "I". Use the business name and your formal name throughout your plan as though someone else was writing about you. This will allow you to separate yourself and describe the business as a separate entity.

Use affirmative words when writing a business plan. Phrases such as "I think," "I believe," "we might" and other such tentative wording don't belong in your business plan. They are good starting points for doing market research but when writing your plan phrases such as "we will," "we know," and "with certainty" give your planning the strength of conviction you need. Your business plan isn't about what *could* be done; it's about what you *are* going to do.

Write about the future. Don't get stuck just describing your business as it exists now or will be on the day you open your doors. State your plans for this business planning cycle of two to three years. Keep the vision of your ideal business of the future in mind.

Write everything down. When you write things down they are captured forever. You can refer to them later. Nothing is inconsequential and nothing should be left unsaid. Details matter. It's better to write more than to write too little. Once you are in the implementation phase of your business, the details will remind you of the reasons why you decided to follow a certain course.

A business plan is both a benchmarking tool, which allows you to judge where you are at any point in time, and a decision-making tool which aids in the day-to-day choices you will confront. As you write your plan, place quantifiable benchmarks throughout so that you can judge if you are on track once you start working your plan. Financial benchmarks are probably the most natural for financial planners, but management, marketing and operational benchmarks are equally as important. State what you will do, when you will do it, as well as how much it will cost.

You are projecting the progress of your business overtime. Most small business owners are comfortable with writing two-to-three-year plans. Each year you'll want to revisit your business plan to review what's happened in the past year, see how it merges into the year ahead, make any changes, and project an additional second year.

At least monthly you should be checking to see if the benchmarks you have written in your plan are being met or hopefully exceeded. When necessary, take time to adjust your plan. Remember, when one plan section is changed more than likely one or more other plan sections will be affected. Business planning is a process, not an event. It starts with writing a plan document, but the process is one of constant review and renewal.

Business Plan Checklist:

Use a business plan outline or tutorial which resonates with you to complete your business plan. It should cover the following:

- Industry and company descriptions
    - Business goals
    - Research and analysis of the overall financial planning industry as it relates to my business
    - Company description, synopsis of business and owners
    - Mission and vision statements
    - Service and/or product descriptions
    - Proprietary positions
- Market Research and analysis: local market
    - Target markets: demographics and psychographics
    - Trends
    - Competition
    - Market size
    - Market share
    - Projected annual sales

- Marketing Plan

    - Overall marketing strategy
    - Pricing policy
    - Marketing tactics
    - Advertising and promotions

- Operations Plan

    - Location
    - Facilities and improvements
    - Operating strategy and plan
    - Personnel and/or outsourcing
    - Technology
    - Compliance
    - Insurance

- Management Plan

    - Business form
    - Organizational chart
    - Key personnel
    - Compensation and ownership
    - Board of Directors, focus group or advisory committee
    - Business exit strategy

- Financial Plan

    - Financial procedures
    - Bookkeeping system
    - Financial assumptions
    - Source and use of funds document
    - Pro forma of cash flow projection
    - Pro forma profit and loss forecast
    - Pro forma balance sheet

- Appendix

    - Supporting documents
    - Future plans beyond this plan cycle

Financing Your New Business

Where to find the start-up capital for a new venture is one of the most often asked questions I receive as a small business coach. Usually, the primary source of money will come from you, the business owner. This can be in the form of personal savings and/or personal lines of credit. Family and friends may also provide early funding. If borrowing from family and friends is one strategy you will employ, it is wise to set up a formal loan. If people believe in and respect you enough to loan you money, show them respect in return by utilizing loan documents with collateral requirements if necessary.

Commercial loans and SBA guaranteed loans might be available as a source of capital, but it is often difficult for new, untested businesses to get a loan. Banks generally want at least two years of business history. It isn't necessary that you be profitable, but a loan officer will want to see a definite trend towards profitability. Service businesses, quite often, have a more difficult time securing bank funding.

A word about grants: in general, they don't exist for start-up, for-profit companies. It is one of the great myths, which seem to forever get perpetuated by the hopeful, that the government has start-up money for small businesses. Grants for businesses do exist, but usually for research and development, within the context of specific federal government department targeted programs and often for severely underserved populations. The Small Business Administration website has information on current grants that are available for most U.S. government departments. Look to other sources for your funding needs.

Employees and Outsourcing

Eventually most businesses, if they are to grow beyond a certain level, require help (there are only so many billable hours one person can achieve in a business). Should your business plan call for hiring an employee or outsourcing some of your work to an independent contractor, there is some basic information you need.

You should become familiar with the differences between an employee and an independent contractor. Employees are under your control. For example, you provide work space and equipment and training, you set pay scales and required work hours, and your employee only works for you. Independent contractors are business owners, just as you are. They negotiate, through contracts, what fees will be paid to them, pay for their own business insurance, do marketing to promote their business, work for several different businesses, and set their own hours. The federal government has a list of 20 areas that define an independent contractor. You can run into some serious trouble, (fines and penalties) should you attempt to circumvent state and federal labor laws regarding who is an employee.

Here is a basic checklist for hiring an employee:

Secure an Employer Identification Number from the IRS
Write your company policy and procedures manual
Determine your pay scale
Write a job description
Write employee handbook
Ensure compliance with federal and state employee laws
Register with your state's employment department
Post necessary employee posters and information where it can easily be seen by your employee
Purchase workers' compensation insurance
Determine if payroll and employee filings will be done in-house or outsourced to a payroll service
Design employee training and evaluation process
Organize furnishings, equipment and office space
Purchase or create an employee application that meets all federal and state guidelines
Create your employee contract and confidentiality agreement, if utilized, and have them reviewed by an attorney
Set up personnel files
Advertise, screen applications and interview
Have employee sign contract and complete a W-9 form

Outsourcing to an independent contractor can be much simpler. You determine the work that needs to be done, design a project, find a qualified person or company to complete the project(s), negotiate what you will pay, secure their company Federal EIN number or Social Security number if it is an individual, and present the contractor with a 1099 form for taxes.

Whether you hire an employee or an independent contractor will be determined by several factors. But, in general, if you require ongoing, dedicated personnel, then employees will benefit your business. For incidental project work, an independent contractor may be best. What's at issue is that your business gets the help it needs to grow.

Most business owners who do hire help wish they had done it sooner. Good help will free you up to do what you do best. Clearly, what you hire someone to do is important. Do you need an additional financial planner in your firm or would administrative help be best? Once again, utilize the business planning process to help you make your decision. Plan for each scenario and see where the results lead you.

Additional Start up Considerations

You will need to choose your business form: sole proprietorship, partnership, LLC, Subchapter S or C corporation. Make your decision based on your personal and business liability risk and tax situation. Enlist legal and tax professionals when making this decision.

Business insurance is a major start up expense. Because of this, many financial planning firms are tempted to go "bare" in the beginning. I did mention that entrepreneurs are risk takers. Business property and liability insurance packages and errors and omissions insurance should be thoroughly investigated before taking on such risk.

In most communities, a business license is required. This applies to home based offices as well as commercial locations.

Organize and furnish your business space with your work needs in mind. Create a space you and your clients will enjoy working in. It should reflect your style as well as the image you want your business to project. Pay attention to the needs of your employees, even if they are future employees. Have adequate lighting, computers, printers, telephone systems, software, file cabinets, storage, tables and chairs (don't skimp on your office chair and your back will thank you). Arrange your space so that it promotes easy, efficient access to what you need when working. Hire an office design specialist if you are challenged in this area.

Purchase the tools that will promote efficient financial planning. This includes software, backup systems, calculators, pens, pencils, paper, folders, etc.

Design an inventory system for supplies. There is nothing more frustrating than being in the middle of printing out a financial plan for a client, having the printer run out of ink and the closest office supply store is miles away.

If your business is named anything other than your personal name, for example, ABC Financial Planning, you may be required to register a Fictitious Name Statement with your city, county or state. Its purpose is to tie a real person to a business name. In most cases it will not protect your business name from another business using the same name. To do that you will need to trademark your business name with the U.S. Patent and Trademark Office, www.uspto.gov. Trademarks can also be registered for your logo and slogan.

You will want to give careful thought to naming your business. I can't tell you the number of hours that new business owners tell me they have spent on coming up with the perfect name. Since it will be something you will live with for years to come and it will be one of the first impressions your company will make on potential clients, make it a name that has meaning for you. So too, your logo and slogan are important. Enlist the services of a marketing specialist to help with these important symbols of your business.

Get sufficient marketing materials printed. These include such items as business cards, brochures, thank you cards, note cards, letterhead and envelopes, appointment reminder cards and client birthday cards. Don't go overboard with the amount you print. You can always reprint as needed. You may decide to change a phone number, fax number, color scheme, etc., and you don't want to be stuck with boxes of outdated material.

Your client contract will need to be written and reviewed by your attorney and compliance consultant.

As a financial planner, you may find yourself writing newsletters, articles for journals, creating workshops and seminars, and designing and writing marketing materials. Depending on your talents, you may even write your own software. Whenever you create intellectual property, it is important to copyright your material. It is easily accomplished by placing the copyright symbol©, the year, and the name of the creator on the document. To get full force of your copyright you should register your materials with the U.S. Copyright Office, www.copyright.gov.

Select your firm's business partners such as insurance agent, banker/loan officer, attorney, CPA, compliance consultant, technology specialist, printer, and webmaster with care. Choose reliable, knowledgeable professionals and develop strong relationships. Throughout your business life you will have reason to call upon these professionals, often at a time of crisis. Ask around in your local business community for referrals.

Where you will open your business bank accounts is an important decision which goes well beyond going to the most convenient location. Review what each bank has to offer its business customers. Check out the fees charged for business accounts. Does the bank offer interest on its business accounts? How attentive is the bank towards its business customers? Is the merchant teller window always staffed? Is the bank a SBA preferred lender? How approachable are the bank manager and loan officer. Does the bank rotate its branch managers and loan officers to new branches on a regular basis? (Not a good thing.) Should you need to apply for a loan, who makes lending decisions and are they made locally? What are the bank's policy and procedures for alerting you and for follow up if there is a problem with your account? Does the bank have safe deposit box availability? Make it a habit to visit with your bank's manager and officers regularly. It can simple as making a quick "hello" each time you go in to make a deposit. You want them to get to know you and your business. Should you need to apply for a business loan, a personal loan or have a problem with one of your accounts, having a good relationship with bank personnel will help smooth the process.

Join financial planning and local business associations and be as active as you can. You will reap the rewards of increased knowledge (gaining status and name recognition, feeling you are part of a larger community, and increased credibility within your community of peers).

Some Closing Thoughts on Business Ownership

Make sure you are ready to become a business owner. Is your temperament suited to the ups and downs that occur, especially in the start-up phase? Do you have the support of the key people in your life? Do you have the resources to start now? Just because now may not be the perfect time, it doesn't mean it won't happen some day. You can start planning and preparing for that time. Set realistic goals that will lead you to ownership.

Take the time you need to start your business correctly. Rushing to get started, leaving some start-up activities for later usually doesn't work well. Somehow, "later" never comes and important needs of your business can go undone. This can cause delays in becoming profitable or worse yet, a failed business. Set a realistic date for your official opening and if you have underestimated your start-up time, set your date back rather than opening without having everything in place.

Starting your new firm should be really exciting. Sure, it is a little scary but your passion for owning your financial planning firm should overcome your fears. Have fun planning and building your business!

Actively ask questions of others. Rely on their experience and recognize you don't have to do everything by yourself. Seek help when needed. SCORE, Small Business Development Centers, local Economic Development Corporations, university and community college programs, financial planning associations, professional coaches and consultants, chambers of commerce, other business owners, friends and family are all available to you. There is no reason to "go it alone."

Network constantly. Don't be shy about telling everyone about your business. Networking is one of the most powerful marketing and business success strategies you can employ. Anytime there is someone to talk to is a networking opportunity. Business associations will provide you with formal networking situations, but you can create your own almost anywhere. You never know when you will find a new professional who can provide you with a needed service and you will be amazed at the number of people who are delighted to have found your unique financial planning business.

Build the business of your dreams!

Chapter 14

Marketing Your Financial Planning Services to the Middle Market Consumer

Contributed by Marie Swift, Marketing Communications Consultant to Sheryl Garrett and The Garrett Planning Network

> *PROFIT IN BUSINESS COMES FROM REPEAT CUSTOMERS, CUSTOMERS WHO BOAST ABOUT YOUR PROJECT OR SERVICE, AND THAT BRING FRIENDS WITH THEM.*
>
> **– W. Edwards Deming**

There's no shortage of marketing information in the business world today, especially in the financial services industry. Peruse any industry discussion board and you'll see a plethora of comments debating the pros and cons of various marketing methods—cold calling, neighborhood canvassing, mall crawling, direct mail, display advertisements, networking, seminars, sales presentations, and more. Attend any industry conference and you'll be privy to a session or two on sales and marketing strategies. Read our industry magazines (or just open your e-mail) and you'll be exposed to a host of tips and assertions about the best way to market your services (and the best services *to help you* market your services).

Each speaker, colleague and writer has his or her own assertions of "what works" based on personal experiences, biases and preferences, training, background, and business model. Wherever you go you'll hear dozens, if not hundreds, of ideas and approaches. Some strategies will make a lot of sense to you, while others may turn your stomach. Are they all worth trying? Are you a wimp if you hate the thought of cold-calling or neighborhood canvassing?

The purpose of this chapter is to share my observations and experiences regarding what works—and what doesn't work—in marketing financial planning services to Middle Market Americans.

Over the years, Sheryl and I have tried a variety of marketing methods and exchanged ideas with numerous successful colleagues (and not-so-successful colleagues) to find out what they do to market their services to glean best practice ideas for specific service models. I'm pleased to have the opportunity to share what I've found to be the best ways to build and sustain a financial planning practice centered around meeting the needs of middle America.

As in any business, there are some basic marketing principles that hold true no matter what your product, service, or business model is. There are, however, some distinctions that make marketing to the middle unique. In this chapter, I hope to help you sort through the various options and opportunities you are likely to encounter as you formulate your marketing plan.

Creating Your Marketing Plan

Once you've decided to target and serve the Middle Market, it will be important to lay a solid marketing foundation and focus squarely on what works. No entrepreneur wants to waste time and resources on high-dollar/low-return endeavors. But, sadly, many entrepreneurs do just that. Why does this happen? How do they get so far off track? In my opinion, they simply lose sight of what matters most. Most likely, they either failed to plan or failed to follow their plan. It's easy to fall for the "strategy du jour" (or the "stock du jour," for that matter) if you lack a long-term, strategic plan.

If you're serious about building a long-term successful practice, you need to have a strategic *written* marketing plan. Putting our goals—and the strategies designed to help us reach those goals—in writing makes them real for us. The subconscious mind goes to work and seeks the target you've written down. We make a stronger commitment to our goals when they are written down because we can measure and track our written plan and determine when we are off track. Of course, the real power lies in not only writing down your goals and how you'll achieve them, but in following through in a disciplined way to *accelerate* the realization of your goals.

Also, much like the process of financial planning, *the process* of working through your marketing plan may be as important as the finished plan and its results. It's the process that forces us to think in terms of "the big picture," not just the individual marketing components. A thoroughly developed marketing plan provides a blueprint to guide us, day-in and day-out, as we create and disseminate the various components. It should also outline how all the components will work together, in a cohesive way, to realize our goals.

Starting to sound a bit like the benefits of creating a personal financial plan or a business plan, isn't it? As we learned in the previous chapter your marketing plan is a subset of your business plan.

Creating the marketing plan will force you to reflect on who you are, who you will best serve, what you will provide, and how you want to do business. It will help you analyze your strengths and weaknesses and should clarify your goals. As you become clear about your mission and personal passion, you will become a better communicator when articulating the value of your services and advice. Finally, if you revisit and refine your plan on a periodic basis, you will refocus and remind yourself of your goals and how you need to make them real. This type of focus will move you closer to your goals and help you reach your desired milestones more rapidly.

Your marketing plan can be simple or elaborate, but it should concretely outline who you will serve (your market), your mission, the services you will offer, why you are different (your message), and how you will reach your clients (your marketing methods). Just remember "the 3 M's"—(1) your *market*, (2) your *message*, and (3) your *methods*. That's the order in which you should think through your plan. Too many advisors jump right to their "methods," without giving adequate thought to their "market" and their "message."

"The Three M's"

Your Market – Define your market. Who do you want to serve and why? Really delve into it. Try creating a detailed composite of your ideal clientele. What do they like to do? Where do they congregate? How old are they? Where do they live? What's important to them? What do they have in common? What do you have in common with them? Write it down!

Your Message – Generate your vision for your practice. Reflect on who you are. What are your strengths? What do you stand for? What are you committed to? Who will you partner with to achieve results? How do you serve your clients? Who have you helped before? What successes have you had? What do you bring to the table that other advisors don't? What is your purpose? How can you communicate that unique purpose? Why do you do what you do? Get passionate! Start crafting your own story. Become the master of telling that story. Write it down!

Your Methods – Consider all the marketing methods and tactics you hear and read about. Which ones seem to make the most sense for you, your defined market(s) and your community? Are you "a natural" at seminars? Are you comfortable using the telephone to spread the word and tell your story? How can you become more active in the circles in which your targeted market(s) travel? Who can you partner with to become known in those circles? How can you create apostles who'll spread the word and tell your story? What do you need to do to create raving fans of your current clients? How can you create media relationships and leverage your press coverage? What's your timeline for success? Where can you best utilize your unique skills and abilities? Write it down!

Marketing Methods Portfolio

Now that you've done the "hard work"—reflecting on yourself and defining your market(s)—it's time to start thinking about your diversified portfolio of marketing methods.

As financial planning professionals, we would never suggest that our clients put all their eggs into one basket; instead, we would suggest a diversified portfolio of investments that should work together over time to realize their long-range goals. Your marketing plan should also utilize a variety of methods that will compliment and build on one another. Sometimes one portion of the portfolio will yield the best results, then the pendulum will swing and another portion of the portfolio will start yielding the best results. Different components of your marketing method portfolio will (and should) mature at different times.

On the other hand, overdiversification (both in investing and in marketing methods) can be detrimental. Strategic focus can be good. Ask yourself which approaches make the most sense *for you* (consider your budget, your temperament and your natural strengths), *your community* (rural or urban, niche markets within the larger market called Middle Market), and *your commitments* (what's your timeline for success, how much fire do you have in your belly?). Then jump in and formulate a portfolio of marketing methods that, *together and over time*, will help you work toward those goals.

A portfolio of marketing approaches might look like the pie chart shown in Figure 14.1:

After you design your marketing methods portfolio and decide how you'll allocate your time and money, then detail the specific activities, expenditures, steps, and commitments connected with each section allocation. (We'll be discussing some of those options and activities later in this chapter.) While some activities will be common to all financial planners, many will be as unique as you and your community are.

Own Your Plan

When all is said and done, you should *own* your market plan. It should inspire and motivate you! If you own your plan, it will be easier to

Figure 14.1

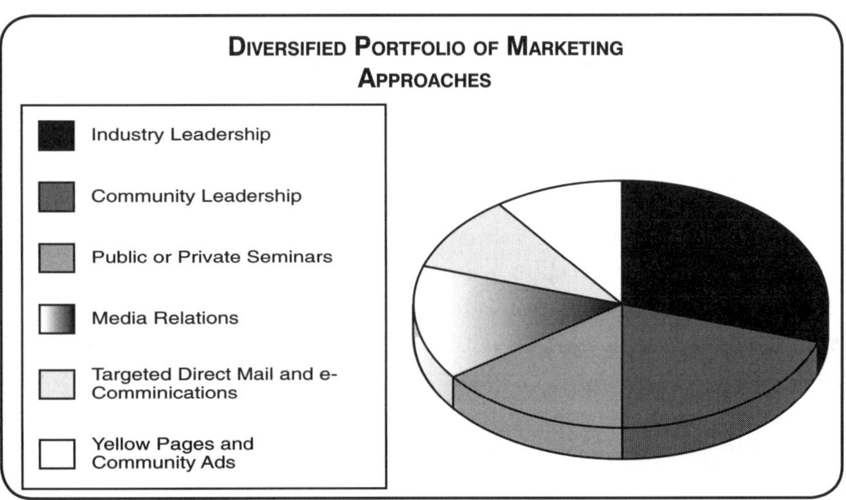

implement the plan, stick to it, and measure its results. But first you've got to own it. One of the traps I see planners falling into is paying a professional, or having an assistant, to produce a marketing plan for them. While some professional market planning and/or staff assistance may be beneficial, there is much benefit to be found in rolling up your sleeves and grappling with some of the tough questions yourself. It puts you in the self-discovery and "ownership" process. Then, if needed, you can partner with a professional or a trusted colleague, or use a staff person, to help you polish, refine and implement the plan.

Work Your Plan

Another pitfall planners may fall into is getting so busy working *in* the business that they fail to work *on* their business. One tip I learned early on is to make an appointment with myself each and every week to spend time working on and/or refining my marketing plan. Initially, we may be good at "working our plan" and getting results. The danger is that we may get busy with our workload or mistakenly assume we have a full and steady pipeline of interested clients and great referral sources.

Marketing is a communications issue, an art form. Building relationships is important, too. We have to work at keeping our relationships intact; that takes time and continued attention. Likewise, we have to work at keeping our marketing program and its corresponding relationships intact. Remember—it's not just *marketing*...it's marketing *communications*.

So, be persistent and committed to building relationships.

When we ignore the ongoing marketing aspects of our business—and the underlying relationships—it may take some time, but eventually we'll feel the pain. We have to keep making deposits to our "community goodwill bank." Just like dollar-cost-averaging, we must religiously invest our time, energy, and money back into our marketing program, through thick and thin, to realize the best results.

Once the marketing plan has been created, it's important to *work* your plan, and to revisit it periodically to fine-tune and improve the plan. Just like a good financial plan, the marketing plan should become a living, breathing document. Don't just write the plan and stick it on a shelf. Take it out, dust it off, and rework it every six to twelve months.

How Much Time and Money Should I Spend?

At a minimum, even when your pipeline is nearly full, plan on devoting 25% of your time to marketing activities.

I'm often asked what percentage of revenues a financial planning start-up should expect to invest into marketing activities in the first one to three years of business, but there are so many variables involved that I can't provide a firm answer in this book. Marketing gurus will tell you to plough roughly 30% of your annual revenues back into your marketing endeavors, but that would be much more than Sheryl or I would recommend. In some cases, however, I've heard of start-up budgets that meet or exceed that guideline due to unique factors related to the advisor and/or the community.

Later in this chapter, we'll discuss the most cost-effective ways to market to Middle Market Americans and do-it-yourselfers.

Marketing Plan Templates

While there are many good marketing plan templates available on the web and for purchase, I've included a blank one-page marketing plan document on the CD-ROM to get you started. Of course, I'd recommend that you do much more than create a simple one-page marketing plan, but this is a good first step. You can see the basic, one-page marketing plan outline in Figure 14.2. My tips for filling it out are explained in the next section, "Steps to Creating Your Marketing Plan."

Steps to Creating Your Marketing Plan

Step 1: Target Market Definition / Parameters

Define your market. Who do you want to work with and why? Describe your ideal clientele. Provide demographics and psychographics. Go to http://www.census.gov to research demographic information. Use your keen powers of observation and personal vision for your business to create your psychographics (i.e., your ideal client composite). In addition to describing your ideal clientele, reflect on and explain whom you will *not* serve and why. Under what circumstances would you turn down a client engagement?

Step 2: Objective / Mission

Generate your vision for your practice. Reflect on who you are. What drives you? What are you committed to? How can you communicate your unique value and purpose? Use passionate, lively words that "light you up." Your mission statement should consistently inspire you. Your *mission* will become a key part of your *message*. Remember to think in this order: (1) your market; (2) your message; and (3) your methods. Think of your mission statement as your personal "lighthouse." Will it send a strong beacon and guide you safely to shore in tough times? Can you enthusiastically share your mission statement with clients as well as allies and/or staff members? Do other people "light up" when you share your mission statement with them?

Figure 14.2

BASIC OUTLINE FOR MARKETING PLAN

STEP 1: TARGET MARKET DEFINITION / PARAMETERS

STEP 2: OBJECTIVE / MISSION

STEP 3: MARKETING METHODS / TOOLS

STEP 4: TIME AND MONEY BUDGET

STEP 5: TIMETABLE / STEPS

Step 3: Marketing Methods / Tools

Now that you've defined *your market* and started crafting *your message*, next start outlining your goals and objectives. (Remember, objectives are more accessible than goals.) This will lead you into outlining *your methods*. How will you reach your market—letters, telephone calls, postcards, business expos, networking, or advertising? Remember, more isn't necessarily better. And you don't have to use every tool. Pick three or four methods that appeal to you (i.e., activities that are a natural fit for your skills and abilities), and start doing them really well. Then branch out so that you have a diversified portfolio of marketing methods. Think of your methods as "your marketing tool belt." The tool belt should contain enough tools to get the job done, but not so many as to weigh you down. You may need a staple gun, a screwdriver, a hammer and some nails to start with. Later, you can add more sophisticated and costly tools to your belt as you become proficient using the fundamental tools (or as your vision guides you).

Step 4: Time and Money Budget

Effective marketing doesn't have to cost a lot of money. Your marketing plan is *yours*. You can choose tools that require you to spend time instead of money. Sheryl and I both feel strongly that the best way to reach middle market clientele is not to spend a lot of money but rather to invest your time networking with other professionals and working with the media. Does this mean we don't recommend spending any money on marketing? No, but we choose to spend far more *time* doing marketing-related activities than we do money. This is a relationship business and relationships generally take more time than money to keep them flourishing. Outline your money budget, your time investment, and parcel that into your schedule. Then stick to that time and money budget religiously.

Time:	
Networking Activities	3 hours per week for 6 months
Direct Mail / Calling Campaign	4 hours per week for 18 months
Seminar Program	2 hours per week for 12 months
Plan Administration	1 hour per week for 24 months
TBD Marketing Tasks	2 hours per week, indefinitely
Money:	
Networking Activities/Dues	$100 per month for 6 months
Direct Mail / Advertising Campaign	$300 per month for 18 months
Seminar Programs/Materials	$75 per month for 12 months
Plan Administration	$0 per month for 24 months

Step 5: Timetable and Steps

For each objective, list the steps needed to attain the objective. Break down all steps to the smallest tasks possible. Determine the order in which you'll do them. For instance:

Week 1 – Gather names
Week 2 – Write introductory letter
Week 3 – Generate and send 50 letters
Week 4 – Make 10 follow-up telephone calls each day
Week 5 – Review and evaluate letter mailing and calling plan

Create deadlines for yourself and stick to them. Pretend your life depends on getting those marketing pieces sent out, telephone calls made, and lunches scheduled (actually, it's not far from the truth!). Find simple ways to reward yourself when you stay on track and, perhaps, more elaborate ways to celebrate your larger successes. Find a committed listener or accountability partner to hold you to your stated goals.

Finally, develop a simple way to track your progress and measure your results. I like working with a specialized way of producing specific, measurable goals called "Bull's Eyes." Over the years, I've had the privilege of working with Bull's Eye's originator and trainer, Tom Werder. (For more information on Tom's book, *The Bull's Eye Principle: How to Lead and Manage People to Extraordinary Results*, go to: http://www.tomwerder.com/1.htm.) Tom's simple yet effective methods have helped me to create and hit many personal and business Bull's Eyes. The beauty of tracking small, specific tasks to measure your Bull's Eye success rate is that you can see in pretty short order just where you need to improve and what you need to refine to achieve your goals. Immediate and constant feedback can serve as a powerful rudder for your enterprise. (Never forget that even if you are a company of one, you are your own enterprise.)

In summary, we have established that it is vital for you to create and maintain a written marketing plan. Whether your marketing plan is five pages or 50 pages, it is important for you to reflect on who you are, who you best serve, what your mission and key marketing messages are, and how you will implement the plan and measure its success. As a planner, you undoubtedly counsel clients that having a written financial plan is the best way to realize success. The same holds true for you, too. Creating a written plan gives substance to your thoughts. A good marketing plan points you in the right direction and gives you a road map to follow, complete with instructions for reaching our destinations.

What is Marketing?

Let's back up just a bit and address the question, "what is marketing and how does it differ from sales?"

The American Marketing Association defines "marketing" as follows:

> *"MARKETING IS THE PROCESS OF PLANNING AND EXECUTING THE CONCEPTION, PRICING, PROMOTION, AND DISTRIBUTION OF IDEAS, GOODS, AND SERVICES TO CREATE EXCHANGES THAT SATISFY INDIVIDUAL AND ORGANIZATIONAL OBJECTIVES."*[1]

The Oxford Dictionary and Thesaurus defines "marketing" as:

> *"ACTIVITY OR PROCESS INVOLVING RESEARCH, PROMOTION, SALES AND DISTRIBUTION OF A PRODUCT OR SERVICE; SELLING OR BUYING IN A MARKET."*[2]

I take the definition of "marketing" one step further:

> *"MARKETING IS ANYTHING THAT IMPACTS A CLIENT'S OR [A] POTENTIAL CLIENT'S VIEW OF YOU AND YOUR COMPANY. IT'S EVERYTHING FROM*

> *HOW YOU ANSWER THE TELEPHONE, TO YOUR SIGNAGE AND HOW YOU [DECORATE YOUR] OFFICE, TO HOW YOU WALK, TALK AND DRESS. IT INCLUDES YOUR COMPANY'S BRANDING AND PRINTED MATERIALS, [AS WELL AS] YOUR WEB SITE AND E-COMMUNICATIONS. IT'S SHAPED BY THE DECISIONS YOU MAKE ABOUT WHAT SERVICES AND PRODUCTS YOU'LL PROVIDE, AND ANCHORED ON THE ESSENCE OF* WHO YOU ARE *AS A PROFESSIONAL. IT INCLUDES YOUR IMAGE, YOUR PUBLIC PERSONA. IT'S EVERYTHING YOU DO TO ATTRACT AND RETAIN BUSINESS."*[3]

When asked how "marketing" differs from "sales," I'll tell you:

> *"MARKETING WORKS ON THE LAW OF ATTRACTION. IT'S MORE ART THAN SCIENCE. TO ATTRACT MIDDLE MARKET CLIENTS, YOU'LL WANT TO CAST A LARGE NET IN STRATEGIC SPOTS WHERE THE 'SCHOOLS OF FISH' LIKE TO CONGREGATE. SALES IS MORE LIKE SPEAR FISHING – IT'S USUALLY A ONE-ON-ONE OR SMALL GROUP ENDEAVOR. IT HINGES ON YOUR PERSONAL COMMUNICATION SKILLS AND WORKS ON THE POWER OF PERSUASION. IT IS MORE SCIENCE THAN ART, BUT CAN BE ELEVATED TO AN ART FORM WHEN DONE RIGHT. BUT BOTH ARE IMPORTANT TO YOUR SUCCESS."*[4]

What style and image reflects your business? How can you best attract and retain Middle Market clients? Let's look at what makes "marketing-to-the-middle" unique.

SERVING THE MIDDLE MARKET

In serving the Middle Market, it is critically important to efficiently reach out to your ideal clients and effectively communicate your key marketing messages in a consistent, confident and easy manner.

People today are simply bombarded with too much information. Time is short. Priorities get muddled. Competing agendas and multiple commitments chip away at our focus. At times life can seem overwhelming.

Average Americans know they need professional financial advice, at least on an occasional or periodic basis. But they frequently don't know where to find help. They may think that no professional independent advisor will work with them either because they don't have sufficient investable assets to meet the advisor's minimums, or simply because they don't want to turn over their assets to be managed.

As a result, many middle Americans and do-it-yourselfers resign themselves to "going it alone"—just doing the best that they can. They don't realize there are professionals who are not only willing, but eager to serve them. Their lack of awareness leads them into the sea of noise and competing interests (e.g., web sites, periodicals, friends and family).

As stated in Chapter 2, this vast, untapped market has been overlooked and underserved for so long that even savvy "Gen-X" professionals may cry out "we have no where to turn for help and advice." See Figure 14.3.[5] (The news release also contains some interesting survey findings about "Gen-Xers" and do-it-yourselfers in general.) This demographic sees the value in having at least an occasional financial check up, and obtaining specific advice on an as-needed basis. Just as they see their dentist on a periodic or as-needed basis and call him or her "their dentist," they'd like to establish a relationship with a trusted financial advisor to round out their advisory and professional services team (i.e., CPA, attorney, doctor, dentist, etc.). Even if they only see you once a year, they will think of you as "their financial advisor."

So, the first thing to do—and what may matter most in all of your marketing endeavors—is to really *want* to serve this market. When you have decided that this is your calling and desire, you will begin to communicate with clarity and passion the many compelling reasons that you are the right advisor for this niche.

The next most important thing is to become active in your community. Look for ways to "see and be seen" by the people you want to serve (and the other professionals who will introduce you to potential clients). Move in the circles where the greatest number of potential clients will see, and get to know you, as a resource for the "average person."

Start saying, "I help average Americans, like you and me, make smarter financial decisions," and then elaborate on just how you do that. Become a good storyteller. People (including the media) love stories! Having a simple, consistent message—a story you can tell and re-tell time and time again—will help you differentiate yourself from other would-be suitors.

Figure 14.3

6750 West 75th Street, Overland Park, KS 66204, Suite 3B. Toll Free: (866) 260-8400
Web: www.GarrettPlanningNetwork.com / E-mail: media@GarrettPlanningNetwork.com

NEWS

FOR IMMEDIATE RELEASE
July 20, 2001

Contacts: Marie Swift, Principal / Impact Communications
Phone: (913) 649-5009 / E-mail: marieswift@impactcommunications.org

Sheryl Garrett, Principal / The Garrett Planning Network, Inc. (GPN)
Phone: (866) 260-8400 / E-mail: media@garrettplanningnetwork.com

SURVEY, ARTICLE SAY GEN-XERS DISTRESSED BY LACK OF FINANCIAL ADVICE

Network of By-the-Hour Financial Planners Seeks to Remedy Situation, Offer As-Needed Financial Planning Services and Advice to All Interested Consumers

(OVERLAND PARK, Kansas) – On CBS.MarketWatch.com, in his July 17, 2001 article "Rich Gen-Xers in Distress," writer Thomas Kostigen says: "Wealthy young adults are crying out for help but are being largely ignored by financial counselors. Two-thirds of Generation Xers, people age 22 to 34, who don't use a financial adviser, want one. Yet, not many investment professionals have focused on Generation X, says a report that surveyed people in this age group with $100,000 or more to invest. Sixty-three percent of those surveyed by New York Life Investment Management said they get their financial information from the Internet. But that's not advice. And a lot want to get their advice from a financial geek rather than a gadget."

Figure 14.3 (Cont'd)

The survey results strongly indicated that Gen-Xers using an advisor felt the relationship provided a satisfying level of financial security and stability, the article said. "Wall Street, however, has been busying itself designing financial services programs and products for the Baby Boomers, the largest and wealthiest segment of the population. But Generation X is no slouch. Roughly one-third of millionaire households are headed by someone between 18 and 39, according to the New York Life report," says Kostigen in his article.

"Most financial advisors have demonstrated little understanding or interest in reaching these investors," says Sheryl Garrett, a CERTIFIED FINANCIAL PLANNER™ practitioner in Overland Park, KS. "Gen-Xers typically want validation of the decisions they make independently. They want help with retirement planning and investment choices," she said. "When I saw this need a few years ago, I began retooling my financial planning practice to reach not only Gen-Xers seeking validation and professional advice, but also any consumer—from the young to the middle aged to the already retired—who wants validation and professional advice without ongoing asset management fees, retainers, long-term contracts or commissions."

"The Marketwatch article says Gen-Xers are in need of advice when it comes to financial planning and that 58 percent of those surveyed lacked a comprehensive plan," continues Garrett. "The sad thing is, too many consumers—from ALL walks of life and income brackets—have been turned away from traditional financial planning and asset management firms with high minimums. Even if the consumer can meet the minimums imposed by these firms, a growing number of more sophisticated investors just don't see the value in paying for an ongoing, contractual financial advisory relationship. Nor can they justify additional brokerage fees and transaction costs. As a result, they have resigned themselves to going it alone. It is my strong opinion, however, that most people need at least occasional professional financial advice to build the brightest financial futures."

According to the Marketwatch article, the New York Life survey shows one-third of those polled will continue to plan and operate on their own, without the help of a professional adviser. The article also points to another problem: being "sold to" rather than being "consulted with" turns off many Gen-Xers and Baby Boomers. Nancy Moore, spokesperson for New York Life, is quoted as saying "Gen-Xers are more focused on trust and an advisor's willingness to communicate and give them advice."

Sheryl Garrett concurs: "Consumers do want an advisor they can trust, but many have had a hard time finding an advisor with whom they feel comfortable. This unfilled need—consumers who want professional financial advice but are discouraged because they don't know where to find the type of advice/advisor they need—moved me to start The Garrett Planning Network. Any consumer, young or old, affluent or struggling, can find an hourly, as-needed planner by visiting the "Consumer Leg" of The Garrett Planning Network site (http://www.GarrettPlanningNetwork.com). As founder of the network, it is my mission to raise consumer awareness and let the public know that there is a nationwide network of Fee-Only planners focused on providing professional financial planning and advice on an hourly, as-needed basis. Now 'average Americans' with more modest portfolios and incomes—and self-managing investors who may have larger portfolios and incomes—have somewhere to turn for professional, timely advice and as-needed, hourly financial planning services."

To stand out in the sea of daily noise and competition, deliver a consistent, simple, passionate message. Emphasize that you *enthusiastically* specialize in working with average Americans and the Middle Market. While you might fear you are beginning to sound like a broken record, repetition of your key marketing messages is essential, both in print and verbal communications.

Help your current and prospective clients understand who you are and how you can help them by speaking simply and directly to their needs and concerns. Then get out in the community and start speaking with missionary zeal about *what* you do, and *why* you do it.

Why Target and Serve Average Americans

I said earlier that it is important for you to *really want* to serve the Middle Market, the Validator and do-it-yourself communities. Sheryl tells the story of her personal epiphany that occurred about seven years into her career. She'd been a registered representative for a major financial services organization, and earned the right to use the CFP® marks of distinction. She'd gotten her "sea legs" serving clients as an assistant to a successful fee-only financial planner, and later as a key staff planner for a large, independent wealth management firm. Eventually she knew she wanted to be an entrepreneur. Over time, she evolved and became a partner in another successful wealth management firm.

While she enjoyed being a trusted advisor to a select group of affluent clients, it always bothered her to turn away the people who did not meet their firm's minimums. After all, Sheryl grew up in a fairly small town, in a disciplined and frugal middle income family with working class values. Her roots simply tugged at her heartstrings until she determined that it was time to "return home."

Having made this decision, she was determined to set up her practice so that she could efficiently serve the underserved, help the Validators, make services affordable to people from all walks of life, and liberate herself from concierge-level responsibilities.

As a result of the changes that she made, she became personally much more satisfied. She made a professional living, and had plenty of time to enjoy her family, friends and leisure time. Sheryl has expressed how pleased she was with the continual sense of satisfaction knowing that she was helping people—just like me—who might not otherwise have access to professional fee-only financial planning and advice. It is not just adding another fraction of a percentage point to a wealthy individual's portfolio. Instead, Sheryl and other like minded professionals are helping "real people" send their kids to college, build for the future, retire worry-free and enjoy a better night's sleep.

Simple is Often Better

Over the years working with hundreds of financial advisors, I've tested simple and fancy marketing materials. What I've found is that Middle Market consumers appreciate professional, but modest, marketing materials and lower-key tactics over slick, high-end materials and high-profile tactics. (Actually, high-end marketing pieces can be a turn off to average folks who may wonder where the money to produce them comes from!). While you want your marketing pieces to look and feel professional, it's important not to appear "overproduced." Average Americans respond better to simple, honest marketing messages and mid-level quality marketing materials. This is good news for the small planning firm or sole practitioner.

While you do need to invest some time and money in developing decent promotional materials, it may not be as expensive as you think to establish a solid presence in your community.

Essential Branding Decisions

The modern notion of "branding" comes from the custom of branding livestock in the American West. Branding cattle conveys to the cowboy a clear and distinct mark of ownership. Branding your company and services should accomplish the same goal: to provide you with a clear and distinct mark of ownership. When potential clients see your advertising and marketing materials, you want them to think, "that's Henry James' company, no doubt about it."

But, while some may think of "branding" solely as the graphic identifier (i.e., your logo) or the tag line, those are only two elements in the branding process. "Branding" is the use of any and all techniques by which a company, organization or product distinguishes itself from others. It's how you express your value and your functions to your target markets.

Just as the cowboy sears his brand onto each of his cattle, your goal should be to burn your message into the minds of your target market. You need to decide in advance what you want your potential client to think or feel when she reads your marketing message, sees your logo, or hears your positioning statement. Over time, your brand should be instantly recognized and trigger an immediate association with your company and its competitive advantages.

So, what do you want to convey to your market? Are you:

- Just another financial advisor?
- The low-cost leader?
- A full-service solution provider?
- A flexible, needs-based resource?
- A comprehensive problem solver?
- An advisor to the affluent or elite?
- A Middle Market specialist serving regular folk?

What type of advisor are you? What type of service and/or focus are you going to use? What type of clientele are you willing to serve?

Branding is the *process* of identifying and differentiating your services to establish your uniqueness. If you've worked through some of the questions and processes described earlier in this chapter (especially in the area of creating your marketing plan), then you've already embarked on the branding and positioning decision-making process. Essentially, you've started developing your "company identity"—a large part of which is *you*!

Branding and positioning affect the messages and the materials we aim at current and prospective clients, the media, and our centers of influence. The essential elements of branding are:

- identity;
- differentiation; and
- uniqueness.

Good branding helps your services be more easily remembered in the community. It provides strong links, and ties together all your promotional and marketing efforts. It unifies your public relations materials, yellow pages advertisements, community advertisements, radio spots, seminar productions, sponsorships, office décor and signage, newsletters and direct mail campaigns, e-communications, brochures, and other collateral materials.

Think of branding as clearly and firmly establishing the identity of your company, product, or services. A "brand" has promotional value and benefits associated with it. Questions to ask yourself during the branding process include:

1. What is *my* distinct personality?

2. What makes *me* different from all the others?

3. What statements can *only I* make in my promotions and marketing communications?

4. What statements do competitors dare not say (or don't bother to say) in their promotional and marketing communications?

5. What ideas, images and motivations can *I* use that will distinguish me from all others?

6. What are *my* personal preferences for style, color, verbiage and image?

Good branding is:

- **Consumer-oriented.** A good brand is credible and sincere, and involves the client. It appeals to the client's self-interest.

- **Focused on establishing one or more compelling reasons for trying your services.** A good brand presents a unique benefit and contains a promise of competitive advantage.

- **Memorable.** A good brand is bold, and leaves a distinct impression. It links your company or name with the key selling ideas.

- **Clear and complete.** A good brand says what it needs to say simply and clearly. It is uncomplicated and easy to understand. There are no alternative meanings or possibilities for confusion.

- **Persuasive.** A good brand moves the client toward action or engagement of your services.

The good news is that just by targeting and serving the Middle Market, you've already established a key way to start differentiating yourself!

When Sheryl decided to target and serve the Middle Market and the do-it-yourself community, exclusively, she and I worked together to create a tag line, logo, mission statement, and key marketing messages during the development of her initial marketing plan. She thought long and hard about what made her different, and how her services and target market were different. We then finalized core marketing messages and produced collateral materials. Over the years, we have continued to improve those materials and refine the delivery of the message. It's a never-ending process, but well worth the investment!

Developing a strong company identity—even if you're just a company of one—is important. Do it earlier rather than later for the best results! We've included a Worksheet on the CD-ROM called "Key Branding Decisions" to help you through this vital process.

Positioning Statements

Every serious businessperson needs a series of positioning statements that can be communicated clearly and with passion—at will. It will take time and some thought to craft the right positioning statements for you. Remember, your positioning statement should be as unique as you are.

As you move through the process of creating your marketing plan and making essential branding decisions, jot down key words and phrases that lend themselves to verbal communications. You'll want to be able to gracefully—and authentically—answer these questions:

1. Who are you?

2. What do you do?

3. What makes you different from other financial advisors?

4. How does your company function? How do you serve your clients?

5. Who do you serve, and why?

6. What's your background? How long have you been doing this?

7. What drives or motivates you? *Why* do you do *what* you do?

8. Why should I trust / do business with you?

9. What benefits and solutions can you provide for me?

10. How are you compensated? What is the cost?

Of course, you wouldn't just plough down the list of questions in all of your interactions—that would send people running! But you need to be prepared to address each of these questions, as needed, in formal and informal settings. Most importantly, you need to *internalize* and, as the humorous Pier One shopping commercial with Kirsti Alley says, "become one" with your positioning statements.

Sheryl admits that she was slow to develop and adapt a *consistent* positioning statement of her own. Eventually, she developed *a series of consistent, compelling replies* that are a natural extension of who she is. It's a great feeling to know your strengths, target market and key selling points so well—and to be able to deliver them in a clear, compelling and consistent manner whenever needed.

Here are some tips to keep in mind as you construct your positioning statement and work on your delivery style:

- When we speak authentically, with forethought, clarity and passion, people are naturally drawn to us. They will either want to engage our services, or help us in other ways (e.g., by referring business to us, or by promoting us in the community).

- When we use lively words and try to draw "word pictures" in the listener's mind, we communicate with vivid power.
- When we anticipate and speak to the listener's needs and wants, we are persuasive.
- When we are sold on ourselves, our services and our business model, we are confident and allow our passion to show.
- When we practice saying our key messages aloud, we become both graceful and credible in our delivery.

I've included a number of other tips on developing a good positioning statement and verbal delivery style in Figure 14.4.

Creating Effective Marketing Communications Tools

Many small business owners think that one of the first things they must do is jump in and start creating their marketing communications tools right away. Financial planning entrepreneurs are no exception. They, too, may feel driven to begin creating and distributing their basic printed materials before they have done the real reflection and thinking described above. However, that is like putting the cart before the horse.

Even your basic collateral materials can help—or hinder—your communication and branding efforts. Every business card you hand out, every telephone call you make (or take), every letter or post card you send out, every seminar you present, every meeting you attend and network at, and every e-mail that you send out means that one more potential client has heard of you.

But what will their first impression be? And how will they remember you?

Make sure that your key messages and value propositions have been fully developed before you create your fundamental materials. You will (and should) evolve those essential messages and materials over time, but you'll want to start conveying the right image from the outset. In addition, it makes sense to start out with a logo and basic suite of collateral materials that you'll feel proud using—and won't outgrow—

Figure 14.4

How to craft a good positioning statement and improve your verbal delivery:

1. Start by typing each question at the top of its own page. Place the pages in a three-ring binder (or in a tabbed section within your marketing plan binder). See the CD-ROM for a set of pre-typed questions in Word format.

2. As ideas and good phrasing occurs to you, jot these words down on the appropriate pages. Hone each reply until you've come up with a precise, compelling and genuine answer for each question.

3. Make an appointment with yourself to work on and improve your positioning statement each week. Re-type and clean up the pages. Create a long and a short answer for each question.

4. Practice speaking your responses aloud. Listen to the sound and rhythm of your voice. Vary your tone and emphasis. Envision yourself speaking to a specific person and intentionally smile while you practice aloud.

5. Use your hands and move around when you practice. Bend your knees. Gesture. Remember to smile. Watch yourself in the mirror.

6. Try out your verbiage on your spouse and other trusted friends and colleagues. Get feedback. Hone your wording and delivery skills.

7. Practice until you are essentially comfortable with your responses and verbal delivery. Notice I did not say "totally comfortable." Most of us never will be!

8. Now, forget about all your answers and preparation. Go out and meet people. Don't worry about "getting it just right." Practice "live," and discover what works and doesn't work. What feels right to you in a real-life situation?

9. Don't worry if you flub the wording when you speak. Let your light shine! It's who you are being in that very moment that matters most. Be comfortable with yourself, and others will be comfortable with you, too. Be more interested in the other person than you are in yourself.

10. Back at the office: Return to Step 3 above. Modify your verbiage and/or improve your delivery style.

for two or three years. Once you're well-established as an expert in your community, you may decide to modify or evolve your brand; however, it is especially crucial in the start–up years to present a consistent visual image and deliver key marketing messages in a strategically-repetitive manner.

Your fundamental marketing tools are your letterhead, envelopes, business cards and brochures. Of course, you can extend that basic suite of materials to include personal note cards and matching envelopes, half-size note sheets, post cards and more. The possibilities are endless, but the good news is that today's technology is making production of these materials timelier and less expensive.

Have your materials professionally printed. You'll probably find that the cost-savings of in-office production dissipate as the quantity of the materials you need to produce increases. You'll want to assess the cost of the paper and the ink (the cost of which will increase for large areas of coverage). You should also factor in your time and the "hassle factor." For instance, if you need small quantities of tri-fold brochures, outputting them on an inkjet printer may be fine. However, if you need to run 50-100 (or more) brochures for a seminar or mailing, waiting for the ink to dry, monitoring the quality, running the second side, replacing the ink cartridge and folding the brochures yourself may be less than ideal.

Another option is using local "quick print" shops (such as Sir Speedy and Alphagraphics) and online "virtual print shops" (such as www.iprint.com and www.vistaprint.com), both of which can also produce decent printed materials. The online "virtual print shops" have basic templates that can be filled in and modified. Their online systems can be used for sending orders directly to one of their print shops. Sir Speedy and Alphagraphics, which have provided traditional walk-in printer's services for many years, now also offer online self-design and/or ordering capabilities. The primary downsides of using these types of templated systems are that the choices may be limited, and there is little (or no) personal guidance. In addition, if you customize or modify the templates too much, you may be undoing the template designer's good work.

A professional's help is very beneficial in the logo design and layout process. Print shops like Sir Speedy and Alphagraphics typically have someone on staff to help you add a bit more flair and polish than you'd achieve on your own. Alternatively, you can visit a variety of online logo creation firms, such as www.logo-mojo.com, and determine whether their skills and design packages seem acceptable to you. Perhaps you know a talented graphic artist who'd be willing to barter design services for financial planning services?

When Sheryl established Garrett Financial Planning, Inc. in 1998, she hired a local graphic designer to help her create her logo and basic printed materials. Together they created an eye-catching, one-color logo. (The logo looked like it was two colors, light green and dark green, but this is a trick that smart designers use called "half toning." Actually, there's just one ink color involved, so printing costs remain low while potential visual impact is high.) She chose to print my materials on a beige colored, recycled paper that retains the characteristic specks most people associate with recycled paper. Sheryl wanted to make a subtle statement about her values and attract clients with similar values, as well as progressive, independent, thrifty and forward thinkers.

A few years later, she decided to have a logo "makeover." At the same time, she adjusted her signature tag line to better suit her target market and service model. Sheryl started by having one of her staff members work-up an idea based on the elements she liked from the old logo; then incorporated a new piece of clip art they had on file. While you won't be able to see the logo color choices in Figures 14.5, 14.6, and 14.7 (because they are printed in black and white), we chose a hunter green for the burst, black for the company name and a deep purple for the tag line.

Figure 14.5

GARRETT FINANCIAL PLANNING, INC.
Hourly, As-Needed Advice for Everyday Life™

~ LOGO #1

THE BURST WAS ORIGINALLY SET IN HUNTER GREEN, THE COMPANY NAME IN BLACK, AND THE TAG LINE IN DEEP PURPLE.

Figure 14.6

~ Logo #2

THE DESIGNER UNCOUPLED THE COMPANY NAME FROM THE BURST, RESET THE FONT TO SOMETHING WITH GREATER IMPACT, RE-FOCUSED THE EYE ON THE MOST IMPORTANT WORD, "GARRETT" AND MOVED THE BURST TO THE RIGHT OF THE COMPANY NAME. SHE SIMPLIFIED THE COLOR SCHEME, KEEPING JUST THE HUNTER GREEN AND THE BLACK INKS. WE PRINT THIS ON BRIGHT, WHITE LINEN PAPER. THIS IS THE LONG VERSION OF OUR LOGO.

Although the elements seemed to work together fairly well, there were a couple of things that didn't seem quite right. (See Figure 14.5 [Logo #1] for the original concept Sheryl's staff provided to the design team. See Figure 14.6 [Logo #2] for the polished design.)

As previously stated, a logo can be simple or fancy text set in a stylized font. It may or may not include some sort of graphic or icon as a visual identifier and branding tool. It can have either a tall or a wide footprint—or there can be two similar versions (one tall and one wide) that allow for many flexible placement options. (See Figure 14.6 [Logo #2] and Figure 14.7 [Logo #3] for samples of how I use both a wide logo and a tall logo.) The third element you may want to include as an integral part of your logo is a tag line.

Whenever possible, include all three elements together: (1) stylized font; (2) graphic identifier; and (3) tag line. If needed, each element can be used separately, in strategic ways. For instance, you may use just "the bug" (the burst graphic) as a watermark on a Power Point presentation or note pad. Alternatively, there are times when the stylized text, isolated from the rest of the logo elements, is what is called for. Mostly, however, I'd use the three elements in tandem.

Figure 14.7

~ Logo #3

Here is what the tall / centered version of our logo looks like. While we prefer to utilize the long / offset logo (see Logo #2) wherever possible, there are times when a long footprint is unwieldy. In that case, we utilize the tall / centered logo. We might also use just the burst or the company name in the specialized font (isolated elements).

A professional-looking, but simple one- or two-color design works well. It's been cost effective, and Validator and Middle Market clients have responded well to these marketing materials. Sheryl shied away from ultra-fancy concepts like gold foiling and embossing because she wanted to communicate to her target market that she's cost conscious yet professional, just like they are.

Before you begin developing any of your collateral items, however, you need to work through the key branding decisions. What image do you want to convey? Progressive and slightly new? Conservative and classic? Old school veteran? Trendy and on the cutting edge? Your logo and collateral materials should help you communicate your company's image. The logo design and color, the layout and motif of your letterhead and business cards, the papers you select, and the tag lines you develop and attach to your logo or include on other items wherever possible—all of these things will work together to convey the type of planner and planning firm you are.

While a graphic designer can assist you by adding the visual flair and polish you might be missing without her help, you must be able to communicate your company's personality and focus so that she can offer appropriate options that communicate your image in the most effective way possible. The logo design process should be collaborative. A good designer will listen to your goals, preferences and mission, and offer several choices that work to bring the concepts into visual reality.

A fourth element in our branding strategy was to incorporate high quality photographs of local landmarks in Sheryl's printed materials and on her web site. When we began building the first web site (www.GarrettFinancialPlanning.com), we created a simple "splash page" that would contain just the company name, logo, tag line and a photo of a quintessential Kansas City landmark. We wanted people to stop—just for a moment—to absorb these four elements and feel a subtle sense of "being at home." Kansas City is known as "the city of fountains" and we were delighted to find just the right portrait of the best-known fountain in the city.

We also had our web team at AdvisorSites create a home page collage of three other easy-to-identify (and easy-to-identify-with) Kansas City landmarks.[6] We carried the water theme over to a specially designed web logo, which included a swish shape reminiscent of a river.

Of course, we learned several lessons in building this first web site (which could be the focus of another chapter in another book). But, the web site continues to prove its weight in gold. Every penny that Sheryl put into it has been returned to her many times over. The web site has served as the quintessential "mega brochure." When prospective clients arrived for their initial consultation, if they've visited the web site they are already "sold" and ready to engage Sheryl's services.

Instead of sending quarterly newsletters, as many practitioners do, Sheryl sent special reports and client letters three or four times a year. We are also big fans of post cards. Sheryl has used them to announce her web site's launch, remind clients that it's time for their financial check-up, and encourage them to visit the web site. Most clients do have Internet access and did visit the web site if prompted to do so.

Here are a few other tips for client communications:

- Find reasons to be in touch with, and to re-communicate your value to, your clients on a periodic basis. Special reports and market commentaries are a perfect way to do this.

- Encourage referrals by simply handing happy clients a business card, brochure or article reprint at the end of every meeting. Ask them to pass it on to someone who might be interested.

- Put a "P.S." at the end of every piece of correspondence that says that you welcome and appreciate their referrals.

- Hold a client appreciation event once a year. Sheryl hosted open houses at her office, complete with appetizers, beer, wine and soft drinks. We also considered hosting computer classes on how to use Quicken to track personal expenses.

Direct Mail and Advertising

As mentioned above, Sheryl and I have used marketing letters, stimulating e-mails, offers for special reports, seminar flyers and postcard campaigns for advertising. Sheryl never mailed "cold" to a purchased mailing list. Instead, she'd put together her own list of names and addresses of people she knows or has met. We call this the "house list." Over time, the list has grown and e-mails and direct mail communications have rippled out to a larger body of people.

Besides purchasing what I think is a pretty darn good yellow pages advertisement (it must be because it pays for itself), Sheryl didn't do any other form of display advertising (although colleagues swear by small display advertisements in their Chamber of Commerce directories, church bulletins, neighborhood newspapers, and other similarly targeted publications).

If you plan to use direct mail or advertising, be sure to budget wisely. You'll need to invest in several mailings to the same list of people in order for it to pay off. You should place the same (or similar advertisements) in the same publication or directory for a number of months in order to build "share of mind."

Other tips include:

- Know to whom you are targeting. Create a compelling message that will appeal to the needs and self-interests of your target clients. Brand your advertisements and/or direct mail pieces.

- Be colorful. Stand out with something different. Have a special offer or reason for them to contact you.

- Work on your headlines and create an active "call out" to attract their attention. You've only got about three seconds to capture their attention, so make those three seconds count.

- Provide options for contacting you—telephone, e-mail, fax, pre-paid reply card, etc.

- Provide your web site address so that your target clients can check you out privately, on their own terms.

- Finally, don't despair if your advertisements and mailings do not produce immediate results. Marketing experts tell us that it takes multiple exposures to your message/offer before a prospective client may call. Ninety-nine percent of the recipients will never call; 1% is a reasonable response rate. However, if you think of direct mail and advertising as just one more tool in your tool belt, and diversify your marketing methods accordingly, you should eventually see your efforts working together over time. Who knows, you may even hit the stellar 3% reply rate that some direct mail companies tout.

- Don't be surprised if you receive inquiries from advertisements, post cards or articles that were sent out many months ago. It's not unusual for people to keep a post card, or tear out an advertisement or article, and place it in the top desk drawer until a need arises.

Kathy Dollard, a CFP® professional who practices near Boston, told me that she consistently hears that people "see her everywhere." Although she uses some small, strategically placed advertisements, they are not the backbone of her marketing communications program. Instead, she focuses on: (1) providing educational seminars in the community (using flyers, postcards, e-mails, catalog listings or targeted advertisements to promote them); (2) networking with allied professionals; and (3) encouraging referrals from existing clients. The direct mail campaigns and display advertisements she uses simply bolster her credibility in the community and help build "share of mind." It's not unusual for someone to show up at one of her seminars clutching a postcard she sent or an advertisement she placed many months ago. Kathy sticks with her marketing and advertising plan, through thick and thin, knowing that it takes time to yield results.

Build Affinity Groups

While e-communications, direct mail, display advertisements and other more expensive forms of marketing communications can bolster your visibility and your credibility, in my experience a key element of success is to find a variety of opportunities to "meet and greet" people with whom you have common interests. If you've done the "hard work" of reflecting on which clients you want to serve and have taken the time to craft the right message, it will be easy to spot right-fit opportunities within your community.

For Sheryl, one of the best places to apply her time and talents was by volunteering in a leadership capacity for key industry groups. Through her activities and the relationships she built via her involvement in NAPFA (the National Association of Personal Financial Advisors), the IAFP (the International Association for Financial Planning), and the ICFP (the Institute for Certified Financial Planners) (IAFP and ICFP were the predecessors to what we now know as the Financial Planning Association), she established herself as "the go-to person" for anything related to serving Validators or Middle Market clients.

Did she have to force herself to take on these leadership roles? No, it was a natural fit for her. She loved being able to contribute to the various committees and task forces. Sheryl also learned quite a bit about working with the media and being in the public eye. A natural by-product of her participation was enhanced visibility among her peers and increased stature in her community. As a result of the relationships she continued to build within her affinity groups, she enjoyed continued referrals from other advisors and clients, repeat business from clients, and continued media interest from local and national press partners.

What are your natural affinity groups? Where can you meet and greet "your people"? Look for ways to meet and greet key people in your community—whether it's serving on a foundation board, doing volunteer work for a non-profit, serving on an FPA public relations committee or in a leadership role with NAPFA, or sponsoring seminars at your local community college or church. Find those people who will introduce you to others—they may, in fact, become your apostles in spreading your key messages. They can open additional (and sometimes unexpected) doors for you.

For example, a colleague of Sheryl's decided that business expositions and community fairs were his "cup of tea." St. Louis-based financial advisor, Dave Ressner, scours community papers and specialty publications (e.g., *Parent and Child*) to find out where opportunities exist. He signs up for the event and pays little or nothing for his booth or table space. Dave may set up just a card table at a Parents' Fair at Babies 'R Us, or he may set up something more elaborate at an Earth Day Festival. The materials he brings for his information table are designed to be a custom fit for the affinity groups and people who'll be attending. He simply thinks about what he'd like to see or receive if he were in their shoes.

At Earth Day, Dave provided literature on socially responsible investing that he obtained from Calvert funds. Of course, he had some additional information to hand out, including a special report branded with his company logo, web site and telephone number. Not only does it "light him up" to attend these events (remember, he's looking for groups in which he has common interests), but he also meets a large number of people who immediately get to know and like him. Frequently, he's the only financial planner exhibiting at the event. Dave uses a clipboard to obtain contact information from people who'd like to hear from him. Many of them check the "call me for an initial meeting" box. Better yet, the folks who come in for that initial meeting almost always engage his services. There's no trick here, but there might be a little "magic" involved—due to the fact that Dave has already established a good amount of rapport and trust just by meeting and greeting these folks at an event tied to a matter they all care about.

Remember, people do business with people they like and trust. Being a model of good citizenship creates a positive image, allows you to get in front of key individuals and groups of people, and makes you a better person in one fell swoop. While it will take some time, you don't need a large budget to make networking and public relations become a large part of your marketing effort.

Public and Private Seminars

One of the most effective ways to maximize your perceived value to current and prospective clients is by delivering informative seminars. Creating an intelligent presentation of thought-provoking material takes time, but it's well worth the effort. It doesn't have to be expensive, especially if you let a host organization provide the room, handle the promotional work, and fill the room for you. An added benefit of a privately-sponsored seminar is that there is an instant implied endorsement of you and your firm.

There are many good financial services seminar modules available for purchase. However, Sheryl and I prefer that you create your own unique seminar modules based on current events or books you like. For instance, Sheryl loves:

- *Your Money or Your Life: Transforming your Relationship with Money and Achieving Financial Independence*, by Joe Dominguez and Vicki Robin.[7]
- *The Seven Stages of Money Maturity* by George Kinder.[8]
- *The Richest Man in Babylon* by George Clasen.[9]
- *The Millionaire Next Door* by Thomas Stanley, Ph.D., and William Danko, Ph.D.[10]

It's easy to come up with a seminar or workshop that focuses on the fundamental messages in books that you love, and it's cheaper and more authentic than buying prepared modules.

Of course, you'll want to give credit to your source. You could even include a copy of the book as a part of the tuition. Or you could sell the books as a courtesy at the back of the room at your cost. What author wouldn't love that? It's a win-win-win situation.

How about creating a seminar based on current events? Possibly tax laws recently changed or the markets are plunging. Clients may be calling—and so might your local TV network affiliate or newspaper.

So what should you do? Step up communications, of course. Offering a seminar on "How to Survive and Thrive in the Current Financial Environment" and posting a related article on your web site is a natural way to be of service to your clients. It also presents a nice marketing opportunity for you. Just letting people know that the article is there—and that you are there to strategize about planning opportunities or coach them through trying times—gives you a reason to send an e-mail message or postcard that can stimulate a visit to your web site or a telephone call to your office. It's also a great way to reach out to the media (more about that later in this chapter).

On one occasion, Sheryl overheard a group of people talking in a small group about the problems couples often have communicating about and managing money. Voila! A seminar was born. She called the proper person at the church, drummed up some flyers, had a promotional blurb placed in the church bulletin and made up a Power Point presentation titled "Couples and Money." What was the result? With just a little work she received a great response, got new clients, made new friends, and enhanced her visibility—all while providing a valuable service.

One rule I always follow in my marketing communications is this: "seek first to be of service and to educate." With a "service first attitude," marketing opportunities and enhanced visibility will naturally occur. People (and especially the media) can smell it a mile away if you have a hidden agenda. My advice to you—don't.

As I mentioned before, whenever possible opt for a hosted seminar instead of a public seminar. Let the host organization do the promotional work and fill the room for you. Then you'll be free to simply show up, present yourself and your material in the best possible light, and provide a valuable and educational handout (which happens to be tastefully branded with your logo and company information). You'll also get instant credibility if a reputable organization is sponsoring your presentation.

A word of caution: don't go overboard on promoting yourself at your seminars, either from the stage or in your handouts. Pressing too hard makes you look desperate and unprofessional, and the attendees will question your motives. Instead, create an information table at the back of the room or in the lobby and provide a variety of interesting handouts or literature for people to take with them. They'll call you if you've made the right impression.

If you feel you must gather names, leave a clipboard out with forms for persons to sign up for your quarterly newsletter or request a special report. Provide a box on the form that says, "Call me to discuss [Topic]," and lines for them to fill in their address, telephone numbers and e-mail address.

Remember: be service-minded first and foremost to reap the best rewards.

When Sheryl spoke to groups, she didn't hand out her business cards. In fact, she didn't even keep them in her pocket. She intentionally left them in her purse. People always approached her afterward and ask for them. Her response is "Sure, just a minute while I get one out of my purse." Even when you need business, don't act like you do. As one major marketing campaign stressed, "never let 'em see you sweat."

Executive coach and consultant Bill Swift points to these truisms:

> *"If people see you need money, you'll never get it. Similarly, if you communicate in any way that you need clients, you won't get them either. You must learn to understand how you show up for other people and improve your public persona. Learn to recognize your own feelings of inadequacy or scarcity as those feelings arise. In this way you can dissipate or compartmentalize those feelings rather than broadcasting your "need" to others unconsciously. Then you can wear the cloak of confidence whenever you engage prospective clients and let your best self shine."*[11]

Create a Busy Professional Persona

Can you still be confident when the pipeline's less than full? With regard to setting up initial meetings or telephone calls with clients, we suggest taking the advice "never look too available" one step further. Here's what Sheryl tells all of the new planners she mentors:

> *"EVEN IF YOUR CALENDAR IS TOTALLY OPEN, BOOK THE APPOINTMENT OUT BY A WEEK OR TWO OR (GULP) EVEN THREE. APPEAR TO BE A BUSY PROFESSIONAL, AND TAKE ON THAT PERSONA. EVENTUALLY YOU WILL BE."*

Is this a "fake it 'til you make it" strategy? To some degree, yes it is. However, if you're focusing properly on the development and implementation of your marketing plan, you should have plenty of "real appointments" filling your week, such as: meeting with other professionals; networking at industry events; scheduling time to work *on* your business (not just *in* it); making telephone appointments with your business coach, marketing coach, mentor or "Dream Team" (more about that later in this chapter); writing an article for the personal finance section of the local newspaper; revising your marketing plan; or preparing for a seminar.

TURN UP YOUR MARKETING RADAR

Another valuable activity is talking to other financial planners who are serving the Validator and Middle Markets. "Pick their brains" to determine what has worked best for them in promoting their services in their respective communities. We also recommend that you attend industry conferences, participate in industry study groups and discussion boards, and read industry periodicals. In other words, learn from the successes and failures of others.

Remember that marketing to Middle Market consumers in rural Tennessee will be different from marketing to Middle Market consumers in urban New York. While middle income folks and do-it-yourselfers nationwide do have common characteristics, needs and sensibilities, every community and market has its own subtle character. *You* also have your own persona, preferences and character, and it's important that you try to match your personality and skills with people who'll quickly grow to like and trust you. In the words of William Shakespeare, "To thine own self be true."[12]

As you go about your daily business, start noticing what makes your community unique. Also take note of what makes *you* unique. Keep a notepad on your desk and jot down your observations for a couple of weeks. Where are the overlapping interests and values that could lead to affinity and opportunity?

Another great idea is scanning the free periodical racks in the front of the supermarket. Read the smaller community publications as well as the larger ones. There are tons of "meet and greet" opportunities you can glean from these periodicals. After a while, what you once saw as "junk" periodicals may take on a golden glow.

Begin attending a variety of business and social functions. Wherever you go, have your marketing radar turned up high so that you will be alert to "right-fit" opportunities. Once you hone this skill, you'll find endless opportunities to talk to people, share your mission, and tell your story.

What Works According to Other Advisors

When asked, experienced advisors almost always list the following marketing techniques in their "what works in marketing" lists. All of these are important to a well-balanced marketing plan, and you might want to test them out in your community.

- Craft several good verbal messages and positioning statements that you can "tap" on demand (based on the situation and with whom you are speaking).
- Speak with friends, family and acquaintances so that you spread the word and get referrals to potential clients and professional allies.
- Actively participate in your local Chamber of Commerce.
- Actively participate in formal networking, civic, and service groups.
- Actively participate in local FPA or NAPFA chapters (or other industry-related groups).
- Write articles or do "Money Makeover" or "Financial Q & A" columns for the local metropolitan paper or smaller community newspapers.
- Produce and distribute an informative newsletter or timely special report.
- Publish a targeted yellow pages ad.

- Establish a good web site—one that is partly educational, and partly electronic brochure.
- Present at privately-hosted educational seminars (a host organization, such as a church, business or community college promotes the event and provides the meeting facility).
- Sponsor public educational seminars (you fill the room and incur all costs).
- Make "warm" and "cold" telephone calls. (*Hint*: you should have a "real" and valuable reason to call.)
- Canvass local neighborhoods with flyers or mailers, in person or using a targeted direct mailing. (I happen to like postcards best because they can be extremely efficient and they have a long shelf life.)
- Place small display advertisements in targeted community newspapers, church and school bulletins, senior citizen center newsletters, etc.
- Do a targeted direct mail campaign (U.S. mail or e-mail) using a "warm" list. (*Hint*: a compelling message/offer is the key here.)

Working With the Media

Getting local publicity is one of the fastest ways to become known in your town. Best of all, publicity is free. All you need is (1) an idea that will benefit the public or the publication's readership, (2) some time, and (3) a bit of writing skill. If you are lacking in the copywriting skills department, a ghostwriter can add the Midas touch. Or perhaps your spouse or a trusted colleague or assistant can help you polish your articles.

A secondary benefit of publicity is that you can use your published items in your sales and marketing materials. Every time you send a letter to a prospect or sponsor a seminar, give out copies of articles that have been written about you (or by you). Nothing builds your credibility faster than your being held up as an "expert" by the local newspaper.

Media coverage, like direct mail and display ads, sometimes has an incubation period before it bears results. (This is one reason why I like postcards. People tend to keep them in the top desk drawer until they have a need for advice, or a stimulating event prompts their call.)

When people call your office asking for information about your services, be sure to include any newspaper articles quoting you as an expert. It's wonderful credibility! And if the articles are not worth providing in their entirety, then create a news summary sheet (or web page as Sheryl had on her web site. With positioning like this, when you make your follow-up call do you think that you will be treated as a solicitor? Or will you be treated as a professional, just as the prospect treats his attorney or CPA?

Another approach is to create a "Dream Team of Advisors," consisting of an attorney, a CPA, a mortgage broker, an independent insurance broker, and, of course, you. You and the other members of your team can write articles together, produce seminars, refer business to one another and ultimately open more doors. You could even add a small business coach, marriage counselor or other non-traditional experts to your Dream Team.

People (including the media) love stories on personal finance and on maintaining balance in life. In fact, just after personal health, personal finance is the hottest topic on many publications' slates. Why would anyone want to write about you? Well, the main reason is that journalists need to fill newspapers with content, and what you have to say can be very good content—especially now that you are focusing on serving the Middle Market (which most likely represents the bulk of their readership).

I've found the best way to start is to simply read a periodical and determine who is writing about what. It's easy to find out how to contact various journalists—either look at the publication's masthead or visit their web site. If in doubt, simply call the publication and ask the person manning the information desk which writer or editor would be most interested in what you have to say. Find out if that journalist prefers to receive her information via e-mail or U.S. mail. Then send a press kit or a letter of introduction along with a story idea and your business card.

Another great strategy: E-mail the writer when he or she has done a good job of writing about something related to your field of expertise. Compliment the journalist in a sincere, non-patronizing way and mention some small aspect that might tie in with the previous article, or that might be a good topic for a follow-up article. And if you're a member of certain industry groups (e.g., FPA or NAPFA), participate in their press partner programs and respond to media requests.

Also, don't overlook industry publications. Focus some of your attention on becoming a resource for periodicals such as *Financial Planning*, *Journal of Financial Planning*, *Investment Advisor*, *Financial Advisor*, *Registered Representative*, *Wealth Manager*, *Morningstar Advisor*, and *Research* magazines. You'll probably be reading these publications and industry discussion boards anyway, so look for opportunities to add your thoughts and insights. Your local editor and other journalists will take note if they see you've been quoted in one of these respected industry publications. They are likely to be favorably impressed and more inclined to contact you the next time they need a resource or story idea. Your clients and referral sources will also be impressed when they see "[Your Name] has been quoted in *XYZ Industry Journal*" in your biography and promotional materials.

Favorite Press Success Stories

Here are a couple of media success stories that I can't resist sharing:

Rich Chambers, a CFP® and colleague who practices in Palo Alto, California, had a goal—a burning desire to be quoted in the *Wall Street Journal*, *Newsweek* or some other major consumer publication. He determined to *religiously read* the personal finance columns in the targeted publications. After awhile he'd compiled a comprehensive list containing the names, titles and e-mail addresses of his favorite columnists. One of them was Jonathan Clements, who as you know writes the "Getting Going" finance column for the *Wall Street Journal*.

Whenever Rich read an article that he agreed with or thought was well done, but could have included some additional insight or piece of information, he sat down at his computer and composed a thoughtful, courteous and brief e-mail to the writer. He was always professional and helpful. Usually, he had a trusted colleague or his marketing communications coach look over his letters to make sure the tone was right, and that the "i"s were dotted and the "t"s were crossed. Most importantly, he didn't write to promote his business; instead, he wrote to provide food for thought or to add a new idea the writer might not have considered. He always ended his e-mails the same way: with a simple sentence inviting the journalist to call him with any questions or for more information. The signature area had his company tag line, contact information and a link to his web site automatically embedded at the bottom of every message.

Within a few months, Rich had the local newspapers calling him for his insight and expertise. He kept a folder of "hot topics," facts, figures, quotes and ideas next to his telephone. If he was caught off guard or was busy when the journalist called, he'd get some information about the article, find out what they were looking for, and determine what their deadline was. He'd ask if he could take 10 minutes to collect his thoughts and compile the information they were seeking. Then he'd call them back, composed and ready to provide his best answers. He practiced speaking in sound bytes and quotable quotes. When the content of the article warranted, Rich would also offer to research additional details and call back within the hour.

The local media coverage enhanced Rich's local visibility and credibility. Clients and other professionals would say, "Hey, Rich. I saw the article you were in" and strike up a conversation; frequently, they'd bring a copy of the article to Rich's office. Within a year of starting his media communications campaign, Rich had been quoted on CBS. MarketWatch.com and featured as a financial planning expert in articles in the *Christian Science Monitor*, *Forbes*, and the *Wall Street Journal*. National Public Radio called, and Rich was one of three planners who provided comments on college funding options.

Rich had more than met his goal. He included reprints of the articles when prospective clients requested introductory material. He mailed and e-mailed copies of the articles to friends, colleagues, and clients who might have missed the article. He noted the media coverage in his biography and on his web site. He placed reprints on information tables when he spoke.

But now the media communications bug was in Rich's system. He just kept reading the publications and sending notes to the journalists.

One day Rich was discussing marketing strategies and joint endeavors with his Power Partner, Steve Bell, a CFP® based in Livermore, California. His cell phone rang and Rich picked it up promptly as always, with a lively "Investors Capital Management. This is Rich Chambers." (Remember, he was meeting with his Power Partner, *not* waiting by the telephone or sitting on his laurels.) When the very pleasant gentleman with an English accent introduced himself as Jonathan Clements and explained that he was working on a story and wanted to bounce some ideas around with Rich, Rich didn't miss a beat (although he *did* think for just a moment that it might have been a financial planning buddy playing a joke on him).

At the end of their discussion, Rich offered to provide some additional information that would help Mr. Clements with his article. He provided the information promptly (via e-mail) as promised, with a brief "thanks for your call, it was a pleasure" preamble. Subsequently, Mr. Clements wrote an informative article that happened to contain ideal content for Rich's client communications, Rich also happened to be quoted in the article. Since then, Rich and Mr. Clements have collaborated on additional story ideas and content.

When Rich told me this story, I almost said, "It doesn't get any better than that!" But then you just never know what can happen with a little thought, some persistence, and the right relationships.

Another favorite media success story is that of colleague, Dean Knepper. Dean hails from the Washington, D.C. area. After practicing for 20 years as a C.P.A. and financial advisor for firms catering to affluent clients, Dean decided to start his own financial planning and tax practice serving middle America; he founded Lifetime Planning in January 2001. Dean attended the Garrett Planning Network initial 3-day intensive training workshop and returned home with a press release to send to his local newspapers. He customized the press release and sent a copy to each of the three periodicals in his community. One of those periodicals was the *Washington Post*. The business editor liked Dean's press release title and story idea so much that he sent a photographer out to capture Dean standing in front of his office signage, complete with his name and credentials in a clearly visible area.

What was so compelling to the Post editor? Consider the title of the article the *Post* ran: "For the Not-So-Rich, A New Kind of Asset—Financial Counselor Changes his Focus." The article began like this:

> *"After years spent figuring out how to manage money for the wealthy, [Dean Knepper, CPA, CFP®] wanted to focus on helping middle-income Americans manage theirs. … Financial planning used to be a term used only by the wealthy. But increasingly, the not-so-rich have sought to follow their example."* [13]

The article went on to describe Dean's practice and detail his services.

A year and a half after the article came out, Dean told me:

> *"I am still getting clients who saw and saved the article. One lady said she had the article on her refrigerator for well over a year before she called for an appointment. It was an added benefit that the article was chosen by the Post for inclusion in a promotional 'Loudoun Extra' section that was distributed to all residents in the county (the Loudon Extra section ran a couple weeks after the main article). I can only imagine what that would have cost if it had been a paid advertisement," exclaimed Dean.*

In addition to enhancing Dean's client acquisition efforts, and helping him to establish himself as an expert with other professionals, the *Post* article—in conjunction with Dean's continued media relations efforts—led to further media recognition. Dean enjoyed multiple quotes on TheStreet.Com. One year later, the *Post* ran a follow up article called "Where Are They Now?"—which again described Dean's practice and how he focuses on serving the Middle Market. A few months later, he was quoted again in the *Christian Science Monitor*.

Dean continued to speak with journalists. Not all of his contributions were used, and sometimes he didn't get quoted at all. Sometimes he'd see his idea or contribution in the article, but without any attribution. No worries, Dean just kept on truckin'. First and foremost, his goal was to become a trusted and valued resource.

One day National Public Radio called Dean looking for a financial planner to interview on a breaking news story. Dean didn't have any experience working with the broadcast media. Having only an hour to prepare, he felt a little gun-shy telling Jacki Lyden of National Public Radio what his clients had been asking—and what he'd been telling them—about the market's recent plunge, and the crisis in investor confidence despite good economic news. It wasn't that Dean would have said something he'd regret; he just wasn't ready for that type of radio interview.

Dean is one smart cookie. You don't have to honor every press request. To Dean's credit, he provided the name and telephone number of a trusted CFP® colleague to the NPR staff person. What a nice surprise Dean's colleague had when NPR called her that day. And I imagine that colleague will think of Dean the next time *she* has a referral or a press request that she'd like to pass along.

But perhaps the nicest surprise of all for Dean was when the writer for *Time* magazine contacted him. The journalist was writing an article on retirement planning issues and how the bear market was affecting baby boomers' and retirees' lifestyle projections. Were people planning to work longer? What suggestions and advice did Dean have? Months passed after the interview, but the article didn't materialize. Then one day, five months after the interview, the writer contacted Dean to let him know that the article would finally be published. Dean would be quoted in a nice-size paragraph summarizing his observations. The article would be *the cover story* for the next issue of *Time* magazine. "The article got shelved before due to a breaking news story," Dean told me. "I thought that was the end of it until the reporter contacted me on Friday and said it was going to print the following week."

There are many more stories I'd share if I had room! But as these stories and my own experience show, once you get rolling with the media, things will start to snowball. Personal finance journalists read each other's articles. They want to know what the others are writing about and whom they use as resources in their articles. One writer will mention your name to another writer, and one day you'll get a (truly surprising) telephone call from a publication. I remember my first such call!

Tips for Working With Journalists

Sheryl started "small" with her local newspaper doing "Money Makeovers" and ended up in *Newsweek*, *Smart Money*, *Kiplinger's Personal Finance* and many more. After many years of personal press success, we've come up with the following tips for working with journalists:

- Be timely. Remember journalists are working on deadlines. Return their calls promptly.

- If you are called out of the blue, ask what's their topic and deadline. See if you may call back in 10 minutes. (Tell them you'd like a few moments to pull together some comments, additional quotes or resources).

- Internalize your message. Say something quotable. Practice speaking in sound bytes. Recognize that quotes often need to be bold statements. You are an advisor, so you must be definitive. Respond to the interviewers questions directly and with conviction.

- Don't be upset if you are misquoted, or if you don't get a chance to proof the article or make corrections before it comes out. Rarely will you have the opportunity to "proof" any of the articles.

- Be helpful. Have a "real reason" to call or e-mail the journalist. (Test: project yourself to the journalist's desk and ask whether *you* would welcome your call?). Seek to be of service first and foremost.

- Be patient. Perfect your style, tone and content to become "media worthy."

The Art of Storytelling

Publicity is by far one of the most effective marketing tools you have at your disposal, but how do you promote yourself to the media so that they will give your growing practice the spotlight it needs? The answer—storytelling!

That's right, storytelling. Ultimately, personal finance stories are human interest stories and every reporter is looking for a good story. Here are the key things you need to give the press to help them tell your story:

Personality. A company is faceless without the people who run it. In addition, personal finance stories work best when you can tell a real-life story about one of your clients and how they overcame an obstacle or realized a better future because of the work you did with them. (Be sure to ask your client ahead of time if you may use their name and story.) You want the personality of the people to come through so that the reader gets a sense of who you are, and who your clients are. As impressive as numbers can be, they aren't the whole story. Real-life examples of how you solved a client's problems bring your story to life. Readers want to hear about real people. Tell the stories behind the facts and provide details that would make someone want to listen.

Facts and Figures. Reporters love facts and figures that anchor a story in reality. Provide a table that supports your key tenets. Give a third-party quote that anchors the article and lends credibility to your assertions. If you prefer not to divulge certain figures about your business, talk instead about its rate of growth. Say something like, "business has doubled in the last year," or "we've already met our objectives for this year, and it's only July." Other alternatives include, "The client makes an executive level salary" or, "he is on target to retire at age 58." You get the picture. Be honest and helpful, but finesse it if you should.

Details that Reveal. Reporters have their antennae up for interesting details about the people behind the companies. Increasingly, that's the approach that reporters are taking so you need to be open and share details with them. Maybe the contents of your refrigerator (or the fact that you work best when sipping tea on your veranda while working from your wireless network) reveals something insightful about your marketing strategy. Perhaps your spouse works with you in the business, or you are active in providing financial literacy classes on a volunteer basis at your local high school. Your motivation and vision for being in business is who you are, and what makes your story unique.

Tie in with current or seasonal events. Every journalist needs support to convince their editor why they should write *this* story *now.* Anticipate this need and provide reasons why the story is timely and should be covered now. For instance, at tax time create a list of "Financial Spring Cleaning Tips." During the holidays, write an article on "Gifts with a Purpose" or "Year-End Tax and Financial Planning." If the markets are turbulent, offer comments on what you're telling your clients, and what they're asking you.

In short, the media needs you! In addition, journalists are frequently just the types of clients that middle market advisors are looking for. Sheryl has heard on several occasions, "it is so refreshing to hear from a financial planner who would actually work with a person making an average salary and driving a Toyota" (they are referring to themselves). Start your media outreach campaign today!

Keys to Marketing Success

I'd like to recap what I consider to be the essential keys in marketing to the Middle Market. To be successful in our marketing efforts we need to:

1. **Define our markets.** Understand our clients' needs and tune in to what makes them tick. Discover and address what's important to *them.*

2. **Gather information**. Look at all the possibilities.

3. **Formulate a written plan**. Set goals. State expected results in words and in numbers.

4. **Make decisions**. Implement the plan. Measure results. Refine the plan.

5. **Own the plan**. Embody our mission.

6. **Know ourselves**. Understand how we are unique and the value we provide. Practice and refine how we communicate our value. Convey benefits, not features.

7. **Become a good storyteller.** Be passionate, courageous and authentic.

8. **Build affinity groups and strong relationships.** To reap the best outcomes, seek first to serve and the benefits will flow to us naturally.

9. **Leverage activities based on our strengths and personal passions.** Pick three or four key marketing methods and then execute them well. The primary methods we select should suit our natural abilities and personalities.

10. **Never give up.** Remain true to your vision and sense of purpose. Be tenacious. Surround yourself with positive, energetic people who support your vision.

A lot of ground has been covered in this chapter, but I feel as though I've barely scratched the surface. An entire book could be written on just the marketing aspects of serving this special target market. But since that is not the sole purpose of this book, I'll save that for another day.

There are many good resources available in the financial planning industry and through general business channels to help you fill in any gaps regarding the effective marketing and day-to-day operation of your practice. I've provided some of my favorite resources on the Resource Pages on the CD-ROM.

ENDNOTES

1. This definition has been approved by the American Marketing Association Board of Directors and is included in the *Dictionary of Marketing Terms*, 2d ed., edited by Peter D. Bennett, published by the American Marketing Association. This definition of marketing first appeared in *Marketing News*, March 1, 1985. See: http://www.marketingpower.com. Click on the link "About AMA," and then click on "Marketing Definitions."
2. *Oxford Desk Dictionary and Thesaurus*, American Edition, p. 485 (Oxford University Press, In., 1997).
3. Marie Swift is the Principal of Impact Communications (http://www.impactcommunications.org/).
4. Id.
5. Thomas Kostigan "Rich Gen-Xers in Distress" CBS.MarketWatch.com (July 17, 2001), at: http://www.CBS.MarketWatch.com. This news release also resulted in a major article written by Cort Smith titled "X Marks the Spot" in *Investment Advisor* (October 1, 2001) at: http://www.investmentadvisor.com.
6. AdvisorSites is an excellent web building resource for independent advisors, owned and run by professional journalist, Andrew Gluck, and web master, Steve Gordonson.
7. Joe Dominguez and Vicki Robin, *Your Money or Your Life*, (Penguin, 1999).
8. George Kinder, The Seven Stages of Money Maturity (Dell Books, April 11, 2000).
9. George Clason, *The Richest Man in Babylon* (Signet, February 2004).
10. Thomas Stanley, Ph.D. and William Danko, Ph.D., *The Millionaire Next Door* (Pocket Books, 2000).
11. The Internet address for Bill Swift is: http://www.billswiftonline.com.
12. William Shakespeare, *Hamlet*.
13. Sarah Schafer, "For the Not-So-Rich, A New Kind of Asset: Financial Counselor Changes His Focus" *Washington Post*, p. T5 (February 8, 2001).

Chapter 15

Growing and Scaling Up Your Business

As I mentioned in Chapter 5, many practitioners are building their businesses along the same lines as their counterparts in the legal profession. There are benefits to remaining solo and there are benefits to growing our businesses and expanding our service offerings. The characteristics most important to you and the type of practice you want to develop are very personal, yet critical decisions. As you work through your business planning (Chapter 13), you will discover those issues that are most important to you.

I see the natural progression for many independent financial advisors to start out as a solo practitioner, and as the demand for their services grow, to begin outsourcing certain services. Many of these options were not available when I wrote the first edition of this book. This area of our industry, with technology, is making things possible that we could not possibly imagine just a few years ago.

By outsourcing everything that we can and should, we can focus on what we do best, meeting with clients and providing financial advice. We can focus on billable work – yet everything critical to running our practice gets done.

Regardless of how much we are able to outsource, there is still a limit to how much quality work a solo practitioner can produce over any given period of time. Once you have mastered your workflow processes, and have delegated as much as possible to various outsource solution providers, you may find that you have the opportunity to take on substantially more clients than you single-handedly can serve.

The traditional next step for practitioners facing this opportunity is to hire a full-time employee. Some of the things we must keep in mind regarding hiring employees involve the fixed costs, such as additional office space, furniture, equipment, licenses, wages and benefits. There is also a time demand: interviewing, hiring, training, managing, and supervising employees. But we must invest this time to glean the benefits employees can provide us.

I recommend the first hire be a paraplanner. Personally, I have never had a secretary or an administrative assistant in my hourly practice. I found that I could hire a paraplanner for approximately the same wage as an administrative assistant, and the paraplanner could provide entry-level assistance and assist me directly with client work.

I don't mind at all if this paraplanner does not have experience working with another financial planning firm. I do care, however, that they have an educational background in financial planning, are eligible or planning to sit for the CFP comprehensive examination, and are self-motivated.

I have had very good success hiring top graduates from local area colleges that offer a CFP Board-registered financial planning degree programs. These talented young people are looking for opportunities to learn from veteran advisors, but often they are not interested in being the rainmaker at this point in their careers. Given that fact, I have found that there are substantial numbers of talented, motivated, yet inexperienced, college graduates looking for this type of opportunity.

As the paraplanner's skills develop they require less direct supervision, and they begin to take on more and more responsibility. I find that within two years, a talented and motivated paraplanner can begin taking on the role of a staff planner. In time, many staff planners desire to expand their opportunities and develop their own clientele. At that point you may give them the title of "lead planner."

Paraplanners are paid a modest salary, but staff planners and lead planners are paid strictly based on a portion of their billable hours. This fee-splitting arrangement is traditional with law firms. Staff planners are typically CFP professionals. They have no marketing responsibilities, and they are paid 1/3 of their creditable hours billed. Lead planners, on the other hand, are CFP professionals as well, but they do have marketing responsibilities. Therefore they are paid 2/3 of their creditable hours billed.

This compensation structure works out very well for the business owner. Staff planners and Lead planners do not get paid unless the boss gets paid. And the more the boss makes, the more the Staff and Lead planners make.

The more work we can delegate to competent professional staff, the more work can be completed, and the greater the total revenues of the firm. This leverage has a direct impact on the owners' net income and on the firms' ability to serve more clients and provides great opportunity to expand and eventually sell the business.

As I mentioned earlier, this type of business evolution is very similar to that of many small law firms. A solo attorney is extremely limited in the amount of work he can complete and the amount of money he can make. We've all heard it – there are only so many hours in the day. On the other hand, a well executed business plan involving multiple professionals can be highly effective – providing that small business, entrepreneurial environment, yet utilizing the leveraging quality of professional staff to maximize opportunities to serve and be compensated. Now imagine a large regional law firm. That is where I see this trend heading for many energetic entrepreneurs.

The following exhibit illustrates income and expense projections for the first four years of a sample financial planning firm's evolution. Please note that in years one and two, the principal has not yet employed a professional staff member. He is working on the business solo. But by the beginning of year three, a part-time, paraprofessional (paraplanner) is hired and begins assisting the principal with billable work. In year four, the paraplanner has evolved into the role of a staff planner and now also meets with clients. A second paraplanner is also brought into the firm in year four. Note the leverage provided when scaling up your business in this format.

Figure 15.1

REVENUE MODEL FOR HOURLY MULTI-PROFESSIONAL PRACTITIONER FIRM

	Year 1 (SOLO)	Year 2 (SOLO)	Year 3 (PRINCIPAL + PT PARA)		Year 4 (PRINCIPAL)	Year 4 (+ STAFF PLANNER)		TOTAL	
Professional's Compensation	$36,180	$48,240	$86,832		$77,184	$35,640		$112,824	**Principal**
Overhead/admin (office space, supplies, etc.	$17,820	$23,760	$24,768		$20,016	$35,640		$55,656	**Overhead**
Staff Compensation			$18,000	PT Paraplanner	$18,000	$35,640	**	$53,640	**Staff**
Total Revenue Needed	$54,000	$72,000	$129,600		$115,200	$108,000		$223,200	**Revenues**
Hourly Billing Rate	$180	$180	$240		$240	$150	***		
Percentage Billable Time	15%	20%	30%		30%	40%			
Working Hours in the Year	2000	2000	1800		1600	1800			
Billable Hours per Year	300	400	540		480	720			

Engagements	Avg Hours	Avg Revenues		Target Number of Engagements (Year 1)	(Year 2)	(Year 3)	Average # of Meetings per Week	Target # of Engagements (Year 4)		Average # of Meetings per Week	
Initial Engagements	8	$1,440	*	38	43	60	1.3	120		2.5	
Hours Breakdown by Pro:								Division of Hourly Billings			
Initial Engagements								3	5		8
Check-Ups								1.5	1.5		3
Check-Ups	3	$540	*	0	19 (apx 50%)	21.5 (apx 50%)	0.4	80 (C/U apx 50% + limited engmnts)		1.7	
Billable Hours:				304	401	544.5	1.7	480	720	4.2	

* At $180/hr average

** Staff Planners paid 1/3 of their gross billings

*** Weighted average billing rate

The following exhibit is an example of my financial planning firms' Employee Handbook.

EMPLOYEE HANDBOOK
HOURLY ADVISOR$, LLC
EFFECTIVE JANUARY 1, 2005

1. Mission Statement of Hourly Advisor$, LLC
   a. Our Mission is to simplify our clients' financial lives and help them to achieve a better quality of life by maximizing their financial resources to best accomplish their personal objectives.
2. Equal Employment Opportunity Policy Statement
   a. Hourly Advisor$, LLC is an equal opportunity employer. Employment is based upon personal capabilities and qualifications without discrimination because of race, creed, color, religion, sex, age, national origin, disability, sexual orientation, marital status, or any other protected characteristic as established by law.
3. Non-Discrimination and Anti-Harassment Policy
   a. Hourly Advisor$, LLC is committed to a work environment in which all individuals are treated with respect and dignity. Each individual has the right to work in a professional atmosphere that promotes equal employment opportunities and prohibits discriminatory practices, including harassment.
   b. Hourly Advisor$, LLC strongly urges the reporting of all incidents of discrimination, harassment or retaliation, regardless of the offender's identity or position. Contact your supervisor or the firm President immediately. An employee's failure to fulfill this obligation could affect his or her rights in pursuing legal action. Also, please note, federal, state, and local discrimination laws establish specific time frames for initiating legal proceeding pursuant to those laws.
4. Americans with Disabilities Act Policy Statement
   a. The firm is committed to complying with all applicable provisions of the Americans with Disabilities Act (ADA). Consistent with this policy, the firm will provide reasonable accommodations to a qualified individual with a disability, as

defined by the ADA, who has made the firm aware of his or her disability, provided that such accommodation does not constitute undue hardship on the firm.

DISCLAIMER

Hourly Advisor$, LLC has established a variety of employee benefit programs designed to assist you and your eligible dependents. This portion of the Handbook contains a very general description of the benefits to which you may be entitled. Please refer to the official plan documents for details.

5. Benefits
   a. Health Insurance
      i. Basic and major medical insurance is provided by company to employee and family. See Appendix A for coverage details.
   b. Life Insurance
      i. $50,000 death benefit is included with Health Insurance Program.
   c. Workers' Compensation Benefits
      i. The firm is covered under statutory state Workers' Compensation Laws. Should you sustain a work-related injury, your supervisor or the firm President must be notified immediately.
   d. Dental Insurance
      i. Employer provides dental insurance for all employees. Employees may elect family coverage and pay the additional premium.
   e. Disability Insurance
      i. Long-Term disability insurance
         1. Lesser of 60% of wages or $6,000 / month
            a. See Appendix B for Certificate of Insurance.
   f. 401(k) Profit Sharing Plan
      i. Employer provides 401(k) PSP administered by State Street Bank.
      ii. Employer matches participant contributions dollar for dollar up to 4% of compensation.
         1. See Appendix C for plan details.
   g. HSA Plan
      i. Employer contributes $3,000 annually to employee HSA account. Employee may also contribute.
         1. See Appendix D for plan details.

h. Vacation
    i. Employees receive 2 weeks paid vacation after one complete year of full-time employment.
    ii. 3 weeks of paid vacation is provided after 5 years employment.
        1. Vacation time-off will be granted on based on seniority and work-load flexibility.
        2. Any unused vacation time is forfeited, under all circumstances. However, employer strongly encourages employees to utilize their vacation benefit.
i. Paid Holidays
    i. One day: Your Birthday, New Year's Day, Memorial Day, Independence Day, Labor Day
    ii. Thanksgiving
        1. Thanksgiving Day and the following day
    iii. Christmas*
        1. The office is officially closed for regular business from December 24th – 31st. However, over that time, staff will share responsibility of checking messages, mail, deliveries, etc. each day.
        2. * Employees participating in any other commonly recognized religious traditions may substitute the equivalent time-off.
    iv. Paid Holidays are in addition to Vacation.
j. Flex-Time
    i. A traditional workweek is 40 hours.
    ii. Employees have some flexibility regarding their work schedule. Options are: starting day at 8am to 10am and completing between 4pm and 6pm. Employees are granted discretion regarding how they elect to allocate their work time over each week.
        1. For example: your work load is very heavy early in the week and would require more than 8 hours per day to manage effectively, you may elect to work 10 hours days Monday through Wednesday and work a short day or two later in the week.
    iii. There may be times of the year or special situations that would require the company to eliminate or restrict the Flex-Time option and set required work hours.

k. Continuing Education
    i. Reasonable and customary expense to obtain required continuing education to maintain CFP® license and NAPFA member qualification are paid by company.
    ii. The vast majority of this CEU requirement will be provided directly to the employee through your membership in the Garrett Planning Network.
    iii. The company makes available the opportunity for each staff member to attend at least one industry conference per year and cover all costs of attendance. Conference selection must be approved by company in advance.

l. Licenses and Dues
    i. Company pays renewal fees to maintain the following designations and memberships:
        1. CFP®
        2. Garrett Planning Network
        3. NAPFA
        4. FPA

6. Compensation
    a. Lead Planners
        i. 2/3 of net creditable billings per month.
    b. Staff Planners
        i. 1/3 of net creditable billings per month.
    c. Paraplanners
        i. Salary (based on market rates).
    d. Interns
        Hourly (based on market rates).

7. Progression
    a. We believe in promoting from within our ranks. Whatever we need, if a current employee has the passion and ability to deliver, any position open for consideration.
    b. Historically we have seen interns become paraplanners and later become staff planners. We've also hired staff planners who wanted to become lead planners, while other didn't. With a small company, such as ours, each of us must be prepared to back up one or more co-workers. If there is work that needs to be done, we all must pitch in. Often times, exemplary performance is illustrated in these situations. Exemplary performance is the key factor in progression.

8. Job Descriptions
   a. Paraplanner
      i. This is the entry level position financial planning position. The ideal candidate will have a four-year degree in financial planning, finance, marketing, or business.
      ii. Without an applicable college degree, or the satisfactory completion of the CFP® Comprehensive Examination, two to three years of applicable experience is required.
      iii. This person should have general computer and typing skills and an ability to work with Microsoft computer programs such as Excel, Word, Access, and PowerPoint.
      iv. We do not anticipate that Paraplanners will have experience using the financial planning, portfolio illustration and summary development applications that we utilize. We provide training on these applications.
      v. Paraplanner will gather Client data and organize this information for input into our financial planning, investment portfolio and summary report software applications.
      vi. They will also make any copies of statements in order to organize them into files and binders for both our firm and for the Client.
      vii. Paraplanner will have telephone and E-Mail contact with Clients to follow up on additional data needed, to clarify data, confirm or schedule appointments etc.
      viii. Paraplanner may also sit in on Client meetings at the sole discretion of the Lead Planner and with the Client's blessing.
      ix. Paraplanners do not have any responsibilities to generate business for the firm.
      x. The ability to think globally while maintaining a strong attention to detail is extremely important.
      xi. Paraplanners are expected to pursue their CFP® Certification if advancement opportunity is desired. Refer to the Staff Planner Job Description for details on the next stage of advancement within our firm.
      xii. The annual salary range for the Paraplanner position is $20,000 to 30,000.

b. Staff Planner
    i. We anticipate that our staff planners will evolve from Paraplanners as experience in financial planning and confidence working with clients is gained, and they have achieved their CFP® designation.
    ii. Staff planners share the same types of job duties; however they should be able to fulfill the responsibilities of their position with very limited supervision. Successful staff planners must be self-directed.
    iii. Staff planners will be compensation at a rate of 1/3 of their creditable gross billings, paid on a monthly basis. Initial billing rate will be $90/hour, without a CFP® designation and $150/hour with a CFP® designation.

9. Quality and Productivity Assurance Procedures for Staff Planners
    a. Objectives
        i. Standardize quality work product.
        ii. Enhance productivity on each project.
        iii. Enhance productivity on each billable Client project.
        iv. Establish systems to ensure staff accountability.
        v. Enable Supervising CFP®(s) to Supervise.
    b. Requirements
        i. All staff planners beyond one year of full-time employment with firm are held accountable to the criteria detailed below.
        ii. Staff planners with less than one year of full-time employment must strive to achieve full accountability to these criteria by the completion of their first year of employment.
        iii. Staff planners failing to achieve this level of accountability within the time frame mentioned above are subject to termination or demotion.
    c. Performance Criteria for Quality Assurance Regarding the Lead Planner and Staff Planner Relationship
        i. The role of Lead Planner is to ensure quality and consistency in work product delivered to Client. It is not the role of the Lead Planner to "proof" data entry, but rather to review the final output, finalize the Summary of Recommendations and meet with the Client.

ii. It is anticipated that Staff Planners will have questions of judgment, or need to clarify Client data with Lead Planner. All other reasonable resource options should be explored prior to presenting questions to Lead Planner. All supporting documentation and notes to the file must be submitted to Lead Planner as soon as practical after question arises. Lead Planner will commit to make himself available to the Staff Planner as soon as possible.

iii. It is the Staff Planner's responsibility to get questions answered in a timely manner, so that they are able to fulfill responsibilities as further clarified below.

iv. Prior to the time the case is submitted to the Lead Planner for review, it must be completed in its entirety, just as if it were being presented to Client. The presentation binder and Client file should be made available to Lead Planner at least 48 hours in advance of Client meeting. All Client notes to the file and notes to Lead Planner must be printed out of GUS and included in Client file. A copy of the Client's detailed billing report form GUS must also be printed and placed in the file prior to review. If by this time the Staff Planner still has questions or concerns of any sort, they must be brought to the Lead Planner's attention in writing.

v. Review of MoneyTree reports, Principia Snapshots, Summary Report and recommendations by Lead Planner should take no more than 20% of the mid-range fee estimate.

    1. Example: Estimated fee range $800-$1,000

    Lead Planner's time should be no more than $180, i.e. approx. 1 hour.

vi. Lead Planner must review all Client work and communications prior to delivery until such time the Lead Planner consistently finds no mistakes of fact. Refer to Requirements section above. Lead Planner must review all questionable judgment decisions.

d. Performance Criteria for Quality Assurance – Additional Staff Planner Responsibilities

    i. Staff Planner should use tutorials, training manuals and prior cases to verify data entry procedures and strategies prior to submitting case for review to Lead Planner.

   ii. Staff Planner must first preview all reports on screen, then print all reports, proof them, know where all data is coming from, and ask themselves "how would this work in real life"? Next, any edits must be made, reports must be reprinted, read, proofed and re-read to ensure accuracy and clarity. Once Staff Planner has reviewed the final output thoroughly the case may be submitted to Lead Planner.

  e. Performance Criteria for Productivity Assurance – Additional Staff Planner Responsibilities
   i. Workflow Checklists must be used as designed and kept in Client's file until case is completed. Time frame guidelines are to be strictly adhered to.
   ii. 100% of time in office and any billable time out of office must be tracked in GUS. Time and billing logs will be reviewed at least weekly. No paychecks will be issued without complete and current time and billing records.

10. Employment Guidelines
  a. All new hires shall complete initial paperwork. See Appendix D for required forms:
   i. Employment Application.
   ii. Employment Contract.
   iii. Confidentiality Agreement.
   iv. Privacy Policy.
   v. Insider Trading Policy.
   vi. W-4.
   vii. I-9.

11. Standards of Conduct
  a. Dress Code
   i. Business Casual on days with clients or visitors in the office. Refer to the Outlook firm-wide calendar for schedule. Any days without appointments scheduled with clients or visitors can be casual days. All attire must be presentable and tasteful.
  b. Oral Communications
   i. First impressions can last forever. We expect all oral communications, whether over the phone or in person, to be conducted in a professional and courteous manner.
    1. Phone

a. Salaried staff will share primary responsibility for answering the telephone during business hours – 9am to 5pm CT, Monday through Friday. If the salaried staff is unable to answer a call after the second ring, anyone available should answer the call, if possible.
b. Answer the phone, "Hourly Advisor$, this is (first name or full name), how may I help you?"

c. Written Communications
   i. Use of letterhead, fax cover page, postage machine, etc.
      1. Retain copies of all written communications in their appropriate place.
   ii. Client Communications
      1. General notes to the file will be retained in GUS electronically.
      2. Letters, faxes, or E-Mails to and from Clients must be copied and one copy placed in the Client file under the communications tab and one copy will be retained in the master Communications (Compliance) file (either paper or electronic) by date.
   iii. E-Mail
      1. Regarding Client communications see above.
      2. Keep personal E-Mail communications to a minimum.
      3. Run Virus Scanning software continually.
      4. Do not open attachments from unknown sources.
   iv. Client reports
      1. See Garrett Planning Network Sample Plan binder for illustration.
      2. Action Plan, Summary Report, Detailed Billing Report and Notes to the File are drafted and retained electronically in GUS, as well as in the Client file.
      3. Financial planning reports provided to clients are the Master Reports list stored in Easy Money, or those components of the Master Reports that the Lead Planner deems applicable to the client case.
      4. Investment portfolios, current and proposed, are illustrated using Morningstar Principia Advanced's Snapshot reports. Morningstar's most detailed individual investment holding 1-page summary reports will also be provided for each position in the

current portfolio and any additions to the proposed portfolio. These reports are printed in color.

5. Client reports will be present in the standard Garrett format, using ½ inch 3-ring binders and with tab sets. The title page for the cover of the binder is printed in color (without 3-hole punch) from GUS.
6. All client reports are to be printed on 24 pound, bright white, 3-hole pre-punched copy paper.
7. A copy of the Client reports shall be retained in the Client file, under the appropriate section and tacked down with 2-hole punch.

12. Payroll and Record Keeping
    a. All employees are paid monthly based on the Compensation outline above. Paychecks are directly deposited into employee's bank account(s) on the 1st day of the month. The pay period ends on the 2nd to last business day of the month.
    b. Financial planning staff paid based on a percentage of their creditable billable time must provide a copy of their audited monthly billing record to the payroll officer by noon on the 2nd to last business day of the month. Billable time for the remainder of that day should be estimated and included on the billing record.
13. Termination
    a. Kansas is an "At-Will" Employment state. Company and employee are both free to terminate the employment agreement at any time, without notice.
        i. We ask that employees provide us with as much notice as possible and grant us the option of having them help train their replacement should they decide to terminate their employment.
        ii. We also request the option of an exit interview.
        iii. In the event company must terminate employment, employee will be given as much notice as possible and appropriate given the circumstances causing the need for termination.
14. Evaluation Process
    a. All employees are subject to a 90-day probationary period.
    b. Periodic informal evaluations and feedback will be provided.

c. Formal evaluations, both for the employee and the supervisor, are performed at least annually, generally on or about the anniversary date of employment.
d. Salaried employees fulfilling the duties of their job description will receive a minimum of a cost of living adjustment. Additional pay increases are based strictly on merit and the ability of the firm to pay additional compensation.

I anticipate exponential growth in the number of practitioners serving clients from *all walks of life* on an hourly basis as our profession continues to evolve over the next decade. I also anticipate that many of these same practitioners will recognize that they desire to develop a financial advisory business employing 2-5 professionals and possibly an equal number of paraprofessionals.

A well thought out, documented business plan, effective use of leverage, and systemized processes are the primary keys to running a successful business.

I hope that the information shared in this edition of *Garrett's Guide to Financial Planning* will help you build that practice of your dreams while you help Middle Market Americans achieve theirs.

Chapter 16

Conclusion

EFFECTIVE PEOPLE ARE NOT PROBLEM-MINDED; THEY'RE OPPORTUNITY MINDED. THEY FEED OPPORTUNITIES AND STARVE PROBLEMS.

– Steven R. Covey

We've covered a lot of ground in this book. In the introduction, I invited you to join me in exploring the many wonderful possibilities that exist in serving the Middle Market. I asserted that you would:

- Gain some fresh perspectives on the financial planning industry and the profession's evolution.
- Learn about different practice models and opportunities.
- Discover a host of financial planning resources.
- Glean key business planning and marketing insights.

Whether or not you join me and become an "All-American Planner," I hope that I have fulfilled these promises. In writing this book, I've tried to communicate a strong sense of purpose and my sincere enthusiasm for serving the Middle Market. Helping to make competent, objective financial advice accessible to all people, is not "just a job" for me – it's a mission!

When I first established my practice, I asked myself a very simple, yet defining question: how would I want to work with a financial advisor if I were a consumer? I built my practice to serve my clients on the same basis I wanted to be served by other professionals – on an hourly, as-needed basis.

Within two years of establishing my practice, I realized that the demand for my services was much greater than I could ever meet on my own. It became clear that my staff and I would be able to affect the lives of only a few hundred people. I received inquiries from people all over the country wanting to engage my firm's services. At times I had a waiting list of up to eight weeks for new client engagements. What made "common sense" to me (i.e., serving people from all walks of life on an hourly, as-needed basis), also made sense to a lot of other people, too.

Now my primary, professional objective is to help make competent, objective financial advice accessible to *all* Americans. While I no longer serve clients on an individual basis I am still very much involved in fulfilling this objective through my work coaching of financial advisors wishing to develop their practice as I did. I've found that "if you build it" – and let people know about it – "they will come." I became an example of this "new breed of planner," the ones who are profitably working with Middle Market consumers and do-it-yourselfers. By succeeding in this market, telling my story and mentoring other advisors, I can accomplish my primary, professional objective – to make competent, objective financial advice accessible to *all* Americans.

Imagine the Possibilities

People from all walks of life need and want to work with you! With the right tools, techniques and mindset, you can make a *huge* difference for your clients and enjoy a different kind of success than you'd ever possibly imagined.

I've heard from many financial services professionals that they have actually dreamed *for years* of establishing this kind of practice, they've just never done it. Unfortunately, the problem has been that too many "veterans" in the industry repeatedly told us:

- "It can't be done."

- "You can't make a living working in the Middle Market."
- "In time, you'll realize that this altruistic attitude must give way to profitability."
- "Go where the money is."
- "You've got to sell products, gather assets, and develop a client base that will provide you with continual revenues."
- "If your approach were doable, people would already be doing it."

At the beginning of the twentieth century, many great minds believed that all of the significant inventions had already been discovered – but since then we've learned that the opposite is true. Like Julius Frontinus (Roman soldier, governor of Britain and author of a history and description of the water supply of Rome in 1st century A.D), some of the world's best thinkers of the early twentieth century also agreed that "inventions reached their limit long ago, and I see no hope for further development."

However, in my opinion Hungarian Nobel Laureate Albert Szent-Gyorgi Von Nagyropolt got closer to the truth when he said:

> *"DISCOVERY CONSISTS OF SEEING WHAT EVERYBODY HAS SEEN AND THINKING WHAT NOBODY HAS THOUGHT."*

We as planners must step outside of the box and redefine our advisory relationship with clients. The problem is not with the clients – it's with the service and delivery model. It's very difficult, if not impossible, to provide the same services, in the same way, to Middle Market clients as we do for affluent clients.

For too long, many of us have deferred not only *our* dreams, but also the dreams of countless deserving and grateful clients. Today, more than ever, *all* Americans need sound financial planning and advice.

Serving the Middle and do-it-yourself markets is not the choice of most veteran practitioners. They have established practices that work for them and their clientele. Many can't fathom working any other way, and that's perfectly okay. Their clients obviously need and want what they have to offer. Fortunately, new or transitioning practitioners have vast, untapped opportunities available in serving the Middle Market.

Not every attorney wants, or needs, to be a high-powered litigator. Not every doctor seeks to be a neurosurgeon or cardiologist. Not every financial planner wants, or needs, to be an asset manager or top producer. Each of these professionals must decide what his or her definition of "success" is. We should, too.

Build Your Business Around *Your* Values

It's actually possible to build your business around your values. At the beginning of this book, I asked you to reflect on your goals and dreams. In the business planning and marketing chapters we also asked you to consider your personal priorities, values, and objectives.

Now let me ask you this:

"What does success mean to you?"

In a recent column on MorningstarAdvisor.com, David J. Drucker said:

> *"Financial-planning media traditionally feature advisors whose success is premised on growth — growth of assets under management, employees, clients, or all of the above. Behind the scenes, though, many of those 'successful' advisors, though admirably client-centered, work long, stressful hours, display less-than-impressive business acumen or organizational skills, and neglect their family and community."*[1]

Three Hints for Happiness

In the August 2002 issue of Investment Advisor, business coach Steve Moeller provided these tips for happiness, saying "There are three things that researchers have discovered were common denominators of happy people...with your help your clients can modify their behavior to increase their happiness." I second his advice but I'd add, "How about you?"

1. **Surround yourself with the right people.**

   Spend time every day with people who make you happy.

2. **Enjoy your work.**

   Do work that is meaningful and a good match for your skills.

3. **Enjoy your environment.**

   Surround yourself with the things and people you like.

By contrast, Dave's column:

> *"SEEKS TO DEFINE THE SUCCESSFUL ADVISOR AS ONE WHO HAS HIS OR HER TOTAL ACT TOGETHER, WHO IS CLIENT-CENTERED BUT WHO HAS ALSO DONE HIS OR HER OWN LIFE PLANNING AND IS MAKING THE TIME AND MONEY FOR ALL OF THE THINGS HE OR SHE TRULY VALUES."*[2]

What about your life planning?

When I took a hard look at my career choices and decided to revisit *my* life planning in 1996 and 1997, it became apparent to me that serving the Middle Market and adopting my current service model were the two missing elements I needed to both build a successful, thriving practice *and* create the type of balance I needed and longed for in my life. I researched other planners who had similar inclinations, penchants and desires.

I became a student of the Middle Market mindset and the validator niche. After experiencing solid financial success and an amazing amount of personal satisfaction within the first two years of establishing my "All-American" practice, I began coaching and mentoring other financial planners with the objective of increasing the number of practitioners who'd embrace with me the idea of providing independent, competent financial planning and advice to anyone who sought it, regardless of income, net worth, investable assets (or anything else). I worked on NAPFA's Middle-Market Task Force and spoke with dozens of industry and consumer journalists.

It's been quite an enlightening journey!

The Success Story Snowball

At first the Middle Market success stories were far and few between. Now, as I travel the nation and exchange ideas with various other professionals within our industry, I hear more and more examples of planners who've built successful practices that not only support their financial goals, but allow them to embrace their personal goals as well.

I personally know hundreds of practitioners who are now (or who are in the process of becoming) "All-American Planners." By doing their own life planning, advisors are making the time *and* the money for all the things they truly value. Many of these planners are meeting, or exceeding, their financial and business development goals. Furthermore, they are happier and more satisfied with their work and their personal lives.

In addition, the industry is increasingly acknowledging and supporting this trend. On August 26, 2002, *Investment News* ran a front page story entitled "Asset-based fees falling out of favor: Competition forcing variation in payments." Writer Jeff Benjamin states:

> *"Fees based on assets under management may be going the way of commissions. The trend now is toward retainers, hourly rates and various forms of a la carte payments for financial advice, according to industry analysts. After pushing for payment in fees for the last few years, independent advisers are evolving toward new payment plans as the demand for new kinds of services mounts. The transformation also is being driven by the economics of the nearly three-year bear market and the need to compete with increasingly fee-based wirehouses, according to experts.*

> *'I don't think the dollar amounts [advisers charge clients] will be changing, but the packaging of the services and the way they are priced will be changing,' says Mark Hurley, CEO of Undiscovered Managers LLC in Dallas. 'It's a logical thing. There's just no rational reason to be charging clients based on a percentage of their assets.' Mr. Hurley compares the pricing evolution to the way medical doctors treat and charge their patients. 'When you go to see a doctor, they don't ask you your net worth,' he says. 'They treat you and send you a bill for the service.'*
>
> *Just as commission-based brokers gradually have given way to fee-based advice, the industry now may be adjusting to an environment in which taking a more holistic approach to pricing and services makes more sense.*
>
> *Matthew McGinness, a consultant at Cerulli Associates Inc. in Boston, has written a research report on the registered investment adviser that includes a perspective on how 'fee structures are in flux. The services being provided are going beyond just asset management, and advisers are trying to align fees accordingly,' he says. 'If an adviser is spending more than half his time providing advice and services beyond asset management, it makes sense to take the focus off of asset management.' McGinness points out that as advisers continue to focus on their clients' 'entire financial picture,' somehow putting a price on the extra services being provided will be important."*

The above quotes summarize what I've been stressing for the last 10 years. I am pleased to see this growing trend within the financial services industry – specifically that:

1. Planners should be compensated for all of the work they provide to their clients.

2. A growing number of planners want to provide services that work for a wider body of clientele.

3. Planners want to achieve a better balance between their professional goals and personal lives.

As Mr. McGinness said in the *Investment News* article, "It's more of an evolution than a revolution." My fellow "All-American Planners" and I expect this trend to continue, and invite you to join us. As Henry David Thoreau said:

> *"Dreams are the touchstone of our character."*

What do your goals and dreams say about *you*?

Follow Your Dreams

As you've made your career choices and business decisions, like me you've undoubtedly encountered various "naysayers" along the way. You'll undoubtedly hear plenty of well-meaning colleagues and mentors tell you that a practice centered on meeting the needs of Middle America is a fruitless and draining venture.

At a conference in 1998, a veteran financial services professional put his arm around my shoulder and with a concerned voice basically told me, "Sheryl, it just can't be done." This colleague was just one of many who voiced their concerns and asserted that:

1. "I couldn't make a living."
2. "Clients wouldn't pay for my services."
3. "I wouldn't be fully compensated for the value I provided."
4. "The implementation wouldn't get done."
5. "I'd have higher liability exposure."
6. "I'd be developing a practice I wouldn't be able to sell."

I'm here to tell you that *not only can "it" be done,* but if you do "it" well – and surround yourself with other like-minded, positive professionals – "it" can be rewarding *both financially and personally*.

And if you're still thinking through the six concerns voiced by various colleagues, please review "Debunking the Myths" in Chapter 4.

This chapter is about inspiring and motivating you to become an "All-American Planner," so remember that:

- If you've got cold feet, remember that you don't have to dive into the abyss alone. Network with other advisors who share the same philosophy. Learn all you can from role models. Find a mentor or affiliate with like-minded peers who support each other.

- If you've still got "how-to-make-money concerns," continue working on your business plan. Through that process you will arrive at the right decision for you. Consider the viability of building your practice around the Middle Market. The opportunities are untapped. Remember, the problem is not with the clientele – it's the service models we use with the clientele.

- Maybe you've decided that becoming an "All-American Planner" is just not a good fit for you. That's okay, too. There's room for all of us. We can all be of service, each in our own chosen way.

But now I want to return to *your vision for yourself* and how you choose to serve people as a financial planning professional. Author Judith Duerk once said, "Sometimes dreams alter the course of an entire life." I concur with that statement, but I'd make the sentence plural to read:

> *"YOUR DREAM CAN ALTER THE COURSE OF MANY ENTIRE LIVES."*

If this dream calls out to you, don't wait another day!

At a recent retreat for financial planners, a fellow advisor took the microphone during the closing session and said words to this effect:

> *"I'VE BEEN A SERIAL JOB HOPPER WITHIN THE FINANCIAL SERVICES INDUSTRY. I NEVER FELT HAPPY WITH WHAT I WAS DOING UNTIL NOW... SERVING THE MIDDLE MARKET, MAKING A DIFFERENCE FOR MY CLIENTS, HAVING TIME FOR MY FAMILY AND FRIENDS, MAKING A DECENT LIVING, WORKING WITH PEOPLE I LIKE AND RESPECT. I NEVER THOUGHT IT WAS POSSIBLE TO HAVE IT ALL. BUT THANKS TO*

MY MENTORS AND THE SHARING WITHIN GROUPS OF LIKE-MINDED PRACTITIONERS LIKE THIS, I SEE NOW THAT I'VE FOUND MY HOME. AND I CAN HAVE IT ALL."

Passion with a Purpose

As you can tell, I'm passionate about sharing my success stories and the lessons that I've learned! If you've read these pages, but you're still on the fence, would you give me just a few more pages to restate my case? And, as you're reading these final pages, would you do me one more favor? Every time I make a statement about proven or potential success in this special market, please plug in this thought:

IF OTHER PRACTITIONERS CAN DO THIS AND ACHIEVE SUCCESS – I CAN DO IT TOO.

Now, let's recap some of the top reasons you should consider catering to the Middle Market and do-it-yourself consumer.

Enjoy Fulfilling Work

Since leaving the wealth management firm to establish my "All-American" practice in 1998, I've been *more than pleased* with the results. The experience of working with a broad spectrum of Americans – each with different needs and characteristics, but with overlapping (and what some would call "common") concerns – is immensely fulfilling. I never tired of "the work." In fact, I hesitate to even use the word "work" because I so greatly enjoyed working with individual clients, Although, I no longer serve individual clients, I continue to be actively involved in helping other practitioners build their practices serving this market. I also want to help spread the word that competent, objective financial advice is accessible to all people. My current "work" allows me to have an even more significant impact on this under served market.

Gain Better Balance in Your Life

Not only can you make a substantial difference for a host of appreciative clients (and not "just another quarter of a percentage point"), but you may also gain better balance in life, too! As I mentioned earlier in this book, in the wealth management environment I felt I needed to be "on call" for my clients 24 hours a day, seven days a week. I also felt increasingly burdened by the amount of responsibility and ongoing commitments required to maintain the level of service that clients would continue to value over time.

With my hourly, as-needed practice, I not only enjoyed my work more, I also was able to help people who really need me, and I had the time, flexibility and mental freedom I needed to enjoy other aspects of my family and personal life. The gross revenues my firm generated and the salary I drew were more than adequate, and grew each and every year.

Doing Well While Doing Good

Bette Davis, a favorite no nonsense personality of mine, once said:

> *"To fulfill a dream, to be allowed to sweat over lonely labor, to be given a chance to create, is the meat and potatoes of life. The money is the gravy."*

This is exactly how I felt about my practice. What could be better than to do work that you love, have time and energy left over to see the folks you love, and do the things you enjoy – and still enjoy a healthy serving of "gravy" on your "meat and potatoes"?

Building a business is much more than building a clientele. It involves building a system of processes that will make it possible to:

1. Provide great service to our clients.

2. Make a fair profit.

3. Enjoy our lives.

To effectively serve the Middle Market, a planner must be very efficient and a good business operator, too. However, with the right systems and strategies, you can indeed capture the Middle Market and increase your profits. And, you'll enjoy virtually no competition. So develop and execute your business plan; refine your processes and systems for delivering your work product; then you can concentrate on your *clients*, their needs, objectives, hopes and dreams.

Planners can make a good living doing work we love if our service model enables us to be compensated for all of our work, and we can work efficiently enough to meet our income objectives.

Keys to success include one or more of the following. Depending on your personal goals and objectives, you may wish to consider incorporating all of them:

- Use technology and systems to their fullest. Streamline and systematize your processes to continually become more efficient.
- Outsource the tasks that are not part of your core competency. Leverage your time and focus solely on the activities that will build the bottom line. Meeting with clients, nurturing press partnerships and building other strategic relationships should always be a part of your job description.
- Add professional staff so that you can serve more clients and receive a portion of their billings. In essence, duplicate yourself.
- Mentor new planners. Surround yourself with self-directed professionals to build a business that will last.
- Contribute to and support other like-minded professionals. You'll be enriched and supported in return.
- Maintain a "service-first" attitude and a clear vision for your practice. Position yourself to "do well as you do good."

Money therapist and author, Olivia Mellan, said in her column in *Investment Advisor*:

> *"When you live your values, your power will be enhanced as clients sense a congruence of your work and your psyche. And deep inside, you'll find that a more integrated sense of self will do wonders for your serenity and self-respect."*[3]

Whether one is building a thriving All-American practice and serving the Middle Market (or even if one is not), perhaps author Ayn Rand said it best:

> *"HAPPINESS IS THAT STATE OF CONSCIOUSNESS WHICH PROCEEDS FROM THE ACHIEVEMENT OF ONE'S VALUES."*

CAPTURE THE MIDDLE MARKET AND INCREASE YOUR PROFITS!

As discussed previously, the overwhelming majority of the American population falls within the Middle Market definition, so the opportunity is indeed vast. There are approximately 105,000,000 middle income households who are *not* the target clients of typical financial planners today. There's little or no competition in this market! Somewhere between 70% and 86% of the American population is being either overlooked or underserved!

The average consumer's awareness of the need for professional guidance with regard to the management of their personal finances is greater than ever. The information age and the proliferation of self-directed, employer-sponsored retirement plans have created top-of-mind awareness and a sense-of-planning urgency for average consumers. But even though the need and awareness are there, average Americans may feel that they have few palatable options for obtaining independent, affordable planning assistance and advice. Those of us who are adopting an All-American focus need to do a better job spreading the word that we are ready, willing and able to help average folks.

One way that I spread the word is simply by making comments like: "I'm a financial planner. I help regular folks, like you and me, make better money management and financial planning decisions." When people hear the words "financial planner" come out of my mouth, I see them go a bit hazy at first – probably because they think they can't afford to work with me, or that I only want to serve an affluent clientele (you know, account minimums and all that). But they usually perk up when I say, "I help regular folks like you and me make better money management and financial planning decisions." At that point, it's as if they mentally sit up and say, "Oh, really? How do you do that? Would you work with me? How can I find out more about you?" and so on. It's an easy conversation to have because I'm prepared with many positioning statement capsules to communicate my value and how I help "All-American Clients" reach their financial goals.

Marketing efforts are also greatly enhanced by the fact that the media loves objective advisors who cater to their readers, most of whom are middle Americans. The financial planning industry's top associations are increasingly supporting Middle Market initiatives and public relations campaigns as well. They're trying to raise public awareness regarding the importance of financial planning for all people.

Opportunities for referrals are greater because the majority of today's independent financial advisors are targeting a more affluent clientele and seeking supervisor-delegator relationships. These professionals are usually relieved to find qualified colleagues to whom they can refer Middle Market and do-it-yourself clients. As financial planners or "specialized participants" (see Chapter 3), we are by nature a group of helping professionals. If we can't help a consumer, we want to refer them to someone else we know and trust.

More and more practitioners are embracing the "All-American Planner" mindset. Although they may choose to structure their individual practices somewhat differently, there is undeniably a small, but rapidly growing movement catering to the Middle Market and the do-it-yourself client. As the trend continues (i.e., as clients tell friends, friends tell colleagues, colleagues tell journalists, journalists tell the world, and so on), the demand for our services will multiply. As the number of "All-American Planners" increases to keep up with consumer demand, our strength and support for one another will blossom and grow. Eventually, conversations about "How to Capture the Middle Market and Increase your Profits" will fade away.

Until then, I'll continue to spread the word that competent, objective advice is accessible to everyone, mentor new and transitioning planners, and "beat the drum" with the media. I look forward to many spirited debates and exchanges with you, and all my colleagues, in the years ahead as we build this new profession together.

Walt Disney said:

> *"If you can dream it, you can do it."*

If you're ready to become an "All-American Planner" now, get going! Start building your own "field of dreams" today.

IMAGINE THE POSSIBILITIES!

UPPER CLASSES ARE A NATION'S PAST;
THE MIDDLE CLASS IS ITS FUTURE.

~ Ayn Rand, American Novelist and Philosopher ~

ENDNOTES

1. David J. Drucker, MBA, CFP®, MorningstarAdvisor.com "Building a Practice Around his Life" (August 21, 2002); see also ***Virtual Office Tools for High-Margin Practice***.
2. Id.
3. Olivia Mellan, "Walking Your Talk," ***Investment Advisor*** (July 31, 2002) at: http://www.investmentadvisor.com.

APPENDIX A

FAVORITE RESOURCES FOR FINANCIAL PLANNERS FOCUSED ON SERVING THE MIDDLE MARKET

BOOKS ON SALES AND MARKETING COMMUNICATIONS

Basic Desktop Design and Layout, by David Collier, Bob Cotton, and Chris Prior (North Light Books, October 1989) (www.amazon.com)

Creative Marketing Communications: A Practical Guide to Planning, Skills and Techniques by Daniel Yadin (Kogan Page, Ltd., February 2001) (www.amazon.com)

Effective Marketing by Peter Hingston (DK Publishing, June 2001) (www.amazon.com)

Marketing Yourself, by Dorothy Leeds (Harper Collins, March 1992) (www.amazon.com)

On Writing Well, by William Zinsser (Collins, Anniversary Edition, May 2006) (www.amazon.com)

Relationship Selling: The Key to Getting and Keeping Customers by Jim Cathcart (Perigree Trade, October 1990) (www.amazon.com)

Selling For Dummies by Tom Hopkins (For Dummies, 2nd edition., 2001) (www.amazon.com)

The 25 Sales Habits of Highly Successful Salespeople by Stephen Schiffman (Adams Media Corporation, June 1994) (www.amazon.com)

Secrets of Closing the Sale by Zig Ziglar (Revell, September 2004) (www.amazon.com)

Books and Publications for Practitioners Getting Started

The Cutting Edge in Financial Services by Bob Veres (National Underwriter Company, 2003) (www.nuco.com)

Getting Started as a Financial Planner by Jeffrey Rattiner (Bloomberg Press, 2nd edition, June 2005) (www.amazon.com)

In Search of the Perfect Model by Mary Rowland (Bloomberg, 2004)

Inside Information by Bob Veres (www.bobveres.com)

So You Want to Be a Financial Planner by Nancy Langdon Jones (Advisor Works, 3rd edition, September 2005) (www.amazon.com)

Books on Personal Financial Planning Topics

Against the Gods by Peter L. Bernstein (John Wiley & Sons, Inc., 1996)

All About Asset Allocation by Richard A. Ferri, CFA (McGraw-Hill, 2006)

All About Index Funds by Richard A. Ferri, CFA (McGraw-Hill, 2nd edition 2007)

Deal with Your Debt by Liz Pullium Weston (Pearson Education, 2005)

The Four Pillars of Investing by William Bernstein (McGraw-Hill, 2002)

The Intelligent Investor by Benjamin Graham (Collins Rev Sub edition, July 2003)

Just Give Me the Answer$ by Sheryl Garrett with Marie Swift & the Garrett Planning Network (Dearborn Trade, June 2004)

The Millionaire Next Door by Thomas Stanley, Ph.D. and William Danko, Ph.D. (Pocket Books, November 2000) (www.amazon.com)

Money Without Matrimony by Sheryl Garrett & Debra Neiman (Dearborn Trade, June 2005)

The New Retire-Mentality by Mitch Anthony (Dearborn, 2001)

101 Tax Saving Ideas by Randy Gardner and Julie Welch (Wealth Builders Press, 8th edition, February 2006) (www.amazon.com)

The Richest Man in Babylon by George Clason (Signet, February 2004) (www.amazon.com)

Saving For Retirement by Gail Marks-Jarvis (Ft. Press, 2007)

Seven Stages of Money Maturity: Understanding the Spirit and Value of Money in Your Life by George Kinder (Dell Books, April 2000) (www.amazon.com)

Think and Grow Rich by Napoleon Hill (Ballantine Books, 1987) (www.amazon.com)

2007 Field Guide to Estate Planning, Business Planning & Employee Benefits by Donald F. Cady (National Underwriter Company) (www.nuco.com)

2007 Field Guide to Financial Planning by Donald F. Cady (National Underwriter Company) (www.nuco.com)

2007 Tax Facts on Insurance & Employee Benefits and 2007 Tax Facts on Investments (National Underwriter Company) (www.nuco.com)

Who Gets Grandma's Yellow Pie Plate? by Marlene S. Stum (Minnesota Extension Service, February 1999) (www.amazon.com)

Winning the Loser's Game by Charles Ellis (McGraw-Hill, 4th edition, March 2002)

Your Credit Score by Liz Pulliam Weston (Pearson Education, 2005)

Your Money or Your Life: Transforming your Relationship with Money and Achieving Financial Independence by Joe Dominguez and Vicki Robin (Penguin USA, September 1999) (www.amazon.com)

Financial Planning Resources

American Association of Retired People (www.aarp.org)

Advisor Intelligence (www.advisorintelligence.com/index_new.asp)

Aging with Dignity (www.agingwithdignity.org)

Ask Search Engine (www.Ask.com)

Bank Rate (www.BankRate.com)

Consumer Credit Counseling Services (CCCS) (http://www.cccsintl.org)

Credit Talk (www.credittalk.com)

EquiFax Credit Reporting Agency (www.equifax.com)

Experian Credit Reporting Agency (www.experian.com)

Insurance Commissioner's Publications: To assist consumers in making decisions about Medicare, health, life, disability, homeowners', auto and long-term care insurance. (http://www.insurance.wa.gov/default_publications.asp)

Medicare Information (www.Medicare.gov)

Money Tree Software -- Easy Money (www.moneytree.com/Products/TOTALPlanningSystem/EasyMoney/tabid/133/Default.aspx)

Morningstar Principia (www. corporate.morningstar.com/us/asp/subject.aspx?xmlfile=41.xml)

The Mutual Fund Education Alliance (www.MFEA.com)

National Association of Insurance Commissioner's Shopper's Guide to Long-Term Care Insurance (www.ltcfeds.com/documents/files/NAIC_Shoppers_Guide.pdf)

NOLO "Your Legal Companionl" (www.NOLO.com)

My Vesta (www.myvesta.org)

Quicken's Debt Reduction Planner (www.quicken.com/planning/debt/)

Trans Union Credit Reporting Agency (www.transunion.com)

USAA Educational Foundation (www.usaaedfoundation.org)

Web Ex Virtual Conferencing Service (www.webex.com)

Groups - Business Associations to Consider

Business Network International (BNI) (www.bni.com)

LE TIP (www.letip.com)

National Speakers' Association (www.nsaspeaker.org)

Toastmasters International (www.toastmasters.org)

Groups - Industry Associations to Consider

The Financial Planning Association (FPA) (www.fpanet.org)

National Association of Personal Financial Advisors (NAPFA) (www.napfa.org)

Groups - Peer Networks to Consider

Alliance of Cambridge Advisors, Inc. (www.cambridgeadvisors.com/web/pages/home/)

The Garrett Planning Network, Inc. (www.garrettplanningnetwork.com)

Web Building Resources

AdvisorSites (www.advisorsites.com)

Custom E-Advisor Pages (www.cepadvantage.com)

Appendix B

Recommended Personal Finance Books for Clients

Bogle on Mutual Funds: New Perspectives for the Intelligent Investor by John Bogle (Dell 1994)

A Commonsense Guide to Mutual Funds by Mary Rowland (Bloomberg Press, February 1999)

Deal with Your Debt by Liz Pullium Weston (Pearson Education, 2005)

The Dollars and Sense of Divorce by Judith Briles, Edwin Shilling and Carol Ann Wilson (Kaplan Business, June 1998)

For Richer, Not Poorer—The Money Book for Couples by Ruth Hayden (Health Communications, September 1999)

The Four Pillars of Investing by William Bernstein (McGraw-Hill, 2002)

Getting a Life: Strategies for Simple Living by Jacqueline Blix and David Heitmiller (Penguin USA, January 1999)

Just Give Me the Answer$ by Sheryl Garrett with Marie Swift & the Garrett Planning Network (Dearborn Trade, June 2004)

The Millionaire Next Door: The Surprising Secrets of America's Wealthy by Thomas Stanley, Ph.D. and William D. Danko, Ph.D. (Pocket Books, November 2000)

Money Without Matrimony by Sheryl Garret & Debra Neiman (Dearborn Trade, June 2005)

The Motley Fool Investment Workbook by David Gardner and Tom Gardner (Fireside, April 2003)

The Motley Fool's You Have More Than You Think: The Foolish Guide to Personal Finance by David Gardner and Tom Gardner (Fireside, January 2001)

The New Retire-Mentality by Mitch Anthony (Dearborn, 2001)

Personal Finance For Dummies by Eric Tyson (Wiley, 5th Edition, 2006)

Personal Finance Workbook For Dummies by Sheryl Garrett (Wiley, 2007)

The Richest Man in Babylon by George Clason (Signet, February 2004)

Saving For Retirement by Gail Marks-Jarvis (Ft. Press, 2007)

Seven Stages of Money Maturity: Understanding the Spirit and Value of Money in Your Life by George Kinder (Dell Books, April 2000)

Simple Asset Allocation Strategies by Roger Gibson and Randal Moore (Marketplace Books, January 2000)

Think and Grow Rich by Napoleon Hill (Ballantine Books, 1987) (www.amazon.com)

The Wealthy Barber: The Commonsense Guide to Successful Financial Planning by David Chilton (Stodardt, February 2002)

Who Gets Grandma's Yellow Pie Plate? by Marlene S. Stum (Minnesota Extension Service, February 1999)

Your Credit Score by Liz Pulliam Weston (Pearson Education, 2005)

Your Money or Your Life: Transforming Your Relationship with Money and Achieving Financial Independence by Joe Dominguez and Vicki Robin (Penguin USA, September 1999)

Appendix C

Frequently Asked Questions

1. **Please tell me about the financial planning process.** Financial planning is a multi-step process that provides you with two important things: (1) An in-depth review of your current financial situation, and (2) a blueprint that shows you how to achieve your goals and objectives for the future. GPN Members believe the financial planning process consists of seven distinct steps (see *Building a Brighter Financial Future* for details on our unique financial planning process). It is important to remember that financial planning is a process . . . not an event.

2. **How do you create this blueprint?** First we focus on your goals, objectives, priorities and values. For instance: the reduction of current and future income taxes may be an immediate goal, funding a quality education for your children and/or grandchildren may be an intermediate goal, and enjoying a secure financial future in your retirement years is likely to be one of your most important long-term goals. Another great goal in life for some people is creating wealth and/or leaving a legacy for your chosen beneficiaries or charities. You may already be on the road to meeting these objectives and simply need a new strategy, professional insight, or to fine-tune your plan. You may just be starting out, or you may be somewhere in between. Whatever your unique situation may be, everyone needs a periodic assessment of where they are on the road to meeting their financial goals. That's why we do an in-depth review of your current financial

situation. Next, you need to know how you can set about achieving (or continue working toward) your financial goals. By focusing on cash flow, investments, taxes, pensions and retirement plans, estate planning, insurance issues, savings opportunities and other general financial matters, we design a customized financial plan for you. Finally, to achieve the intended results, you must implement and monitor your plan.

3. **Sounds like a lot of work!** It may seem like that at first, but the good news is, if you follow your plan and maintain a disciplined approach, you can rest well knowing you can reach your stated goals. GPN Members try to make the process as easy as possible for you. In addition to receiving professional advice on your most important financial concerns, we can also provide implementation and ongoing asset management services, if appropriate for your needs.

4. **Who can benefit most from your services?** Any individual seeking financial peace of mind can benefit from our services. We serve people at all income levels, from all walks of life. Clients have the flexibility to work with us on either a one-time, as-needed basis or an ongoing basis. We welcome clients who simply need a one-time financial consultation or a second opinion, as well as those who need comprehensive financial planning and possible ongoing asset management services. In addition, any corporation or organization seeking quality, unbiased financial education for their employees or members can benefit from our financial education programs

5. **What is "Fee-Only" financial planning and why should that be important to me?** Because we are Fee-Only financial planners, all conflicts of interest regarding compensation are removed. We do not accept sales commissions; we work solely for our clients. Because we do not sell financial products such as investments and insurance, there are no third-party relationships or outside influences to color our thinking and financial recommendations. For more information on Fee-Only financial planning, including our Code of Ethics, Fiduciary Code and member requirements, please visit www.NAPFA.org.

   In addition, all GPN Member firms are Registered Investment Advisors (RIAs); RIAs must comply with a host of regulations designed to protect the consumer. One important question you should always ask when considering a financial planner's services: "May I please have a copy of your ADV Part II?" This document contains important information about the planner's qualifications, fiduciary duties, history of any past violations, etc. Any GPN Member would be happy to send you a copy of their ADV Part II.

6. **I understand the benefits of working with a Fee-Only financial planner, but I might need to obtain financial products. How will I be able to do that?** While we do not sell financial products, we will offer specific recommendations and opinions regarding the purchase of the various financial products that may be appropriate for you. So, if you need to obtain an insurance policy or a new mortgage, invest into a portfolio of mutual funds, or find an estate planning attorney or tax professional, we can direct you to the resources you need and/or help you obtain these products and services. If appropriate, we can also help you implement your plan and set up your accounts.

7. **Do GPN Members provide only comprehensive financial planning?** No. Although a comprehensive financial plan can provide the greatest benefits, we can limit our advisory services to your specific needs, such as cash management and budgeting, investment analysis or college education funding.

8. **My spouse and I are just beginning to build for our financial future. There is so much to learn! We need help and guidance to get started. Will you accept us as clients?** Yes. Some firms have income levels and/or net worth minimums but GPN Members realize that everyone has financial needs. We are proud to work with people from all income levels, and all walks of life. Remember, "You don't have to have a fortune to start building one." Click the *Find a Planner* button and get started today.

9. **I have already accumulated substantial assets and think I am doing quite well. But as I progress and build for the future, things seem to be getting more complicated. I want to be sure I am on track, but I don't always have the time or inclination to manage the myriad details by myself. Can you help me?** Yes. People who need more sophisticated financial planning or advice will find our services appealing and beneficial. If you have a desire to simplify your financial affairs, one of our Ongoing Client Programs may be right for you (see *Building a Brighter Financial Future.*)

If you are looking for a professional review or a second opinion to ensure you are on track, we can provide that, too.

10. **I'm in charge of the retirement plans and employee benefits at my firm. I would like to increase the number of employees who participate in our benefit programs. How can you help us?** Corporate education is key in building employee participation. Our financial planning team can help your people understand the benefits of your programs. Please call to discuss your specific needs. We can custom-build an educational program for your company.

11. **What types of securities do you provide advice for?** We provide advice for all types of securities, including mutual funds, stocks (as they relate to your portfolio holdings), bonds, bank deposits, variable and fixed annuities, limited partnerships and tax shelters. We also provide advice on mortgages, budgeting and cash flow issues, 401(k), 403(b) and other retirement programs, stock options, life and disability insurance, etc. If it has to do with money and finances, we can provide counseling, guidance and/or resources for you. Because we want our clients to know that they can call on us with any and all of their financial concerns, we have developed the slogan "Financial Planning and Advice for Everyday Life." Clients are encouraged to call us when they have a major life event, such as a new job, a baby, a marriage or divorce, or if they are planning to buy a new home or start their own business. We also encourage our clients to call us with more common everyday questions, such as: "How should I invest within my 401(k) or 403(b) plan?" "How can I reduce my taxes?" "What advice can you offer on refinancing my home?" "How can I maximize my Flex Spending Account, Cafeteria Plan or Section 125 Plan at work?"

12. **If I use a GPN Member to develop a financial plan, am I obligated to purchase the recommended products?** Absolutely not. We will offer recommendations which in our professional opinion will meet your needs and objectives, but you are under no obligation to purchase them. In today's competitive market, it makes sense to shop around for the best available product or service. For instance, if you need to obtain a life insurance or disability policy, we will suggest the kind of policy, which riders and what amounts may be best for you. We will then direct you to a choice of companies that can provide a quality product at competitive prices for you. If you wish, we can

help you purchase investments and/or set up your accounts with a third-party custodian such as a discount broker.

13. **Tell me about your investment philosophy.** As financial planners and investment consultants, we believe in the following fundamental principals with regard to designing an investment portfolio and making specific recommendations: The purpose of a client's investment portfolio is to fund current and/or future financial objectives. The design of the portfolio must take into account the client's financial objectives, tolerance for risk, needs for current income or liquidity, and special considerations such as income and estate taxes. The important thing to remember is that *no one can predict the future.* It is difference of opinion that makes a market. Investment and economic "experts" provided with the same information often come to different conclusions. We do not suggest that we can, or that any of the money or mutual fund managers that we recommend, will make the correct decision every time. We do believe, however, that studying the historic trends and relationships of investment classes and the philosophies and approaches of successful investment managers can provide valuable insight. The appropriate allocation of investment assets for your goals and risk tolerance is the most important component in developing an investment portfolio. We believe that having a diversified, well-balanced portfolio, following long-term buy-and-hold strategies, and having patience, will increase the likelihood that one will achieve their long-term financial objectives.

14. **How do you select investments for a client?** Before we recommend any investment, we consider the current economic conditions, the outlook for that asset class or type of security and how this investment fits within your portfolio given your objectives and tolerance for risk. For equity investments, we focus primarily on the philosophies, experience and track record of the management team. With fixed income investments, we look for the best yield available for a given quality of security. As fiduciaries for our clients, we strive to obtain the most appropriate investment vehicles to meet your objectives, while being very conscious of total expenses and risk exposure.

15. **How do you price your financial planning services?** The fees are based on the actual time involved in meeting with you in person or over the phone, researching and analyzing your current situation,

and providing specific recommendations and implementation assistance (if appropriate). Hourly rates vary from one GPN Member to another. An estimate of fees will be provided at the end of the Get Acquainted Meeting, when your needs have been fully identified.

16. **How much will my financial plan cost?** Financial planning fees are determined on a project basis; the total fee for a financial plan will vary from client to client based on the specific needs and complexity of your situation (please see our diagram *Building a Brighter Financial Future* to learn about our financial planning sequence and the client service options available). An estimate is provided after the Get Acquainted Meeting, when your personal needs are fully identified. Once your financial plan is complete, there are generally two or three levels of client/advisor relationships available to you (for more information, see *Building a Brighter Financial Future* diagram).

17. **Are your fees tax deductible?** Yes. Section 212 of the Internal Revenue Code permits an itemized deduction for tax and/or investment advice in the miscellaneous section of Schedule A. It is subject to a 2% floor of the adjusted gross income on a personal tax return.

18. **Once my financial plan is completed, will our relationship end?** Depending on your client track, the actual engagement of services may end (please refer to *Seven Steps to Building a Brighter Financial Future*), but the majority of our clients choose some sort of Continuing Client Program. Because financial planning is a *process*, not an event, we offer ongoing services, periodic reviews and day-to-day consultations as requested and/or needed.

19. **How can I get started?** The first step is an initial inquiry from you. Call us, toll free, at (866)260-8400 or email us at service@garrettplanningnetwork.com. Or, click the *"Find a Planner"* button on this site. All GPN Members offer an initial, no-obligation Get Acquainted Meeting, either on the phone or in their offices. For Get Acquainted Meetings, appointments are scheduled based on availability during regular business hours of 9-5, Monday through Friday. Expanded office hours are available to accommodate special needs or emergency situations. Should you decide to engage a GPN Member's services, they will discuss which of their services and

client tracks is appropriate for you. Most clients find the financial planning process to be stimulating and enlightening. The end result, of course, is greater peace of mind. We look forward to helping YOU build a brighter financial future!

http://www.garrettplanningnetwork.com/whatwedo.asp?SPID=1770&Title=Frequently+Asked+Questions&OrgID=116

Appendix D

Seven Steps Flowchart

Building a Brighter Financial Future ™
Create your Financial Blueprint

Advisor Actions / Responsibilities	Financial Planning Sequence	Client Actions / Responsibilities
When you contact us, we'll provide a brief description of our services, philosophies, methodology and fee structures. We'll direct you to our web site or mail you an introductory packet to help you learn more.	**Step 1: Community Outreach or Initial Inquiry**	If our services appear to fit your needs, we'll schedule a Get Acquainted Meeting (can be done on the phone or in person). You can review our introductory materials, or visit our Web site if you wish to learn more, then contact us for Step 2.
The Get Acquainted Meeting or Teleconference is an opportunity for us to exchange information about your needs and objectives, and further discuss which of our services are right for you. We will also provide an estimated fee quote.	**Step 2: Get Acquainted Meeting or Teleconference**	When you decide to engage our services, we will give you a list of additional data or information which we will need to begin formulating your financial plan. One-half of the estimated total fee is due at the time of this engagement.
When we receive your information, we begin to review and develop your financial plan. We prepare initial reports to discuss at our Step 4 meeting.	**Step 3: Data Gathering and Initial Preparation**	In Step 3, you gather the data requested, and complete your cash flow worksheet and risk tolerance questionnaire. You may fax or mail this information to us before our next meeting. Upon receipt of it, we will schedule our Step 4 meeting.

Advisor Actions / Responsibilities	Financial Planning Sequence	Client Actions / Responsibilities
In this interactive meeting, we discuss and clarify the information you have provided thus far. We continue to refine your financial goals and objectives.	**Step 4: Interactive Goal Setting Meeting or Teleconference**	In this Interactive Goal Setting Meeting, you have another opportunity to clarify your current situation, financial goals and objectives. Come with any additional questions or concerns you may have.
We edit the initial information as needed and run additional scenarios if applicable. We conclude our research and analysis, and produce final reports for your personal financial plan. We add our observations and recommendations to the plan.	**Step 5: Analysis and Plan Formulation**	As we move into Step 5, you simply schedule a meeting or teleconference 1 or 2 weeks after our Step 4 meeting. The ball is in our court in the interim. Revisit our web site to stay current on the changing world of personal finance and investments.
In Step 6, we present and review your personal financial plan. We discuss all reports and provide you with a written summary of our observations and specific recommendations.	**Step 6: Presentation of Your Financial Plan**	Congratulations! At this point, you will hold a personalized blueprint, custom designed to meet your financial goals. Full payment of the balance for actual fees incurred is due at the conclusion of your plan presentation meeting.
If you need and desire our help with plan implementation and follow up, at the conclusion of Step 6 we will discuss what might be an appropriate ongoing plan with you. Periodic update meetings and reviews are also recommended.	**Step 7: Plan Implementation and Follow Up**	Proper implementation is crucial to reaching your financial goals. Whether you now implement and monitor the plan yourself, or engage us to provide a portion or all of these services for you, we urge prompt action.